Leslie E. Stern

TotalRecall Publications, Inc.
1103 Middlecreek
Friendswood, Texas 77546
281-992-3131
www.totalrecallpress.com

All rights reserved. Except as permitted under the United States Copyright Act of 1976, No part of this publication may be reproduced, stored in a retrieval system, or transmitted in any form or by any means electronic or mechanical or by photocopying, recording, or otherwise without prior permission of the publisher. Exclusive worldwide content publication / distribution by TotalRecall Publications, Inc.

Copyright © 2015 by Leslie E. Stern   All rights reserved
ISBN: 978-1-59095-099-9
UPC: 6-43977-60992-2

Library of Congress Control Number: 2014937194
Printed in the United States of America with simultaneous printings in Australia, Canada, and United Kingdom.

FIRST EDITION
1   2   3   4   5   6   7   8   9   10

This is a work of fiction. The characters, names, events, views, and subject matter of this book are either the author's imagination or are used fictitiously. Any similarity or resemblance to any real people, real situations or actual events is purely coincidental and not intended to portray any person, place, or event in a false, disparaging or negative light.
The scanning, uploading and distribution of this book via the Internet or via any other means without the permission of the publisher is illegal and punishable by law. Please purchase only authorized electronic editions, and do not participate in or encourage electronic piracy of copyrighted materials. Your support of the author's rights is appreciated.

To my mother who is my best friend and will always know how much I love her.

Addictive as in drugs,
Addictive as in love,
Addictive as in reading,
This book is Addictive, Addictive. Addictive.

Special thanks to my mentor and dear friend, Rosemary Daniell and her Zona Rosa writing group.   Without her love and support, this book would surely never have been written.

PROLOGUE

October 2008

Dr. Emma Weiss sat in a comfortable chair in the atmosphere of a psychic's lair. The office had been transformed into a parlor with antique furniture, books on the occult and mystical creatures surrounding her. Emma had been referred to Mary Hoggins by a friend. Mary only accepted referrals, as she was too busy with her important clients to make time for just anyone. Though Emma was skeptical of such metaphysical endeavors, she was desperate. Coming here was a last resort, and Emma silently prayed this woman could help her. She sat quietly, waiting for Mary to do all the talking, a strategy Emma had chosen before she entered the room. If Mary was all Emma had been told she was, then Mary would sense what Emma needed.

"You're in a relationship but you're troubled," Mary paused, her ringed forefinger pointing its deep red polished nail straight up. "He's going to use drugs again during the holidays. And you're wondering if he'll get caught. Yes, dear, he will."

Emma's heart dropped into the pit of her stomach and she found she could no longer concentrate. As Mary spoke and continued to scribble in an unknown language, all that had happened during the past year since she had met Jake flooded Emma's mind. She thought about the first time she had realized Jake was using cocaine, only weeks after he had come into her life.

"Where the fuck have you been?" Emma's previously angelic mouth had shouted at Jake.

He'd been four hours late coming home and told her his truck had broken down and he'd had to walk two miles. By then she recognized the signs and knew he'd been out scoring coke. Emma had been ready to kill him. She had demanded they go to the drug dealer's house to retrieve the truck. His words echoed in her head as she remembered that night and looked blankly at Mary, who was still talking, but the words were muffled by Emma's own memories.

"Baby, we can't go into a neighborhood like that," he had said, trying to hang back as she grabbed his arm and tugged him toward the garage.

She hadn't cared if the drug dealers shot at them. She only hoped they'd hit Jake and not her. She also remembered how scared he'd been. But was he afraid of the drug dealers, of losing the woman he claimed to love—or of just losing his meal ticket?

Mary's words shocked Emma out of the past, and for the moment, she was back in the present. Mary began telling Emma personal information about her late father—information no one could possibly know. She listened intently and was amazed at the accuracy of Mary's words.

Mary continued to tell Emma about her late uncle and even told her about the child her mother had long ago aborted. Emma tried to pay attention to Mary's words but her mind kept drifting back in time; this time to an incident only weeks prior to this trip to Atlanta. She began to relive a night after Jake's arrest and his idiotic run from the police. Emma had heard a noise in the house and reached into her nightstand for her pistol. It was gone. Because of Jake, every drug dealer in Savannah and Garden City knew where she lived, and the son of a bitch has stolen her gun. How stupid could he be? Emma had asked herself. He was on probation, running from the police, and had taken her gun to a pawnshop where he had been fingerprinted and given his name. After she had cursed him out, he had called three times a day, begging her to forgive him. As she sat across from Mary, she couldn't believe she had forgiven him and still more unbelievable to Emma was she still loved him.

As Emma wrote the check for the fifty dollars her friend had told her was Mary's fee, Mary stopped her.

"Emma, dear, the fee is a hundred and twenty five dollars. But I'll tell you what. You give me that check and dump this guy of yours now, and we'll be square. If you dump him now, you might be able to save yourself."

Emma knew Mary was right, but she also knew she couldn't break it off. She just wasn't ready. She had hoped Mary would be the miracle to give her the strength to end it, but she hadn't. Emma wrote a second check for seventy-five dollars and slid it across the desk.

"I'm sorry, Mary. I can't do it. I'm just not ready."

Chapter One

Dr. Emma Weiss sat nervously in her navy Donna Karan suit, signing page after page of papers at the Law Offices of DeLesseps and Carney. It was an unusually chilly day in December of 2005, even in the usually tepid southern city of Savannah, Georgia. Emma was surrounded by strangers in a strange city at a large oak table. At twenty-eight years old she tried to look confident, but inwardly she was shaking. The closing attorney, Hank Carney, sat at the head of the table. His reading glasses were perched on the end of his nose as he babbled something about each paper he handed Emma to sign as the buyer of her first house. The seller of the house Emma was about to own sat directly across from her. His wife sat next to him. They were an elderly couple who were from Savannah, and it was whispered that they owned half of the city. Emma's realtor sat next to her, supposedly for moral support. She didn't offer any, but Emma assumed this was just the way closings worked. Odd, Emma thought. I moved to Savannah, Georgia, for the small-town charm and hospitality, and I get a brash, New York Jewish realtor. What are the odds?

The strangers around the table looked at Emma with curiosity. They assumed she was just a rich, vapid, Yankee heiress by looking at her. They didn't know she had her PhD in Psychology and was a member of Mensa. They just saw a beautiful young woman with a cashier's check made out for the entire amount of the house. The voices around Emma just became a distant hum, and before she knew it, the keys to her new house were passed across the table to her with a vague explanation of which key fit which lock. Everyone stood, shook hands, and left the room. Emma walked down the Victorian staircase, to the cobblestoned street, and into her Lexus SUV knowing her life was about to change. She just didn't realize it would change forever.

Emma had been born in Chicago, and her parents divorced when she graduated high school at sixteen. With her grades, she could choose any college she wished. Her mother and her new stepfather wanted to move to Phoenix where his family lived and her father chose sunny Fort Lauderdale where he could enjoy his passion for sailing all year long. Emma chose to remain in Chicago to attend Northwestern and finished her dissertation in Psychology at twenty-three (the youngest PhD the university had ever bestowed). Emma then moved out of the cold winters to Fort Lauderdale, where her father lived. She sailed with her father on weekends and worked as public relations director for a major advertising agency in Fort Lauderdale all week. She had a wonderful job and a nice apartment. She had a loving golden retriever named Tasha. Her life was happy and productive. She was lonely due to the lack of eligible, intelligent, attractive single men in Fort Lauderdale, but she was spoiled and overprotected by her father. It was not an exciting life, yet Emma was content, despite the lack of sex.

When her father, David, suddenly died right in front of her of an abdominal aortic aneurism, Emma was stunned. She was bringing their fifty-six-foot sailboat from the boatyard back to the dock behind her father's house with a mutual friend of theirs, John, and she threw the mooring line to her father on the dock. When they arrived at the dock behind David's house, he pulled the mooring line of the sixty-five thousand pound boat to cleat it off, and David dropped to the wooden planks of the dock. Literally. He died right there, on the dock of his house. By the time the paramedics arrived, it was too late.

Although they were Jewish, Emma's father wasn't a formally religious man and wanted his ashes thrown into the ocean he loved. She held a small reform Jewish service at her apartment, and she and John took her father's ashes and gave him to the sea.

With her father's death came both responsibility and freedom. Emma had to settle his affairs, which was a big responsibility. But she could finally live where she chose, and she could be the full-time literary writer she always dreamed of becoming. In her spare time, she had nearly completed her first novel, but it had taken her five years to write it. With her father's sudden death, she was rich and would never have to work again. Everything her father owned was already in trust in Emma's name, so she immediately had access to all his holdings. Emma splurged and replaced her eight-year-old Buick with a fabulous two-year-old Lexus GX 470 SUV that was under Lexus warranty. It would take six months to settle her father's affairs, and even after her own shopping, Emma still inherited over a million dollars in cash.

The first time she had visited Savannah had been on her way

to Fort Lauderdale from Chicago when she was twenty-three. Emma had immediately fallen in love. The moss-laden streets, the historic antebellum homes, and the Southern charm had enraptured her from the start. She had gone back on her birthday every year after that.

So Savannah it would be. While Emma was busily settling her father's finances, she drove up to Savannah every two weeks to research and house hunt. She met with the local Mensa group, checked the prices of insurance, and visited the Jewish Community Center. The consensus was positive about Savannah being a great place to live, except for one minor problem. There were few single men in Savannah—especially Jewish men. Emma rationalized that the larger city of Charleston was close, or once she settled, surely someone would introduce her to an eligible bachelor. She was wrong.

During Emma's research trips and house hunting, she found a cleaning woman who would work for her once she moved. Emma had hired Miss Ellie from the motel at which Emma always stayed when she was traveling back and forth from Florida. Miss Ellie was the only one of the staff there who would clean Emma's room with her dog in it. She was an older woman and loved Tasha, Emma's golden retriever. So Emma cornered Miss Ellie one day and asked if she would clean her house for her when she moved to Savannah.

"Oh, Miss Emma, I'd be pleased to do that. You just let me know when, and I'll be there on my Wednesdays off," she replied.

"Thank you so much. I'll let you know when I'm here permanently, and you can start every week." And that was the beginning of a close relationship between Emma and Miss Ellie.

Emma was obsessed about owning her own house and making it a sanctuary—a house where everyone wanted to hang out and no one wanted to leave because it was so much fun there. Emma had always rented apartments, so home ownership had been her dream. After looking at every available house in her price range, Emma finally found one with a great deal of potential in the perfect location. It was a corner lot and bigger than she needed, but by God, it was exactly what she wanted. The house she found had four bedrooms, two baths, a formal living room, and an enormous great room, a pool and huge private patio, priced right, and it was in Ardsley Park! Five minutes from historic downtown Savannah and five minutes from Southside's modern shopping. She was elated. It would need some work to make it her dream house, but it was still a great deal.

After six months of driving back and forth to get the new house perfected to her standards and settling her father's estate, Emma was ready to become a permanent resident of Savannah. She joined the Mensa group in Savannah and made some good friends. She went to a Passover Seder at her realtor's house and met Kathy Stein, who would become her best friend. Emma learned that her friend John, in Fort Lauderdale, had a sister in Savannah. John had told her, "Oh, you'll love Joey!" and he was right. They became quick friends. Jo introduced Emma to her friends, and they all got together. Her neighbors, Mark and Sheila Turner, were wonderful people and welcomed her with open arms. Emma also quickly learned that gossip spread as swiftly as kudzu in Savannah. Once she moved in, all the southern busybodies in her neighborhood had to see what she had done with the house.

Of course, it didn't hurt Emma's social life that she was not only brilliant but beautiful. She had thick, natural blonde hair the color of a wheat field that flowed nearly to her waist and had large, expressive cornflower blue eyes. She had full lips that were usually glossed. Her skin was flawless, so she never needed foundation. At only five-foot-four inches tall, she was still all legs and ample cleavage. But Emma's kindness—which would be her downfall—kept any potential jealousy at bay.

For the first time in her life, Emma joined a writing group. Whether it was short stories Emma had already written about her family or chapter after chapter of the novel she'd been working on for the past five years, the group was always supportive. Emma also became close friends with one of the other writers. She was a fun woman of Emma's age named Dana Rosenberg. They got together to talk about their writing, men, and anything else that might cross their minds.

During her frequent trips to Savannah, Emma had found a quiet, local restaurant called Jaycee's Café near her house. She quickly befriended the manager there. Ray was an affable, funny fellow, and he and Emma hit it off immediately. Emma was still renovating her house after she moved in, and she was having problems with the master bathroom. She was using the guest bathroom because the master bathroom was already gutted and no one seemed to be able to finish it. She had gone through five contractors and was becoming annoyed. One day at lunch, she asked Ray if he knew of any good contractors.

"Yeah, I do," he laughed. "And she's sitting right over there. She also happens to be my wife." He introduced Emma to Samantha, who quickly began the work on her bathroom. Within two months, Sam transformed the gutted bathroom into a soothing oasis. Ray worked on his days off from the restaurant with his wife as a painter, so he was at Emma's house frequently at the end of the job. Ray and his wife, Sam, attended all of Emma's parties, and Ray was always the joker. Sam was solemn most of the time, until she got some booze in her; then she became downright vivacious.

Only months after Emma moved permanently to Savannah, she had a fabulous Fourth of July party with her new friends and their kids. She had become good friends with the manager of her bank, Jenny, so she came and brought her husband, Mac, and their little boy. Emma's closest friend, Kathy Stein, brought her two small children. Ray and Sam brought their little girl. The kids splashed around in her pool while Emma grilled burgers and hot dogs on her gas grill and served white wine sangria to the adults.

By December of 2006, she had a huge Christmas party, and for the first time since she was a child, she actually had a Christmas tree. Screw the Jewish neighbors who whispered behind her back, "and it was right in the front window where everyone could see it!" It was her life, and she was going to live it as she saw fit.

And Emma was right about her house. No one wanted to leave. She had purchased a pool table for the great room and had a full-length wet bar built in. Okay, so Emma didn't really drink much but she loved to entertain. She and her friends played pool or sat by the fireplace listening to music in the winter, or sat outside on the large patio where they could smoke and hear the music from the wireless speakers Emma had strategically placed everywhere. They watched the fountain pour into the pool and were treated to the fairy lights Emma had wound around the columns and trees outside in the back. On the side street, she had turned an area that had been just dirt into a lovely courtyard. She had thick grass planted to cover all the dirt, and she installed a black stone fountain of Bacchus in the center. She bought black stone pavers with dragonflies leading to the fountain and a bench to sit and look at the fountain. She had planted a beautiful flower bed that bloomed with pink and white impatiens and black wrought iron window boxes for more flowers. The ugly and somewhat cockeyed brick wall that surrounded the courtyard had been hand-built by the original owner in 1950. Emma wouldn't dare tear it down, so she planted Confederate jasmine that would cover the brick once it matured, which was quickly. It smelled heavenly in the springtime and especially at night. The outdoor areas were the perfect sanctuary Emma imagined.

Emma was also quickly learning the ways of Savannah. When she had Confederate jasmine planted, she tried to joke with the landscaper.

"I know! Why don't we plant Confederate jasmine on one side and Yankee jasmine on the other side and see who wins this time," she teased. Not even a smile. Clearly, Emma realized, they have no sense of humor about the War of Northern Aggression, as it was referred to in the South.

When she had been in the process of moving, Emma had strolled into an antique shop in the historic district downtown and saw a dining room sideboard she wanted. She walked up to the owner and asked the price. The man barely looked up from his paperwork.

"Oh, I think it's sold," he drawled without even acknowledging her.

"Well, is it or isn't it?" Emma pushed for an answer. She really wanted that sideboard.

"I think it's sold," he repeated.

"Can I ask how much?" she gently pried.

"Thirteen hundred dollars," he muttered.

"Okay. Here's my card. If they change their mind, please call me," she placed her personal business card in his hand.

"Yeah, sure," he dismissed her.

Emma happened to have dinner with Jo and Jo's friends the next night, so she relayed the story to them.

"That's the Savannah way, Emma," Jo's friend, Ken, had told her. "That was Ben you talked to. You just tell him I sent you," Ken winked at her. First thing Monday morning, Emma was at Ben's store and told him that Ken Carlton had sent her.

"Oh," Ben instantly brightened. "You know Ken Carlton? Well, darlin', of course it's for sale. It's thirteen hundred dollars. And I'd be happy to deliver it for you," he smiled. "I know just where you live." This incident woke Emma up to the ways of Savannah. You had to know someone or be kin to someone to accomplish anything.

Emma adjusted. After all, she was intelligent and logical. Okay, so she was a little naive. She knew she had been overprotected by her father and her life had been easy for her. Emma Weiss had everything going for her. She was rich, brilliant, beautiful, had friends, and was settled. She only lacked a love life. Her research had been right about that. But life was good—for the first year. Then she made what turned into life-altering, fatal mistake. She bought a new mattress.

It seemed an innocuous purchase. Emma had owned the same mattress for—ever. Knowing little about mattresses, she had just automatically moved hers along with her other belongings. But she began to notice that when she awoke, she felt a pain in her hip from the old springs poking her. Her closest friend, Kathy Stein, recommended a local mattress shop called The Mattress Depot owned by Joe Sherman. Joe was usually referred to as Big Joe, and when Emma walked into the door, she knew why. He was huge; jolly, kindhearted man who couldn't do enough to help her. Together they walked the showroom, and Joe asked all the pertinent questions.

"Well, beautiful, are you a back sleeper or a side sleeper?" he drawled.

"A side sleeper, sir."

"Oh, honey, don't you 'sir' me. I'm just Joe," he said with such southern charm, Emma couldn't resist him.

After he made Emma lie down on each one to get the feel of them, they picked out the mattress that would best suit her. He said he would have it delivered the next day and the deliveryman would take her old mattress with him.

This simple act of buying a mattress would change Emma's life. In late March of 2007, just a year after moving to Savannah, he walked into her house. Mattress on his back, sweat running down his massive, manly chest, a gorgeous man delivered the bed.

"Good afternoon, ma'am," he drawled and then smiled, showing straight white teeth and dimples in his cheeks.

"Hello. Come on in," Emma invited. Wow! Where did you

come from, was all Emma could think. He had to be six-foot two and what an ass! As Mr. Gorgeous hauled the mattress inside, her fingers ached to run them through his thick, dark hair. His sparkling bottle green eyes had a smile in them and were surrounded by thick dark lashes. Okay, Emma thought as she ushered him into her boudoir, I can deal with this. She couldn't help but watch his broad shoulders as he took the old mattress off and gently set it aside like it weighed nothing.

"My name's Jake," Mr. Gorgeous smiled. "Jake Stanton."

Chapter Two

Mr. Gorgeous, a.k.a. Jake Stanton, entered Emma's life to deliver a mattress. For the first time in a long while, Emma was overwhelmed. She could barely find her tongue to utter a word. As this muscular hunk of a man set up her bed, she finally got her brain to re-engage.

"I'm Emma," she replied. "Do you like music? I just got Monty Python Sings in today's mail and haven't listened to it yet. Do you mind?"

"Oh, my gosh! You're kidding! I love Monty Python. I didn't think anyone else did," Jake answered enthusiastically. "At least not in Savannah."

He went to his truck to get the box spring while he hauled out Emma's old mattress, and Emma put on the CD. There was a speaker in the bedroom, so the entire time Jake was setting up her bed, they listened to Monty Python and laughed. Jake sang along with "Always Look on the Bright Side of Life." They talked about their common interests. Movies—mostly comedies—playing pool, playing Scene-It (a movie trivia game on DVD). They found they had a great deal in common. But Jake left with a smile and a handshake. No "can I call you?" or "let's get together." He just swaggered back to his truck.

Oh, he would call every so often to joke with her. He left a message on her answering machine with a spot-on English accent saying, "Good day, M'Lady. This is Sir Jake. I just wanted to check on you." He was funny and charming that got to Emma. But he never asked her out.

Emma found excuses to see Jake, though. If he wasn't going to pursue her, then she would put herself in his way. He had offered to do any basic chores that she needed, so she paid him to fix this or plant that. He always charged her half the price he was actually at her house because they spent more time laughing and talking than he did working. Emma particularly enjoyed the planting chores. Emma and Jake would drive to Home Depot together and pick out plants. They would stop for lunch (which she paid for) and then came the good part. Watching Jake strip down to his tank top and use all those sinuous muscles to dig the holes for planting the flowers. As he worked, she looked at the colorful gardens Jake was planting. What a view, Emma thought. And the flowers were pretty, too.

In August, Emma flew to Phoenix to see her mother. Jake continued his humorous calls on her cell phone while she was away. Each time, it made her smile. She visualized that perfect body, the little dent in his chin, the sparkling green eyes, and she would smile. She believed he cared about her, and she thought maybe when she got home something would evolve in their relationship. She thought it would only be a temporary romp but definitely fun. Emma never saw any serious potential with Jake. After all, he had a totally unstable job making very little money and didn't have future prospects. She didn't for a moment think of him as a long-term relationship. He was not an avid reader or well educated. But he did make her laugh, and after years with a father who was excessively deep and pensive, laughter was a tremendous relief to Emma.

It wasn't until early November that their relationship changed. Jake turned to Emma in crisis. She knew it was unkind, but she was glad he was turning to her.

"Emma, I'm really sorry to tell you this, but my house burned down, and I have nowhere to turn." It didn't dawn on her that he couldn't own a house on his meager pay and that if he did, he would have insurance. She just bought his story. Yeah, she was naive.

"Well, Jake, you know I have a spare bedroom. Why don't you stay here until you find a place," Emma replied. Although she had ulterior motives, she wanted to help. Okay, she was thinking with her glands. But she also liked the idea of being kind to someone who needed it.

"Oh, I couldn't ask that of you," he said meekly.

"But I have to go to Chicago to see my grandmother for Thanksgiving. She's in the hospital after breaking her hip, so I have to go and take care of some paperwork. And you could take care of my dog for me," she added. "It would be a big help to me, and you could look for a place from here."

"Okay," he conceded. "But it should only be a couple of weeks. Just until I find a place of my own."

"No problem."

And Jake moved into Emma's lavish house. They watched Kevin Smith comedies on her forty-five inch television, played pool, played Scrabble, and Jake cooked dinner. Emma lent Jake five hundred dollars to pay off his storage unit, and he signed an I.O.U. swearing he would pay her back. She was also paying for his gas, car insurance, and all the food he was cooking—and eating. He was a bottomless pit and ate like a twelve-year-old. She never believed she would see cans of Spaghetti-Os in her pantry. Her mother would never have allowed her to eat that kind of junk when she was twelve, let alone at thirty. But she figured she was being supportive and considerate. And it was cheap. Besides, that's what they did in the South. They looked out for one another. And she had plenty of money, so why not help this fantastically gorgeous guy. After all, she hadn't had sex in—how long had it been? Oh, God! Three years! She hoped that having Jake in her house would lead to such activity.

Emma left to go to Chicago after only a few days. It never occurred to her not to trust Jake. He seemed sweet and kind and knew exactly how to treat a lady. And with all the people in town who knew Jake, no one told her anything negative about him. Only that he had a big heart and a kind soul. To Emma he was charming and respectful. She never thought about the simple fact that she was leaving a stranger alone in her house with all her belongings. Because she was honest, she trusted others. Jake's sister, Cheryl Rosenberg, was good friends with Emma's best friend, Kathy Stein. Kathy told her that Cheryl was married to a prominent member of the Jewish community and that Cheryl had converted to Judaism when they got married. Since Jake's sister was technically Jewish, at least he wouldn't be anti-Semitic. Somehow that sated Emma.

While Emma was in Chicago, Jake called three or four times a day to check on Emma, to check on her grandmother, and to update her on home.

"Tasha is fine," Jake would report about Emma's beloved golden retriever. "She's such a sweetie. And I've kept the fountains full and the flowers watered. I just miss you."

And that was how it all started. Emma believed that Jake said what he meant and meant what he said. He misses me, she cooed to herself. That's so sweet. Her cousins in Chicago gave Emma sage advice.

"Jump his bones when you get home," Lucy told her.

"I can't do that!" Emma blushed.

"Sure you can! Just go into his room and jump him! He sounds yummy and you need a good fuck!" her cousin Jean responded with her typically bawdy laughter.

"Amen to that!" Emma admitted.

"Then just do it!" Lucy nudged.

That was all Jake meant to Emma in the beginning—an amazing hunk of a man who might fulfill her physical needs.

Only a couple of days before Emma was preparing to come home from Chicago, she received a phone call from Jake. These constant phone calls were beginning to annoy her. She would be in the middle of a conversation with her family, and her cell phone would ring. She would be standing outside indulging in a cigarette in the freezing temperatures, with snow falling, and her cell phone would ring. The odd part was that he rarely had anything to say. He just sounded lonely. Of course, Emma interpreted that to mean he missed her, specifically. She didn't read any more into these calls. This particular call was a rather strange one.

"Hi, Emma," Jake started, "how are things going there?"

"Fine. I should be able to leave on Saturday. I've been going nuts trying to get everything organized with the nursing home, going through Grandma's stuff at the apartment, and getting all the financial information to my mom. I'm ready to pull my hair out!"

"Don't do that," he calmly replied. "It's such beautiful hair. If there's anything I can do to help, just let me know."

"Right now, just be there when I get home," Emma sighed.

"You don't have to worry about that. Umm. I have a favor to ask," Jake stuttered.

"What is it?" Emma asked.

"Well, my cousin and his girlfriend are going to be in town for the night. They came from California and they have no place to stay. Do you mind if they stay here?"

"Absolutely not!" Emma demanded. "No one in my house except you."

"I understand totally," Jake answered. "I'll tell them no."

"Thanks, Jake. I'm really sorry, but I don't know them from Adam and don't want strangers in my house while I'm gone," she reiterated. "I'll talk to you later and I'll let you know when I'm leaving." But wasn't Jake just that—a stranger—she thought. Yet for some reason, she trusted him.

"Okay, darlin'. Just be careful," Jake said pleasantly.

Two days later, Emma was finally able to leave the cold of Chicago and drive home. It was the Saturday after Thanksgiving, the end of November. She was ready to be home. She'd had a week of arguments with family, cleaning out her grandmother's apartment, digging through paperwork to find important tax and income information for her mother, and visiting assisted-living facilities that might accept her grandmother. Due to her broken hip, her independent grandmother would never be able to live alone again. Since Emma's mother was in Los Angeles and led a busy life and Emma was an only child, all the responsibility fell on her shoulders.

During the drive home, her cell phone rang constantly. She was sick of having her Bluetooth attached to her ear, sick of all the fighting with family members, and hoped she'd done all that was required of her. Had she sent her mother everything she needed? Had she been supportive enough to her grandmother? Had she been strong enough? Her ears were ringing, especially with the last question of herself. Her mother, Rose, had harped on her forever about how Emma needed to "grow a set of balls."

"Stand up for yourself," Rose would preach time after time, year after year. "Don't let people walk all over you. I know, honey, you're Pollyanna incarnate. But you just can't live your life like that."

"Mom, I like who I am. I like the fact that I see the world as a beautiful place and see the best in people," Emma would defend herself. "I don't ever want to be bitter," like you, she almost added but resisted. After all, it was her mother she had the most difficult time standing up to. Frankly, she was scared to death of her mother. Rose had always been hardened to the world, and she never stopped lecturing Emma about her innate softness.

After stopping for the night, at a random halfway point between Chicago and Savannah, Emma had to check in with everyone before eating dinner or unpacking. She had to call her mother, her grandmother, Jake, and her two cousins in Chicago. When the "I'm at a motel somewhere in Tennessee and I'm fine" calls were over, Emma unpacked for the night, ate dinner, and unwound for a little while in a hot tub and then wrote in her journal. For Emma, that was relaxation. She went to sleep early so she could get an early start. After driving through Atlanta to get to I-16 to Savannah, she called Jake to update him on her progress.

"I'll be waiting for you!" he said happily. "Call me when

you get through Macon."

Emma finally arrived at home—and what a word. Home! She pulled into the driveway instead of the garage, where Jake's truck had been parked. She was amazed and delighted when she saw Jake sitting at the black wrought iron table in the courtyard waiting for her. He rushed to get all her luggage from the car and carried it all into her bedroom. He had let her dog, Tasha, into the courtyard with him. Emma ruffled her fur and hugged her, all the while Tasha's tail was wagging like mad and she was licking Emma. "I love you, too fur face," Emma crooned.

"God, I missed you," Jake grabbed Emma into a hug. Hmm. That was the closest he'd been to her. Maybe she wouldn't have to jump his bones after all. Maybe he'd—and her thoughts stopped as his mouth devoured hers. There was a humming in her head as she stood on tiptoe to reach his luscious mouth.

"I missed you, too," Emma managed.

"You, um, must want to unpack and settle in," he stammered.

"No, this is a much better housewarming."

Chapter Three

Jake carried Emma to her bed and gently laid her down on her side of the bed. He pulled the comforter down and started tossing pillows off the bed. He took her mouth slowly and patiently. His patience left him at that point. He began pulling off her pants and then her sweater. He muddled through and then got to work. She was so excited just looking at him, she nearly had an orgasm. Caressing his broad shoulders and strong chest, finally running her fingers through that curly brown hair, and looking deeply into those green eyes, Emma was already hot. He was gentle and caring. A bit shy, she noticed but all in all, worth the three-year wait. She couldn't fathom why he would be self-conscious. He kissed like an angel and knew exactly how to pleasure Emma. As for Emma, it felt so marvelous to have a man inside her again, especially such a fine one, she overlooked his insecurities.

Emma didn't want to make his oddities into a big deal. After all, it was their first time together. But he was as quirky in bed as he was out. He immediately jumped out of bed when they were finished and went into the bathroom to clean up. No pillow talk, no snuggling, nothing. Just into the bathroom. He's just being considerate, she thought. He doesn't want me to sleep in a wet spot. That's all. But even after the bathroom break, he started getting dressed. Emma was concerned.

"Is everything all right?" she finally asked.

"It's great," Jake said and kissed her. "I was just, I guess, I was nervous. Was it okay for you?"

"Absolutely!" Emma tried to boost his ego. "I wasn't sure we would ever do that."

"I just don't deserve you," Jake confided. "You're so beautiful, and classy, and smart and I'm a nothing. I've wanted you since the first time I saw you, but I just never thought you'd actually go out with me."

"Why wouldn't I? You're gorgeous, intelligent, and funny. You have everything going for you. You'll find your niche in life," Emma encouraged.

"Thanks. So what would you like for dinner?" Jake changed the subject and walked into the kitchen. "Why don't you go and unpack and I'll make spaghetti with sausage for dinner."

"Sounds great, Jake. Thanks." Emma had to make her own salad because Jake wouldn't eat salad. Since he was in kindergarten and ate a salad he didn't like, he hadn't eaten a piece of lettuce. His eating habits were strange for a thirty-year-old man. Spaghetti-Os, hot dogs, and pizza were his staples. He used no condiments for his hot dogs or hamburgers. No mustard, no ketchup, no nothing….other than hot sauce. Jake could find a way to put hot sauce on just about anything. And he was as addicted to food as he had admitted he had once been to cocaine. He just couldn't stop. He inhaled his food as though someone was going to take away his plate before he was finished. Then he burped energetically again and again when he was finally done eating. This symphony could go on for hours.

They had dinner together and watched television. Of course, even as large as Jake's first plate of spaghetti had been, he was compelled to take seconds and thirds. Then they played Scene

It. They laughed and played. Emma went to take her evening bath, putting on nice lingerie and softening her skin with body lotion. When she came out of the bathroom, Jake was still in the great room watching television. She opened her satin bathrobe a bit to reveal the black teddy underneath. He just said good night and turned off the television. Jake slept in the guest bedroom, and they didn't make love again that night. Emma was shattered and confused. Why would he do that? Forget it, she thought. I'm not going to torment myself. So she went into the guest room and asked him.

"What's wrong?" Emma urged.

"Nothing, why?"

"Well, you're sleeping in here and I'm sleeping alone. And we're not making love. Why is that?" she reluctantly asked.

"Oh, baby, nobody can sleep with me. I toss and turn, I talk and yell, and I've actually hit somebody accidentally."

"Well, I'd like to try. And I hoped we would have sex again."

"I'm not a machine, honey. I ate too much and I feel bloated and full," he explained. "I'll do better tomorrow. I promise. I won't eat so much, and we'll try sleeping together," he said with finality.

"Okay, sure," Emma said, already feeling the tears welling up in her eyes. She took off the sexy teddy she had worn for him and put on flannel jammies. She quietly wept into her pillow.

Days went on and Jake never found a place to live or a better job. He was out a great deal of the day, telling Emma he was doing bed deliveries and looking for a better job. When he came home, he was just happy to be home with Emma. But he kept to a strict schedule of lovemaking. Ten o'clock at night was his time. They slept together and Jake moved his clothes into her closet. She emptied two drawers in her dresser for him. They were really together but he was right. He was a restless sleeper. He sometimes yelled in his sleep, he talked in his sleep, and he kicked or elbowed her more than a few times. He also snored incessantly. She solved some of the problem with two arthritis-strength Tylenols and an antihistamine. That helped, although there was still the occasional screaming in the middle of the night, which scared the hell out of Emma.

But they had fun. They were getting to be able to read each other's thoughts, and the longer they were together, the more they had in common. They enjoyed or disliked the same movies, and they could finish each other's sentences. They both related to life in terms of movie lines, and since they enjoyed the same movies, they always got the connection.

Emma's best friend, Kathy, finally met Jake. Kathy had converted to Judaism when she was eighteen for no reason other than it just felt right. She had been born in Alabama and loved to refer to herself as trailer trash. She claimed she went into her Baptist church and just didn't feel she belonged. But someone took her into a Jewish synagogue, and it just clicked. She quickly converted and was a more devout Jew than Emma had ever been. Kathy had two small children who were attending the local Jewish private school, which was how Kathy knew Cheryl, Jake's sister. Her children were in the same classes with Cheryl's. Kathy's soon-to-be ex-husband was a prominent doctor, and when she left him, she bought a house that was only eight blocks away from Emma. Kathy came over one sunny afternoon in early December to meet "Mr. Gorgeous." Jake gave her a big hug and told her how happy he was to meet her.

"Oh my God!" Kathy mouthed when Jake's back was turned. Jake went into the kitchen to fetch some sweet tea for Kathy. Emma had learned to love the Southern delicacy of iced tea that was three-quarters sugar and one-quarter tea. While Jake was in the kitchen, Kathy giggled and looked at Emma.

"Wow, Em! Definitely fuckable!" she laughed quietly.

"Yeah, isn't he just! And he's damned good at it!"

"I'm so happy for you!" Kathy flung her arms around Emma in a warm embrace. "I love you, sweetie, and I'm just so glad you found someone. Jake's great!"

"I didn't find him, though. He found me," Emma laughed. "I was just minding my own business, and he delivered my bed. From the mattress store you recommended! So thanks for that!"

The next time Kathy came over, she brought her children, and Jake was in heaven. He played with them and tickled them. He adored her little girl, who was five. But he roughhoused with her little boy, who was three. Since both children were in the same classes with his own niece and nephew, once Kathy's kids knew Aunt Emma and Uncle Jake, the word spread through the Jewish community about the couple.

Emma made a Chanukah dinner for Kathy and her kids. Jake loved it; the tradition, the lighting of the candles, and the latkes. Emma even made sure to buy a kosher chicken and bake it in tin foil, since she knew Kathy tried to keep kosher. Jake started to put butter on the chicken, and Emma caught him just in time.

"No!" she yelled. "You can't mix milk and meat."

Kathy went to the Conservative synagogue, but she still kept kosher. It was a bit of a challenge for Emma, but dinner worked out great. They exchanged gifts, mostly for the kids, and sat by the fire in the formal living room. Emma had forgone the Christmas tree her second year in Savannah because she learned the hard way that she was allergic to pine. Her Orthodox neighbors, of course, believed it was fate. "See, God will get you for being Jewish and having a Christmas tree!" they all taunted her. But Jake fit right in—with the children, with the Jewish traditions, with Emma's world. He even decided to convert. His sister had been nagging him to convert for years, but now that he had met Emma, she was more insistent.

Just after the Chanukah dinner on December fifteenth, Jake came home and nervously asked Emma to go out for a fancy dinner together, on him. He had just been paid for a delivery and wanted to take her to dinner. Emma was a bit apprehensive, so she picked a restaurant that was her favorite but wasn't too expensive. She dressed up to match Jake's suit, and together they drove in her SUV the few blocks from her house to Toucan Café. Since she had frequented the restaurant, the manager gave her a hug and kiss when she came in. Emma introduced the manager to Jake. They were seated at a quiet corner table. Jake ordered two glasses of wine and quickly took a big gulp of his own. He seemed uneasy. Actually, he was shaking.

"What's this all about?" Emma asked innocently.

"Well," Jake said with a definite quiver to his voice. "I have something in my pocket."

Oh, God, was all Emma could think. He couldn't be. He wouldn't be. We've only really been together for a month. And before she could get her thoughts together, he produced the little jewelry box.

"I love you, Emma. Will you marry me?" he asked.

Now, in this situation, many women would fling their arms around the man's neck and weep with joy. Emma just put her fork down and thought—huh? This was supposed to be a fling. He'd get a place to live and a better job and move on. This was definitely not supposed to get serious. And there were problems. She couldn't put her finger on them, but they were there. She knew his overprotective mother had coddled him and he could get away with murder with her. She knew he had once had a drug problem, but he had been clean for months. She knew his father had died when he was little and he was the one who found his father lying on the floor. As she was lost in thought about his issues, Jake was waiting.

"Umm. Is that a yes?" he asked hopefully. She looked at the platinum and diamond ring and was swept away by the moment. "I had hoped it would be an easier answer," he added.

"Yes, Jake," she answered hesitantly, and he leaned over to her and kissed her. The waiter watched the event, as did the manager. They both came over and congratulated the happy couple.

"Jake," Emma asked when they were alone again, "how did you afford the ring?"

"Well, I paid part of it myself from tips, and the rest I put on your credit card," he confessed. "When I was gone all day and you gave me your card to get gas for my truck, that's where I was."

"Uh huh," Emma tried to smile. "Well, I guess that's okay." Was it? Emma was in such shock, she couldn't think.

"I bought it at a pawnshop, so it wasn't too expensive, but it is platinum and it's a carat and a half of diamonds."

They finished their dinners, though Emma could barely eat, and they went home to make passionate love. It was their best sex yet. Maybe the glass of wine loosened him up, she thought. But they definitely celebrated.

The following day, Emma e-mailed everyone and called everyone to announce she was engaged. Kathy came running over to see the ring. She beamed with happiness for her friend and jealousy for her choice.

"I want to do the bridal shower," Kathy exclaimed. "It will be fabulous! Just get me the list of who you want to come and I'll take care of the rest!"

"Thanks, Kat. You're the best! We aren't planning on the wedding until next spring," she added. "Oh, God, I wonder if Jake has called Cheryl yet? He probably has. I know his mom will be thrilled. She's already said I'm the best thing that's ever happened to Jake. Mrs. Stanton spoiled him rotten, but she's an amazing person," Emma babbled giddily to Kathy. All of her logic and intelligence went out the window every time she even thought about Jake.

Emma had already planned her first Christmas party with Jake for the eighteenth of December. It had turned into a combination Christmas/Engagement party, and for the first time in her life, Emma threw a party in her own home with a handsome man at her side all the time. Emma prepared an enormous spread of food from traditional Savannah peel-n-eat shrimp, which was pretty much against Southern law to omit from any major gathering, to meatballs in a beef stroganoff gravy, to a whole ham. She designed cream puffs to be pulled off of tree-shaped cones, just like they had in Victorian times. There were various dips and cheeses placed strategically throughout the house and outside. Emma found a fabulous recipe for what was called "witch's brew," a concoction of rum, orange juice, and spices, including ginger and cinnamon. She used her large punch bowl, and all two gallons were gone by the end of the night.

All of her friends happily attended. The author Rosemary Daniell, Kathy and her new boyfriend, Jo and her husband and their friends, Emma's amazingly kind next-door neighbors Mark and Sheila, Dana, Ray and his wife Sam, and Jenny and Mac. Ray and Sam were always among the first to arrive and help Emma set out dishes or clean up afterward or pick up ice on the way. Dana brought a friend of hers, a computer expert named Steve, who was gay. Emma and Steve clicked immediately and they would become close friends. Cheryl showed up briefly, dressed to the tens, but her husband called every five minutes, so she didn't even have time to eat. Even Emma's hairdresser, Reid, showed up with his significant other. Reid was tongue-tied when he met Jake. He had remembered a time when he tried to seduce Jake many years ago. When they met at the party, they both realized this was not the first time. Jake had only been fifteen years old when they first met, but the recognition was there. Reid wandered around muttering to himself the whole evening.

"Fifteen years old! Oh my God, fifteen years old!" Every

time Emma would see him that night, those were the only three words that came out of his mouth. He just couldn't believe he had tried to seduce a fifteen-year-old child.

The party was a tremendous success for Emma. All her friends had finally met the beautiful and sweet Jake Stanton and congratulated Emma on becoming Mrs. Stanton the following spring. They asked about the wedding, and Emma and Jake would stand arm in arm discussing the possibilities.

"I'd really like the whole Savannah deal," Emma said. "A horse-drawn carriage to the gazebo in Whitfield Square would be perfect for the ceremony. I think that would be so romantic."

"Then we could just have the reception here," Jake kissed Emma.

"That would be perfect. Not too big and just personal enough," Emma agreed.

Emma showed off her engagement ring and gave out small gifts to her closest girlfriends for Christmas. Everyone had a great time, and on these occasions Emma was so glad she chose her house. There was plenty of room for everyone, she had fires blazing in both fireplaces, and her fairy lights on the patio were a festive place for smokers to congregate comfortably. Her guests stayed late listening to the Christmas music and jazz on the stereo throughout the house and outside, played pool, and nibbled on food wherever they stood. Emma's witch's brew was a big hit, but she also had beer, wine, and soft drinks for those who wanted something else. Life couldn't get any better than this, Emma thought.

Emma and Jake spent Christmas Eve with Jenny and Mac

and their family on Wilmington Island. Their house was right on the marsh, so the children played outside and fed the ducks that waddled right up from the water onto their large backyard. Jake and Mac had become quick friends; being Southern boys they could laugh themselves silly farting at each other while they were outside sneaking cigarettes. Emma and Jenny talked in the kitchen while Emma helped get food on the table. Jenny looked picture-perfect with her long, platinum hair flowing over her Christmas red jumpsuit, which accentuated her voluptuous curves. Her lips, fingernails, and toenails matched her jumpsuit—all in Christmas red. Her bright, Caribbean green eyes seemed to be chosen to match her Christmas colors.

Jenny's idea of hors d'oeuvres was Ritz crackers with cheese whiz and salami but who cared. Jenny was a Southern belle from her drawl to her food. Her side dishes for her ham were mac and cheese, broccoli and cheese casserole, and of course, fresh biscuits. Mac made his famous banana pudding—another Southern delicacy—and there was apple pie. It was a night of family and friends that Emma enjoyed.

Jake and Jenny seemed to get along fine, hugging each other and wishing each other a Merry Christmas. The more of her friends who befriended Jake, the better Emma felt about her life.

They spent part of Christmas Day with Jake's mother. They didn't exchange Christmas presents because Jake's mother had no money. Emma bought some slipper socks and foot cream for Jake's mother from both of them. Marjorie Stanton was in a nursing home, after suffering three strokes at only seventy-two years old. Jake would give her foot massages and polish her toenails for her. But Marjorie, for all her pain and anguish over the loss of use of her legs and right side, and her speech impairment, always had a smile on her face. She was happy to see her baby boy and was thrilled with the engagement ring and the news. She was sharp and kind. And she was another person who thought Emma was the best thing that could happen to Jake.

Emma didn't quite understand why everyone who knew Jake felt he was so lucky to have found her. He seemed to have so much going for himself and he had overcome drug abuse. He had run a lucrative restaurant with his mother for ten years, but they had just recently closed it. Emma got conflicting stories as to why it closed, depending upon who told the story. Jake said his sister ran it into the ground because he had burned out. His sister said it had been Jake's drug use that destroyed the restaurant and his embezzlement of thousands of dollars. His mother said it was just finances and legalities that closed the restaurant. Emma figured it was Rashamon. Each person's story held some truth to it.

Chapter Four

Emma's mother asked her to go back to Chicago to find some more papers she needed in order to get her grandmother situated when she got out of the hospital. Emma decided that since they could stay at her grandmother's apartment, that Jake should join her to meet her family. They could take Tasha with them, and with Jake sharing the drive, they could make it in one day. So on December 26 they drove to Chicago together. It was the first time Jake had really been in the snow, so Emma had to buy him a winter coat and gloves and a hat. They went to a thrift store to buy some sweaters.

When they arrived in Chicago, they immediately went to her grandmother's apartment (Emma had kept the spare keys from her first trip), and they unloaded the car, walked the dog, and left Tasha in the apartment. They went immediately to the hospital to see Emma's grandmother.

Emma's grandmother had always been sexy and voluptuous. Emma's cousin, Jean, had told Emma stories about phone calls from her grandmother about her boyfriend and how they were having sex four times a day at eighty-five years old. Emma and her younger cousin Jody had often joked that their grandmother was getting more action than the two of them combined. Emma had been twenty-three and Jody only twenty. They both knew from whom they got their sex drive. Now Emma looked at her grandma and saw a tiny, frail woman of ninety.

"Hi, Grandma," Emma entered the room and kissed her on

the cheek. "How are you feeling?"

"Oh..." (There was always an audible pause after she said 'oh'). "I'm all right. And this handsome young man must be Jake," she said as she looked past Emma.

"Jake, this is my grandmother, Francis Kay."

"It's a pleasure, ma'am," he drawled politely, as was his custom.

"Isn't he just handsome," her grandmother flirted. She just couldn't help it. It had been her way for too many years to flirt. She had outlived two husbands, Emma's grandfather and then her "Papa," Grandpa Kay. There hadn't been a time in her life when Emma's grandmother didn't have a handsome man on her arm. "Oh, the nurses will go crazy for him," she crooned.

"Yeah, but he's mine," Emma laughed.

After a lengthy visit, during which time Jake left the room a half-dozen times to go out for a cigarette or just wander around, they left the hospital to have dinner with Emma's two favorite cousins. They both hugged Jake and welcomed him to the family. Jean especially mouthed the "Oh My God!" behind his back. Jean was thirty-eight and had already been married twice, both times to younger men and also both times to pretty boys. But now, for the first time that Emma could recall, Jean actually had a boyfriend who was older than she was. However, he had a bad back, so sex together was—shall we say—infrequent. As soon as Jake went outside for a minute for that much-needed smoke, Jean started.

"Oh, Em! He's gorgeous! Those dimples when he smiles! And what a great ass!" she rasped through a voice that was strained from so much use. Jean was known in the family (and probably everyone else, too) as the type of person who, if a thought went into her head it came out her mouth. Actually, thoughts probably didn't get sifted through her head until two days after they came out of her mouth. But Emma loved Jean tremendously, in part because of that honesty.

"Yeah, and he's great in bed!" Emma teased.

"Oh, sure...go ahead and brag!" Jean laughed raucously.

"He seems to really love you," Lucy added. "I just care that he doesn't hurt you and that he treats you right. He said he had a drug problem. Are you sure he's clean?" Lucy questioned.

"Oh, yeah. He assures me it's been months since he used," Emma confirmed.

"Well, just be careful," Lucy warned. "He had two beers with dinner. Is he also an alcoholic?"

"No. He won't have any more and doesn't need any more," Emma defended.

"Oh, Lucy," Jean prodded, "leave her alone. She's happy and he seems like a great guy."

"Oh, don't get me wrong, Emma. I think Jake is a great guy, too. I really like him. I'm just worried about you. I love you, Em. I mean, does he have a job? Is he helping out at all with the finances?" Lucy asked.

"Not yet but he will," Emma was still on the defensive. "He said he would love me if I didn't have a dime."

"I think he would," Jean agreed. "I think he really loves you."

And that was the consensus of most of her family, including her grandmother. He exuded tremendous Southern charm, he was handsome, and he treated Emma with respect and love. Emma was pleased because the Jewish family grapevine was about as short as the Savannah southern grapevine. News would get back to her mother that Jake was accepted.

During their trip, however, Jake drank at every meal with her family. He hadn't been drinking at home, except for the one glass of wine when he proposed to Emma. That concerned her. She gently urged him not to drink, but he assured her it was fine. Even when they went out with Lucy to her favorite bar and he had two cosmopolitans, he reassured her. Finally, Emma just decided to go along, and she had two cosmopolitans herself. Of course, since she rarely drank, she got silly drunk. But after the silliness came great sex when they returned to her grandmother's apartment. As far as Emma was concerned, that was just fine.

Their trip was successful. They worked together cleaning out her grandmother's apartment. Her family adored Jake, and that was a relief to Emma.

Once they returned home, Emma and Jake's relationship didn't remain in a blissful state for long. Jake had become wary of a big wedding in Whitfield Square and wanted to get married at Emma's house, which disappointed her. Since Jake had decided to convert to Judaism, they both agreed to have her massage therapist, who was really an Orthodox rabbi, to officiate. Ephraim Cohn was the sweetest man they both knew. He lived across the street from Emma, so he just wheeled the massage table over to give her a weekly massage. Ephraim was small in stature, but his kindness, intelligence, and depth of spirit made him larger than life. His curly red hair and freckles didn't seem to fit the yarmulke-wearing rabbi. He looked more like a Christmas elf. But his children were friends with Jake's niece and nephew, and he was beloved in the community. To their great dismay, Ephraim couldn't perform the ceremony. Not because he was Orthodox and Jake would be a Reform convert but because he still had Canadian citizenship. They were both crushed when they learned this news.

Not long after Christmas, Emma decided to pay off Jake's truck. Her decision seemed clear until she went to the sleazy car lot where he had purchased the truck with no money down. She had been making the payments on the piece of junk truck, so she thought it was the financially intelligent decision to pay it off. They had done a search online for its value, and according to Kelly Bluebook, its value was higher than the payoff amount. The moment they arrived at the lot and she realized what she doing, she regretted her decision. She knew it was foolish, but it was forty-two hundred dollars and at the rate she was making payments, it would have cost her ten thousand dollars to pay off the piece of junk. The truck was supposedly worth five thousand dollars, so it made some amount of sense. But Jake was certainly not bringing any money into the house, and in the heat of the moment, it seemed logical. She would own the truck, so at least she could sell it to recoup her losses if need be. Even Jake begged her not to do, it but it was her money and she did it.

A week later, Emma went into her closet as she did every day, but this time she was looking for a purse. She wasn't looking for any particular purse for any particular reason; she just slid one of the bamboo boxes in which she stored her designer purses in their protective bags off the shelf. The box felt light. Her pink leather Prada was missing. Then she started going through all of her storage boxes. Three of the six Prada purses were gone, but only the two pink ones and a white one. Four of the Louis Vuitton purses were gone. One of the two Prada totes was gone, as well all the Louis accessories. Then she looked through her jewelry drawers in her vanity. At least half of her jewelry was gone. It was as though someone had gone shopping in her bedroom. Gee, I like this one. I don't like that one. I like this ring, not that one. She immediately turned to Jake.

"What the hell happened in here?" she demanded.

"What do you mean?" He sounded so innocent and ran into the walk-in closet.

"I've been robbed!" she shouted. "Someone went into my bedroom and took a ton of stuff," she whimpered.

"Let me see," he said angrily.

"The pink Prada purses are both gone. And my favorite Louis Vuitton purse is gone. You want to know more?" she yelled.

"You don't think I had anything to do with this, do you?" he answered indignantly.

"Well, who else? You're the only one with access to my house."

"Emma, honey, I wouldn't know a Prada from a—I don't know what. Coach? Is Prada more expensive than Coach? And I don't know what a Louis Vuitton even looks like!"

"Yes, Jake. It's about a thousand dollars difference in price. This," Emma shoved a purse into him, "is a Louis Vuitton. See the LVs all over it?"

"Okay but why would I take it?" Jake sounded genuinely baffled.

"I don't know. To pawn," she yelled at him. "What about the jewelry? You could have taken them piece by piece while I was out of town and pawned them individually, hoping I wouldn't notice. Have you been using drugs again? Please, tell me the truth," she demanded.

"Emma, no, I haven't. I didn't do this. You know who probably did? My cousin! When he and his girlfriend came from California. I know you said they couldn't spend the night, but they were here for a while. Then I passed out on the sofa. And when I woke up, they were both gone. It was like two in the morning. Maybe his girlfriend did it."

"I told you not to let anyone into my house!" Emma replied with total frustration.

"I know and I'm really sorry. I just wasn't thinking…" he started.

"What's new?" Emma muttered.

"I know I shouldn't have let them in, but I just thought they'd stay a little while and would leave early," his eyes shifted, and if Emma had understood anything about lying, she would have seen it in his body language. But being naive, Emma believed him.

"Well, then give me their names so I can call the police," Emma demanded.

"I can't do that. They're family," he replied sheepishly.

"Okay, now I know where your loyalties really lie!"

"I love you, Emma. Don't think that. It's just, my cousin has a police record, and they would put him away. Besides, I don't even know his girlfriend's name, and she's the one who probably did it."

"Fine. Whatever. I'm calling my insurance agent, and I'll

call the police and explain what happened. That we don't know her name." Emma felt betrayed and angry. She called the police first and filed a report. Then she called her insurance agent, a man who was kind and had a generous and humorous nature.

"Hi, Paul, It's Emma Weiss," she tried to sound cheerful. "How are you?"

"I'm just fine, Emma. Everything all right with you?" Paul asked, knowing that people didn't often call their insurance agent for kicks and giggles. But he was always friendly and never sounded bothered, even if his true feelings must have "oh shit, what now" when a client called.

"Paul, I was burgled," Emma said plainly. And she explained the bizarre circumstances of the theft. "It was like someone went shopping in my closet," she explained. "No. No windows were broken. There was no forced entry, according to the police. Yes, I'll fax the police report over to you," she answered his questions.

"Well, Emma, we'll take care of the purses and all, but you'll have to go through your jewelry policy for that part. You have your jewelry scheduled, remember? Y'all will have to work that part out separately."

"Okay, Paul. I'll go through everything and compare what's here with the pictures and hope I can remember what I had and what was stolen. Thanks. How long will it take on your end?"

"Oh, as soon as we get a list and the prices and then verify them, it shouldn't take but three weeks altogether."

"Well, you've got pictures of everything on file and their prices. I'll do the rest," Emma sighed.

And it all got done. There were some difficulties. The Louis Vuitton purse wasn't made anymore, since they sometimes only make a given style for one season. The same with the Prada purses. Emma had taken pictures of everything she owned and copied it all to her agent, so that helped her job. But she still spent hours online, getting newest prices on all of the valuables that had been stolen. Some were irreplaceable; family heirlooms that had no monetary value high enough to compensate Emma for their loss. It felt like what she had heard about robberies—a type of rape. Especially this one. This wasn't a professional burglary. This was an individual pawing through her most personal possessions. Emma had one sigh of relief. She wore a size five shoe. Thank God, she thought, this female burglar didn't touch her shoes. She would have killed someone if her Chanel boots were gone.

The total amount of the theft was over sixteen thousand dollars, and Emma recouped all of it. She went to Atlanta to Neiman Marcus to replace the Louis Vuitton purse and accessories and took Jake with her. He helped her pick it all out. Of course, he also tried to finagle something for himself, to which Emma just laughed and said, "fat chance." She had to replace the jewelry, as opposed to receiving a check for the amount of the loss. So Emma spent two hours shopping at Levy Jeweler's in downtown Savannah with six thousand dollars of credit. Jake helped her pick out pieces that he thought would look good on her. She especially liked the John Hardy bracelet he chose. Emma might not have picked it, but once it was on her slender wrist, he was right. Again, he tried to finagle something for himself. This time it was a watch. She relented. There was a watch that was only one hundred fifty dollars that

Jake liked. She figured if he had a watch, he might actually come home on time. Of the six thousand dollars, Jake got one hundred and fifty for a watch.

Emma was still unsure as to Jake's part in the theft. But it did look like a female had committed the robbery. The choices were too feminine. But it would always prey on her mind. Did he have something to do with it? Eventually, she would find out. But in the meantime, she put all her valuable jewelry either in her safe at home (changing the combination to a number he would never know) or in her safe-deposit box at the bank.

Chapter Five

Life with Jake was turning from bliss to drama. Emma told her friends about the robbery, and most were understanding, but the skepticism in their voices was clear. Emma had become friends with Jake's sister, Cheryl. Cheryl looked nothing like Jake, though that was probably because they had different fathers. Jake looked exactly like his father, and Cheryl looked like their mother. She was five foot ten and slender, even after having two children. Cheryl was ten years older than Jake, but she had been a model and was still gorgeous. She had her mother's big, expressive blue eyes and perfectly coifed hair. After being a model, Cheryl had become a hair stylist, so her hair was always cut perfectly and she liked to change it. She had gone from blonde to dark brown to medium brown. Emma had seen many incarnations of Cheryl's hair, both in life and in photos. But regardless of the color or style of her hair, Cheryl was still a strikingly beautiful woman.

One day, while Jake was making a delivery, Cheryl called Emma.

"He's using again," Cheryl told Emma after the preliminary courtesies.

"Using?" Emma asked naively.

"Drugs," Cheryl answered curtly.

But when?" Emma said incredulously. "He's with me most of the time or he's delivering mattresses for Joe."

"Emma, I know my brother. He's using again. He came to

me for money."

"Oh my God! I had no idea. What are the symptoms? I mean, I've never used cocaine, so I don't even know what it's like," Emma pleaded. "I've never known an addict before."

"Does he make up absurd stories about where he's been? That's the first sign. He's a terrible liar, and he has to cover up what he's done." Emma thought about this.

"Since we've been back from Chicago, he came home really late one night and said he had to walk eight miles because his truck broke down. It sounded pretty silly at the time."

"Yep, that's Jake. He gave his truck to a drug dealer to use for the night. He's done that to Mama before. The drug dealer had it for two days before Jake got it back from him. It was dented and the mirrors were broken when she finally got it back."

"Between you and me, Cheryl, that's my truck. I paid it off because I was sick of making the payments on it. Stupid me! Okay, what else? What else should I look for?" Emma asked with growing frustration.

"Well, he won't eat after he's used. That should be pretty obvious since he's such a pig most of the time. And he'll be achy and tired for the next couple days. He'll probably sleep a lot. He'll be too out of it to have sex," she added. "Also, check your liquor cabinet. He needs alcohol to come down from the cocaine." Cheryl explained.

"Shit, shit, shit!" was all Emma could say and, with the cordless phone to her ear, walked over to the wet bar. "I'll check. Damn, Cheryl. He drank my whole bottle of Grand Marnier! And my single-malt scotch is gone!" she told Cheryl as she looked at her bar. "I'm going to kill him!"

"Emma," Cheryl tried to calm her down, "he really loves you. He tells me everything, and I know he truly cares about you. I talked to Joe and we've both told Jake not to fuck things up with you like he has with everyone else."

"Well, he has!" Emma raised her always soft voice. Emma didn't have a temper. It took a great deal to set her off, and even then, she usually walked away from confrontation. But this was too much.

After she hung up the phone with Cheryl, Emma took a quick inventory of her house. For the first time, she checked her wallet. Forty dollars was missing. She checked her bar. She had bought a twenty-four pack of beer and left it in the mini-refrigerator in the wet bar for friends and her own occasional consumption. There was one left. She had special-ordered two bottles of expensive Jewel of Russia cranberry-infused vodka that couldn't even be purchased locally. But as little as she herself drank, they would last so long, it was worth it to her. It made perfect cosmopolitans. The open bottle was empty, save an inch. Luckily, she had hidden the second bottle.

She immediately called Joe at the mattress store. She needed some honesty.

"Hi, Joe, it's Emma," she started.

"Hey, darlin'. How are you doin'?" he asked.

"Is Jake really on a delivery?" she asked bluntly.

"Yes. But that was this morning. He delivered a queen, which should have taken him an hour plus the drive time to Wilmington Island. He should have been back by one or two o'clock."

"Was he paid in cash?" Emma asked.

"Well, he usually gets tips on top of the paycheck from me at the end of the week."

"Joe, Cheryl thinks he's using again," she told him. Joe was a father figure to Jake, and he needed to know.

"Shit. He loves you and I know he doesn't want to lose you. He can't stop talking about you," he said. "He's told me how sexy you are and how perfect your breasts are."

"Oh, jeez! Okay, that's enough."

"Yeah, well. He's told me everything."

"Obviously!" Emma laughed.

"Well, sweetie, good luck. He'll straighten out. He's got a big heart and he's a good boy. He wants to do right. And I think you're just the girl to make that happen." Joe ended the call. Those were the most destructive words he could have said to Emma. With Emma's savior complex, those words hooked her even deeper.

It was six o'clock by the time Jake came home. He looked guilty and tired.

"Where the fuck have you been?" Emma demanded. She couldn't believe how often and to what degree she cursed at Jake. No one had been able to elicit that degree of temper from Emma. No one. Ever.

"I was delivering a mattress. What do you think?" he retorted.

"Bullshit! I just talked to Joe. You were finished four hours ago! Where have you been? And where's your truck?"

"It, um, broke down and I had to walk two miles! I'm exhausted and filthy. I need a shower," he demanded and tried to sneak off to the bathroom.

"Get in my car," Emma yelled. "We're going to see your dealer and get my truck back. Then we'll talk."

"What are you talking about?"

"I know your game, honey. You gave my truck to your drug dealer to use. Well, we're going to get it back right now."

"Okay, you're right. I fucked up. I'm really sorry. I swear it won't happen again but don't do this. These are bad people."

"I don't care! Get your lying ass in my car! I found out about the money you stole and all the booze you drank. I don't give a shit about the drug dealer. We're getting the truck!" Emma unlocked her Lexus and waited for Jake to get in. She threw the SUV in reverse, and the wheels screeched. "Where are we going?"

"Honey, calm down," Jake tried to get Emma to at least drive safely. He gave her directions, and she was flooring the gas all the way there. "Please, Emma honey, you're going to get a ticket or kill us," he pleaded.

"Fuck you!" she replied indignantly. In her entire life, Emma had never said that to another human being. Sure, she would use the word occasionally, but never directed at someone. She was actually shocked to hear it come out of her mouth. Jake, too, got very quiet. He spoke only to give directions. He hadn't seen this side of Emma, and he was scared. Whether he was just afraid he would lose his meal ticket, lose his home, or lose Emma, she wasn't sure. But he was scared. When they arrived at the house, he pointed. There was no truck there.

"Call him," she demanded. "Tell him to get his ass home now."

"I'm telling you, honey, I can't intimidate these guys…" he trailed off, seeing the fury on her face.

"Just call." He called and reported to Emma that he would be back in twenty minutes.

"We'll wait," she said firmly.

"But..." He couldn't get the rest of the sentence out.

"Listen to me, Jake. You're going to get my truck back, and then you're going to pack your shit and get out of my house."

"Honey, calm down. I don't even want to wait in this neighborhood at night. Let's go home and talk about this. I'll have the truck back by morning. I promise," he said calmly.

"Fine. You just make sure you do." They drove home in complete silence. Jake was afraid to open his mouth, and Emma was so angry, she couldn't find the words. When they arrived home, Jake was as sweet as he could be. Or as her new Southern friends would say, sugar would melt in his mouth. He talked and talked until Emma relented.

"I have no place to go, honey. I know I fucked up, and I know I don't deserve a second chance. But I swear, Emma, I love you and I couldn't bear to lose you. I won't ever go into your purse again for anything. And you can hide the liquor. I won't touch it anyway. I think that it all started in Chicago. I started drinking, and it just spiraled me downward. Then I couldn't help but take that next step. But I swear I won't do it again. No drugs, no drinking. Nothing. Please, let me just take a shower and get a good night's sleep. I'll be fine tomorrow, and everything will be back to normal."

"Okay, Jake. But one more fuck up and you're gone. Get the truck back and stay clean and I'll give you one more chance. But you are sleeping in the guest room. I don't want to be near you tonight."

"I understand completely. I love you, honey. I can't lose you." With that, his cell phone rang. He walked in the other room for a moment and came back. "That was him. He's going to bring the truck here and get a ride home. He'll leave it in the driveway."

Emma was so relieved that the truck would be returned, it didn't even cross her mind that if the drug dealer brought the truck to her house, he would know where she lived. That one little fact just flew right past her. When morning came and the truck was in the driveway, there was only the thought that all was back to some sort of normality. They had a long talk when Jake was finally sober enough to think clearly.

"Emma, the truth is that Joe is part of the problem. He's given me money for drugs," he started. "He's gay and I lived with him for a while. I let him, um, do things to me for drugs," he told her hesitantly. "I mean, he only did it a couple of times, and I told him I couldn't reciprocate. That I just didn't like dick. I tried to do him once and I just couldn't." She could tell this was information he really didn't want to share. "When I was a kid, I was so fussy about my hair and my clothes, the other kids called me queer," he went on. "When I was fifteen, Cheryl took me to Club One (the famous drag club in Savannah). We hung out backstage with Lady Chablis and the others. We were all doing lines of coke and partying."

All Emma could think was "poor Jake." He's been through so much trauma. It's amazing he's as normal as he is. Joe, his father figure, was actually destroying him. His sister started him using drugs and had him hanging out in drag clubs. With her stability and normal upbringing, Emma was sure she could teach Jake the basics of how to deal with life without the use of drugs.

"Okay, honey. It's okay. First, you've got to cut off Joe. He's nothing but bad news for you. He's undermining your recovery. You'll have to find another job, but I want you to quit working for Joe immediately. Just being around him is a trigger for you," Emma counseled.

"You're right, honey. You're right. He's just a trigger," he parroted. "I really know I can stay clean if I don't see Joe."

"I know you can," Emma showed every inch of her compassion. "I believe in you. I have faith that you can overcome this."

"If I just keep close to you, I know I can do it. If I'm not out of your sight, I can. You're the best thing that's ever happened to me, and I won't lose you."

"Okay, Jake. Let's try to put this behind us. But we can't just be together twenty-four/seven. I need to write and do my stuff, and you need to get a real job. One that you have to punch in and punch out. Where you have to account for every minute," Emma explained to him.

"I agree. After I sleep this off, I'll get to work looking for something," Jake promised. "I'm still exhausted, so I'm going to take a nap," and he walked out of the room.

Chapter Six

The new year brought a month of fun, frolic, and frustration. Emma was afraid to let Jake out of her sight, and Jake was afraid to be out of Emma's sight for fear he would get into trouble. She was determined to be the strength behind the man. Emma knew she had a savior complex, and Jake desperately needed saving. She believed in her enormously giving heart and her logical mind that she could achieve her goal. She could be the one person who could guide Jake into her world of reality and consciousness. Although some felt he was a hopeless addict, Emma saw the potential of the man hiding behind the mask of a spoiled child. Emma taught Jake everything she knew. She patiently explained her father's philosophy of "giant killer," believing this would be the crux of Jake's overcoming his weaknesses.

"What's giant killer?" Jake asked.

"Well, the belief structure is based on David and Goliath. The difficult we do immediately, the impossible takes a little longer," Emma patiently explained.

"Okay, say that again," the genius asked.

"The difficult we do immediately," she purposely paused, "the impossible takes a little longer. It means you do the things you don't want to do first, then do the easy ones. You build your confidence if you follow that concept. You see, if you pick the chore you really don't want to do and actually do it first, you will feel an inch taller by tackling it. By doing that one thing—whatever it is—it will give you the confidence to do the next thing," she explained.

"Wow, that's really deep. But it makes sense. How do you do that?" he asked. To Emma it was simple, but to Jake it was like figuring out which day of the week didn't end with a Y.

"It's called using your mind instead of just doing. That's your major problem, Jake. You just act. You don't think first. You're so spoiled, Jake. Your mother always did your thinking for you, and you let her. It's time you started thinking for yourself. If you stopped and used your logic before going to get drugs, you wouldn't. When you get the urge—and I know you will—just stop. Get out of your truck and take a short walk. Just wait fifteen minutes before you act and use that brain of yours. Think it through to the conclusion. Not just give in to temptation, which is the easy way. We all want to take the easy way. Giant killers take the high road, the more difficult path. You need to not just see what you want but see what the outcome will be." Emma was starting to get excited. If Jake would just hear her words echoing in his head, maybe he really could stay clean.

"Now you know why I love you, Emma. You're so smart. That's such a good idea. If I get the urge, I'll do exactly that. I'll just take a walk before I do anything. Or I'll call you. Is that okay?"

"Of course. I would never be angry with you for having a craving. I'll only be angry if you act on it. So, if you would actually call me, I can help you through it." Emma was so pleased. She was sure he would trust her and call her before he went and got drugs. What she didn't understand was his need. She had no real understanding of addiction. He had to want to be talked out of doing cocaine. What she would learn was most addicts don't call their sponsors because they know they'll be talked out of their bad decision and that's the last result they want.

Jake told Emma he would no longer speak with Joe, and she believed him. Every time Jake's cell phone—which, of course, she had bought for him and paid for each month—would ring, she would glare at Jake. She was always afraid it was either a drug dealer or Joe. But it was usually Cheryl with words of warning to him. Or at least that's what Jake told Emma.

So for most of January, they played pool or Scene-it or hung around together watching movies. They laughed and joked and made love when Jake was in the mood at ten o'clock every night. Jake did as many chores as he could. He made their meals; cleaned house, kept the fountain filled, watered the plants, and just did whatever he could to make amends. They worked on a top-notch resume, and Emma let him out of the house for job interviews, but she insisted on calls before and after and kept an eye on the time for every second he was gone. He found a job waiting tables at a local restaurant. He had a bit of help because Emma's close friend, Ray, was the manager there.

Ray had done the painting in the bathroom, his naturally outgoing personality even got Emma's cleaning woman to fall for him. When Miss Ellie first started working for Emma, they went through some rough patches while Miss Ellie was getting used to Emma's quirky requests. Like, her bed had to be made exactly the way she wanted it, pillows facing a certain direction. But between Emma's sweetness and Miss Ellie's straight talk, they quickly overcame any obstacles. If Emma was in her way, Miss Ellie would just tell her.

"Okay, everybody git!" Ellie would say with a hand wave toward the bedroom. "You and the dog gotta go in the other room so's I can clean in here!"

Miss Ellie adored Emma's friend, Ray, from the start. Ray was still manager at Jaycee's Café, but on his days off, he worked with his wife, Samantha. Ray did the painting and finish work, and his first job was to help complete Emma's master bathroom. He was painting one Wednesday while Miss Ellie was cleaning. She would tell Ray how tough Emma was and how much she loved her. Ray, in turn, would needle Miss Ellie no end.

"What if I just take my paint brush and shook it?" he teased Miss Ellie, while miming shaking his wet brush all over the floor.

"Oh, you're a devil child, Ray! Don't you do that. Miss Emma will blame me for the mess…and you know Miss Emma. If I doesn't make her bed just so, she make me redo it." Ellie drawled. Miss Ellie was the penultimate Mammie from Gone with the Wind. Tough as nails and the biggest heart on the planet. While she complained or talked to herself about how picky Emma was, she would kill someone who tried to cross Emma. But Ray could always make her laugh.

"I'll just tell her you did it," Ray tormented Miss Ellie with a laugh.

"Oh, you bad boy, you. I'll slap you silly! You know I will," she chortled.

With that, Ray entered the hearts of Miss Ellie and Emma. Emma adored Miss Ellie, and she enjoyed the bickering battle between her and Ray.

When Ellie had been working for Emma for a year, she walked in on Wednesday morning and congratulated Emma on her anniversary.

"What anniversary?" Emma asked.

"Why, our year anniversary I been working for you," Miss Ellie beamed. Emma's sixty-four-year-old cleaning woman took her work seriously and knew how picky Emma was regarding her house. When Jake moved in, Miss Ellie liked Jake at first.

"Ooh, Miss Emma! Isn't he just handsome!" she had said. "And so neat. He always asks me what I want to eat for lunch. You never do that," she chided.

But Miss Ellie saw the changes in Jake firsthand. She became very quiet, which was a change from the norm. Emma and Ellie usually had wonderful conversations while she was working, but when Jake had used cocaine, he had left beer cans in the bathroom, cigarette burns on the furniture, and ashes all over the floor. Miss Ellie just kept her mouth shut.

With Jake by her side, some doors were more opened to her among her friends. So many were couples, and it was easier to get together with them as a couple. Ray would never consider getting together with just Emma because he was married. But once she was with Jake, Ray would stop by the house on his way to work just to play a game of pool.

Emma had become close friends with Jenny, the manager of

her bank, but since Jenny was married, they could only get together for lunch before Emma met Jake. Once Emma was coupled, Jenny and her husband, Mac, would meet them for dinner. They all had a great time, until they went for Mexican food, and then there were pitchers of margaritas. This, Emma knew, was dangerous for Jake. After that particular night, Emma kept elbowing Jake to slow down. It was easy for Emma to nurse one margarita, but Jake kept refilling his own glass. Jenny kept pouring and got happily sloshed, while Mac drank soda. But they enjoyed Jake's company and the way Jake treated Emma. As a close friend, Jenny only cared that her friend was happy. She didn't care one way or the other about Jake, only how he interacted with Emma.

When Emma got up from the table to go to the ladies' room, Jake looked at Jenny and Mac and said, "Isn't she the sexiest lady alive? Especially in those jeans."

Mac, a good ole boy from his balding head to his beer belly, blushed in response. Jenny, a gorgeous woman with platinum blonde hair nearly to her waist and freshly manicured coral tipped nails, drawled, "But of course she is, darlin'!" Jenny liked Jake immediately—until Emma began to confide in Jenny, which would prove to be Emma's undoing in Savannah. She would make the mistake of confiding in too many people.

Emma was the person in which everyone confided his or her problems. They trusted her.

Emma's door was always open to her friends. Her house had become exactly what she dreamed. The house no one ever wanted to leave. But after a year, Emma was starting to realize this might not be the dream she actually wanted. It had seemed like a good idea at the time, but Jake was not easy with new people, and with all of the drama between she and Jake, she wasn't always pleased to have people dropping by unexpectedly. As she had originally dreamed, they didn't want to leave. It was becoming more of a nightmare.

Jake was finally working at Jaycee's Café during the day. Emma thought that with this freedom, she would be able to finish editing the novel she had already finished in Florida and get some of her own chores done. But even with all of her own giant killer ingrained in her, she realized she missed Jake. She missed the playing together and she missed the sharing. She found this rather shocking.

Despite trying to accomplish her own goals and the longing she felt for Jake when he wasn't home, Emma worried while he was gone. Her concern made it difficult to concentrate on herself. Was he really working? Was he getting into trouble? These fears plagued her all day. He would check in every couple of hours, and that kept her from total panic, but it also kept her from accomplishing much. When he came home, she watched him carefully. She checked his appetite, his energy level, and his sense of humor.

Emma's naiveté was beginning to diminish. She was starting to analyze his habits. She began to observe that when his sense of humor became cruel, it could be when he used drugs or was craving them. He picked on her, rationalizing that he only picked on people he loved. He could become an obnoxious, petulant child. Emma's logic told her that when he used drugs or overindulged in alcohol, he felt guilty and angry at himself for doing what he knew was wrong. Thus, he would become mean to those around him.

It didn't take many days before her fears were realized. He came home late one afternoon, acting as if all was fine. He kissed her and immediately told her he was going to take a shower.

"It's been a long day, honey," he said and just walked out of the room toward the shower.

"Oh, shit," Emma muttered. She sat on the sofa and stared into nothingness. She had been hungry—until he arrived. She listened intently. Emma knew that when Jake was clean, he sang in the shower. He had a good voice, and she could start to read his mood by his song choice. If it was Sinatra, he was feeling loving and kind. Presley was happy; Beatles was guilt; oldies from the 50s or 60s was silly. But no singing at all was dangerous. As Emma listened, she heard nothing. She saw him walk past the great room into her bedroom with a towel around his waist. He didn't say a word. Emma began to panic. She checked her purse for cash missing. She checked her credit cards. Bingo. Her Visa card was missing.

"What do you want for dinner, honey?" Emma asked Jake as he got into T-shirt and pajama bottoms. This would certainly be the acid test, she thought.

"Oh, I ate at the restaurant," he lied.

"You selfish, lying bastard," Emma muttered and just started crying. She couldn't bear to look at his handsome face or his shoulders in the tank top. She just cried into the throw pillow on the sofa -- quietly sobbing.

"Honey, what is it?" he asked as though he were innocent.

"Do you think I'm an idiot?" she sobbed. "I know you've used."

"Why would you say that? I have not!" he defended.

"Oh, stop it. Please! Give me some credit."

Jake sat on the love seat across from her and began to cry. Tears dripping down his face, it was pathetic. He looked so guilty and so full of self-hatred.

"Okay, first. Where is my credit card?" she demanded.

"Here," he handed it to her. "I'm sorry. I filled up my tank with gas," he told her.

"Right," she muttered as she grabbed the card.

"Second, have you even been to work?"

"Of course. Well, two days," he admitted. The tears were still flowing. "I got fired because I came in late one day."

"God, you really are pathetic. You used your tip money for drugs instead of helping fill your bottomless pit of a stomach. You only think of yourself. You didn't think about the fact that I would be hungry tonight, just because you snorted a line or smoked crack and you wouldn't be hungry. You really are a piece of shit. And don't even think of telling me you love me. You have no idea what the word even means," she began to sob again.

"Yes, I do. I just have a problem. I know you can help me, Emma. You're the only one who can," he pleaded.

"Not me, Jake. I don't deserve this. I have done nothing but be kind to you. I've given you advice, which you don't listen to. I've given you ridiculous amounts of money to help you get back on your feet, which you've never done. You're a lazy piece of shit."

"I know I am, but I know I can beat this. Joe told me I'd fuck up," he let slip.

"So you've been talking to Joe?"

"Yeah, at least once a day. He's like a father to me," tears fell down his cheeks.

"Tell me the truth, if you know how. Does Joe really have anything to do with this?"

"I don't know. I don't know anything anymore," he whined. "I just know I can't live without you. And I don't mean the money. I couldn't live without you if you were living in a trailer and were dirt poor. You're the classiest, smartest, most beautiful woman I've ever been with, and you're right. I don't deserve you," tear continued to drip down his face.

"No, you don't," Emma agreed, still crying into her pillow. "Get out."

"Okay, I'll leave."

"Give me the key," Emma held out her hand. Jake took her key and remote for the alarm system off his key chain and handed it to her. He skulked out the door.

"Lock the door behind me, honey," he said as he closed the door.

Emma locked the door and then just sat on the sofa and sobbed. She slowly got to her feet and went into her bedroom. She brought a box of trash bags in with her. She began slowly filling the trash bags with all of his clothes. Without thinking or caring, she methodically sorted his clothes. Underwear and T-shirts in one bag, shirts in another, pants in another, shoes dumped into another bag. Then she went into his bathroom with a bag. She tossed all of his toiletries into a bag. She dragged all the bags to the door and, one by one, put them on the patio at the side door to the courtyard. Then she opened a bottle of merlot and poured herself a glass of wine. She let hot water and bath salts fill her jetted tub. With wine in hand, she turned on the jets, got into the tub, and sobbed.

Chapter Seven

Emma lazed in her tub, surrounded with fragrant lavender candles, sobbing. She had soothing Irish harp music playing and a second glass of wine sitting on the tub surround. She tried everything to relax. When the tears finally subsided, she stepped out of the tub, and after moisturizing her face, she put on flannel pajamas. With a tissue in her hand in case the waterworks started up again, she went into the great room to turn off the lights. She couldn't stop herself from looking outside the beveled glass in the door to see if Jake had picked up the bags. His truck was parked in her driveway. She turned around and went into the kitchen to open the back door for Tasha's evening constitutional and made coffee for the morning.

Not surprising to her, the phone rang. She looked at the caller ID, and of course, it was Jake. Tears began to fall silently again. Everything in her wanted to ignore the call. Emma felt so betrayed and angry, yet she still loved Jake. She still believed she could save him, and that led her to answer the phone.

"Hello," she answered coldly.

"It's me," Jake replied, clearly not knowing what to say.

"I know. What do you want?" Emma tried her best to sound distant, but she knew he could hear the tears behind the words.

"I want to come home, Emma. I love you so much, and I'm afraid if I lose you, I'll die. My only hope to be the man I can be is you," he began to cry. "I can't live without you."

"Why in God's name should I give you any more chances?" she asked. She really hoped—she didn't know what she hoped. She knew she was conflicted. Emma didn't understand addiction at all, so she still believed Jake was in control of his actions. She had only to get through to his empty head and fill it with the right information. Then he would be able to make the right decisions instead of always making the wrong ones.

"Because we were meant for each other. We're soul mates," he answered. "And I need your help to overcome this."

"I swear, Jake, this is your last chance. You use drugs one more time and you're out for good. No drugs, no alcohol. Nothing. This is it."

"I'll go to NA and AA. I promise," he pleaded.

Emma went to the door and opened it, her eyes staring at the ground. Jake came in and took her in his arms. Oh, those strong arms! He held her tight to his chest like he would never let go. She only reached his armpits, but the feeling of being held was too powerful for her to resist. She looked up. And that was her downfall.

She saw his green eyes full of tears and guilt. His perfect long fingers stroked her hair. Then his lips caught hers. He kissed her tenderly and with need. The passion in Emma was always present, but with Jake, it soared. He silently took her into her bedroom and began slowly taking off her clothes. He kissed her neck, her shoulders, and slowly moved down toward her breasts. Emma was fully aroused. He pulled her pajama bottoms off, and his kisses moved down her torso. As his tongue got busy, Emma was ready for him. He pulled off his boxer briefs and—nothing. He was totally flaccid.

The look on Emma's face told Jake everything. Disappointment, rejection, and pain. He actually took his limp penis and shook it as though it was its fault.

"I'm so sorry, honey. I...well, you know what drugs do to me. You know I wanted to. Can you imagine how I feel?" he whined.

"I don't care," she sobbed. "You did this to yourself and hurt me in the process," she turned away from him, put her pajamas back on, and curled into a ball to cry into her pillow. "Good night, Jake."

"Good night, honey." And Jake took his pillow and went into the guest room.

Two weeks went by and the laughter returned. Jake went to Narcotics Anonymous meetings and Alcoholics Anonymous meetings. Emma even joined him a few times. He stayed clean and sober and put in applications all over town; from Home Depot to restaurants.

Emma started getting her charge card bills and found discrepancies. She called her credit card companies and told them about the fraudulent charges, never telling them who had used them. They deducted the charges from her bill, so it didn't hurt her. She only felt betrayed by Jake. She had to destroy the card and wait for another one. But when she received her cable television bill, she went ballistic. Pornography! Talk about betrayal! He implied he could only get it up once and sometimes he couldn't at all, and yet he would watch porn and jerk off all night! That hurt. When she confronted him with the fifty dollars worth of porn, he stuttered and stammered.

"Five of them on my bill, you shit!" Emma threw the cable

bill at him. "How could you? How could you humiliate me like that? And this last one was the night you couldn't get it up with me. But you could get it up for an eighteen-year-old cheerleader?" Emma had never even seen a pornographic movie, but the titles he chose said it all.

"No, honey. I was just as frustrated with them. I just…I went into the guest room and was so angry with myself that I couldn't perform with a beautiful woman like you. I just, I don't know…I guess I kept trying. I hated myself."

"Good. Do you have any idea how this makes me feel? No, of course you don't. You never think of anyone but yourself. You don't consider the cost to me. I've already cancelled almost all the movie channels to cut back on my bill, and what do you do? You add fifty dollars to it! My God, you have no morals whatsoever. My credit card bills, my cable bill. You just steal from me every which way you can."

"I'm so sorry. The meetings are really helping. I mean, I've stayed clean. And I won't order any more porn. I promise. It just makes me feel worthless anyway," he assured her. "Call Comcast and have them blocked."

"I will. Right now." And she picked up the phone to call the cable company. She blocked all the porn channels and walked into the other room to put a childproof code on the television. That, she figured, would solve one problem. It didn't solve the most serious problem, but at least Emma could use her favorite four-letter word on the porn issue—D-O-N-E. Okay, Emma thought, at least that issue wouldn't reoccur.

"Can you just explain it to me?" Emma coaxed him to think; a tough job on a good day. "What does watching pornography do for you? I mean, you have an attractive, willing woman that you can have sex with any time you want. You certainly have no control over your other desires, and you're horny several times a day. Why would you have sex with me only once a day and watch four hours of porn?"

"Uh..." Jake's brain was quick when it came to movies, but actual depth of thought was not his strong suit. After all, it was Jake who complimented Emma on her winter hat. "I like the bidet, honey," he had told her.

"Darling. Light of my life. It's a beret. A bidet is something that cleans your ass not something that sits on your head," Emma had laughingly corrected him.

"Oh, yeah," he chuckled. "I always confuse those two."

So his answer to the porn question was just as vague and moronic. It was just a method to get out of trouble, not the depth Emma wanted to hear. Jake talked in circles about his love for her and how sexy he found her. Porn was just different. It was more of an addiction.

"I don't really even enjoy it," he proclaimed.

"Then why would you spend so much of my money on it? Sneaking off to watch other people have sex that's not even real when you could have sex with a real, live woman?" she pushed.

"I don't know," was his only answer, and it was supposed to satisfy Emma. It didn't.

The irony was Emma and Jake were soul mates of a sort. They enjoyed the same movies, remembered the same lines from movies, and laughed together. They had the same quirky sense of humor. When they went to a store, he held her hand and, when no one was looking, grabbed her ass. In public, he acted like he was totally in love with her. He was also the consummate Southern gentleman. He always opened doors for her; he lifted any heavy objects, and automatically reached to get something down from a high shelf. And Emma loved seeing him get the double takes from all the girls who ogled him. She felt lucky that this gorgeous man was hers. She knew she was attractive, but girls that were much younger than Emma would lust after Jake. She could smell it around her.

However—isn't there always a however?—there were annoyances. Putting aside the cocaine addiction, the stealing to pay for it, and the compulsive lying to cover it up—not easy to put aside—there were other frustrations. His selfishness and self-indulgence, which Emma believed were the basic reasons for his more serious problems. Nevertheless, his overall attitude about life was that he was entitled. That had come from his mother.

Since his father had died when he was only a small child, his mother felt some sort of guilt for not giving him a father. As a result, Marjorie Stanton had indulged Jake's every whim. She coddled him his whole life. He actually slept with her until he was ten years old. The stories she heard from both Cheryl and Jake added to Emma's understanding of Jake's obsession with his mother. And Emma had become fairly close to Marjorie, called Mimi by her family. Mimi's astrological sign was Cancer, which to Emma said it all. Not that Emma was an astrology aficionado. She wasn't. But damned if there weren't some accuracies. Most Cancers seemed to have similar temperaments. They were possessive, controlling, and protective. Those Cancer claws described them. Maybe that wasn't the only reason Jake turned out as he had, but it was certainly an element. Mimi was assuredly all those elements.

Once Jake had started using drugs at fifteen years old, he began stealing from his beloved mother. Jake idolized her in every way. Yet when Jake became a teenager, she slept with her purse hugged tightly to her body every night. He still managed to steal money from that purse. He stole her medication, pawned her jewelry, and anything else he could get his hands on. When they opened their successful restaurant, Jake embezzled thousands of dollars from their profits. He actually put her into debt. Because of Jake, Mimi went from being financially sound to a point that she couldn't afford to keep up her life insurance policy; a life insurance policy that ironically would have left Jake five hundred thousand dollars when she died. For all he did to her, his mother consistently forgave him. He had always lived with her unless he was imprisoned on drug charges (for eighteen months) or went into rehab (several times). But as soon as he was released, he moved back in with her. Even when he had been engaged two years before he met Emma, they lived with his mother. He had never been on his own; never stood on his own two feet. At thirty, Jake visited his mother in the nursing home daily.

Emma was sure these stories she had been told were true because Jake's personality bore them out. He acted like the little prince who was always given his way. His mother had clearly indulged him. This made Emma think of her own upbringing. She would never have gotten away with that type of leniency. Emma's mother was gentle and kind but a strict disciplinarian. She was punished for wrongdoing, without exception. She was never allowed to wrinkle her nose at food. She had to taste everything. She wasn't fussy because she was raised to be open-minded. Not so with Jake.

On the one side of his personality was the spoiled child who just—did. Wouldn't think about the consequences because there were none that he had to pay for. The other side of his personality was the result of the first. He was insecure and had an inferiority complex. It drove Emma crazy. He made it so difficult for her to save him when he didn't feel he was worth saving.

Part of his feelings of sexual inadequacy came out in another of the horror stories Jake had told Emma. He confessed to her late one night that he had been sexually assaulted by his gym teacher when he was a boy. His older sister, Cheryl, had become a beautician, and she always styled his hair perfectly. In his early teens, Jake always went to school perfectly coifed. Adding to his sexual ambiguity, Jake had been diagnosed as obsessive-compulsive and ADHD as a child and had been given Ritalin, so he was fussy. Combining all these factors together made his sexual security questionable. He admitted to Emma that he felt almost more comfortable among gay men than women because at least he knew he was attractive to gay men. They always boosted his ego. But he was unsure of his appeal to females, so Emma worked very hard to stroke his masculine ego. Any time her girlfriends mooned over his good looks and charm, she told him about it. She always praised his sexual prowess in bed and chided him when he complained that his penis wasn't big enough.

"Big enough for whom, honey? It does a great job for me, and isn't that all that counts?" she would tell him.

"But I want an injection to give it more girth," he constantly and irritatingly would complain. He was rarely satisfied with his performance, regardless of Emma's reassurances.

Emma also did everything she could to impart her wisdom to Jake. When he was willing to have an actual conversation, which was not often, she would try to enter his realm of reality.

"Jake, there is one way to be more in control of your mind that works for me. That's to keep a journal. Write down your feelings. That will make you aware of what's going on inside you," Emma would feebly attempt. "You don't have to show it to anyone, including me. It's just for you, and it would really help." She even bought him a journal. That didn't work. He never wrote a word.

Emma went to the grocery with Jake and bought salmon. She knew it was risky because Jake had never eaten fish, unless you count shrimp as seafood. But her idea was to douse his salmon with lemon pepper, his spice of choice. She fixed green beans (the only vegetable he would eat) and rice with soy sauce. To her utter amazement, he finished it all. Emma actually went to see Mimi the following day and told her.

"Mimi, I don't want to give you another stroke," Emma started with a laugh, "but your son actually ate broiled salmon!"

"Oh my God! You're right. It might have! I just can't believe it. I knew you were the best thing that's ever happened to my baby," she said smiling. It was difficult to understand her speech because of her condition, but Emma certainly understood those words.

Emma was trying to improve Jake. To make him a man. She didn't tell him what to do because that was what had ruined him. He had never been forced to think for himself, and Emma was going to do just that. He always asked her for advice on critical issues in life.

"Honey, what should I take for a cold?" was one of such critical questions.

Emma wanted to say, "What are you, five? What, you've never had a cold before, you moron?" But she didn't.

"What do you think you should do?" Emma would reply with patience. Then she waited for his brain to adjust to the shock. And God forbid he should catch a cold or have a pain. Emma dreaded his ailments like the plague. Jake became mean, selfish, and cruel when he was sick. She just tried to avoid him. He didn't want to be helped, but if she didn't find all the answers to his ailment and provide them, he was cruel.

Jake was a hypochondriac and that didn't help. Not only was there always something wrong—constipation, diarrhea, a bruise, a hemorrhoid, or he was coming down with a cold from which he was sure he was going to die—but he was graphic about all his ailments. He discussed every bowel movement, every itch, every rash, and every bit of phlegm in great detail. When Emma complained that they needed a bit of mystery and she really didn't want to hear the details, he got angry.

"I could tell my mother everything," he would complain.

"Well, honey, I'm not your mother. I'm your lover. It's different," she would try to explain. It didn't work. They actually got into an enormous fight one night when he left the door open to the bathroom while he was urinating.

"Please, Jake. Close the door. It's just not proper for me to watch you peeing," she said gently.

"Why not?" he asked, as he continued the stream. "It's natural."

"Because it's in poor taste," she explained, adding some heat to it. "Only trashy people would go to the bathroom in front of their girlfriend."

"Oh, really? Well, my mother didn't raise us that way. She always left the door open," he screamed. Now Emma was in a jam. How could she convince him that it was wrong if his saintly mother had approved?

"Well, Jake, your mother was wrong. Classy people just don't do that."

"Oh, so my mother wasn't classy?" he yelled louder. Okay, Emma thought. How do I get my foot out of this one? Just let it lay.

"Fine, Jake. Whatever. Let's just leave it that I wasn't raised that way and it was different. No right or wrong. Just different." There, Emma thought. That should do it.

"Fine. Whatever. Back at ya," he brooded. At least the screaming match was over. That counted for something.

These differences in upbringing produced difficulties, but Emma and Jake got through them. He still hadn't started the conversion classes with the synagogue, which was annoying Emma. He kept saying he wanted to convert, but he also never did anything about it. She didn't know if was because he really didn't want to convert or if he was just lazy. Or the worst possibility, was it just a con to keep her in his life? The last seemed awfully skeptical and against Emma's innate nature. So she didn't consider it with much vigor.

Knowing Jake's background, Emma still felt sorry for him. After all he had done to her, all he had taken from her, and all he did to hurt her, she still believed she was going to be the one to save him. She still believed that there was a good man hiding beneath what Emma saw as just a facade. The side of Jake that was hurt and indulged was the aberration, not the funny and kind side. Emma didn't understand addiction and only knew the power of her own mind. She believed the power of the mind and spirit overcame all adversity. She just had to get Jake to accept it.

Then, one day while they were just sitting in front of the TV, they came up with a great idea that could change Jake's life. The concept just flew into the room out of nowhere. Jake could start his own business. He was having a difficult time finding a job, and working for Joe just got him into trouble. Once Jake had the idea, together they became obsessed with Jake starting a restaurant consulting business. It was the first time Emma had seen Jake giddy with enthusiasm. After ten years owning his restaurant, he could coach others on cutting costs and maximizing profits. With Emma's background in public relations and marketing, she did the basic design of the brochure and business cards, and Jake worked tirelessly writing the copy. She was actually quite surprised. He was a good writer. She designed a logo, and all she had to buy was premade business cards at Office Depot and paper stock. They spend two weeks designing the forms he would need and contracts his clients would need to sign, and Emma created a questionnaire form that would help Jake when he got nervous during initial meetings with potential clients.

They did a few tests of their own. They went out for dinner at local restaurants that he already believed needed his guidance. There was a small, family-owned Italian restaurant that Emma thought had fabulous food, but it was always empty. As they waited for a table, Jake took a quick inventory of their flaws. Emma took notes on all his findings. They had a delicious meal, but Jake found more flaws in the way the restaurant was being managed.

"They're using two fourteen ounce pieces of chicken," Jake noticed. "They should be using two eight ounce pieces. They'd save a fortune. I'd have to go into the kitchen to get a real feel, but I'd say I could really help these people."

As they left the restaurant, Jake set up an appointment with the owner. Unfortunately, he didn't get them as an account. But Jake was right. The restaurant closed within two months. If they had hired him and done as he recommended, they would probably be open and making a profit.

If he could close even one consulting job a month, it would bring in two thousand dollars. He told Emma it would make him feel like a man if he could just bring in a good paycheck to her. They were both equally enthused at the prospect. Once Jake was ready, Emma lent him her briefcase and he dressed in a suit. He began visiting every restaurant in Savannah. He started with restaurants he knew were in financial trouble or were owned by people he knew. Every day he spent hours on the streets looking for clients.

Chapter Eight

For the first time, Emma went with Jake on two of his monthly errands. Jake was on probation with both city and county on old drug charges, so there were two stops each month—and two cashier's checks each month. The first stop was at the city probation office on Habersham Street.

Habersham Street ran from Bay Street downtown, all the way to Southside Savannah shopping, a good five miles or so. There were portions of Habersham that were residential with houses built in the 1950s at the southern end and through Ardsley Park where Emma lived, portions that were commercial with restaurants and enchanting stores, and eventually Habersham wound around historic squares of downtown all the way to the north end of Savannah at the Savannah River. The particular portion of Habersham on which the probation office was located was charmingly called the Victorian District. In English, that meant the Dumps.

The Victorian District of Savannah did have original Victorian houses, but most had not yet been refurbished to their original splendor. Most were crack houses and flophouses, which upset Emma every time she drove through the area. The basic bones of these houses were magnificent. She could envision their stately charm despite the termite infestation and overall unkempt current state. What was amazing to Emma was the interspersion of renovated Victorian homes that were worth upwards of seven hundred thousand dollars with Jaguars in the driveways. Yet next-door would be a broken-down crack house.

She used her powers of observation to mentally take pictures of this depressing setting. The probation office was situated next to a barbeque joint and clearly a seedy section of town. From the street, it just looked like any office. Jake asked Emma to stay in the car and lock the doors. That was certainly a hint. She had already gone to the bank to get the one hundred and twenty five dollar cashier's check he would need to pay the monthly stipend due them. She had been giving him these checks every month, but this was the first time it became a reality.

Although she waited in the car, Emma tried to peer into the daunting office where criminals were forced to report to their keepers each month. She couldn't see a thing through the tinted window. So she just watched people enter and leave through what appeared to be just another door to just another office. But this particular door was for frightening, dangerous-looking characters with no teeth and dirty hair or low-slung jeans and a bandana around their head. When she saw Jake open the door to walk out, she couldn't help but think he didn't fit in with this rough group.

Jake quickly got into the car, and they proceeded to the county probation office. This was downright terrifying to Emma. It was in the worst section of town, and the building was surrounded by wire fencing. It might as well have been barbed wire, it looked so daunting. There was little parking, and the existing parking was far from the actual door. Huge areas of partial sod and partial mud acted as a mote between the street and the probation office, a clear field of demarcation between the criminals and the rest of humanity.

From the moment they pulled up, Emma got the heebie-jeebies. This was a world Emma had never seen and never thought she would see. She never wanted to see this world. Yet here she was, watching men and women who looked like hard-core criminals coming in and out of the oppressive building. She stayed in the car and circled the block until she saw Jake coming out. Once again, he looked out of place. He was clean-cut, attractive, and most importantly he carried himself like the privileged man he had been. He got into the car so quickly, he startled Emma. He looked nearly as frightened by the place as she was.

"How'd it go?" Emma asked once he was seated calmly.

"Fine," he said shortly.

"Come on, what happens in there?" Emma prodded.

"Honey, it's just a horrible place. You want to know? Okay. You sit in a waiting room full of badass criminals—mostly violent crimes—until your name is called. Then when they call you, you go through a metal door that locks behind you. Then you meet with your probation officer. Mine is Mrs. Grant. She usually drug tests me and then asks me a few questions. She's really pretty nice, but that's because I'm nice to her and she knows Mom. They're just checking to be sure I'm keeping out of trouble."

"So you go into these places and lie through your teeth," Emma said without thinking.

"Thanks, honey," he replied and stared out the window.

She knew it was unkind, but she just couldn't help it. She was losing patience with him. Emma was already trying to sell some of her more expensive jewelry on eBay to recoup some small amount of the money she was spending. She chose pieces she didn't often wear but were valuable. She decided on two beautiful, large John Hardy diamond pendants. She took them out of the safe and placed them discretely in a John Hardy flannel pouch on a corner of her desk so she could answer online questions if they were asked of her. If no one knew there was something in the pouch, it looked inconspicuous. Emma was sure Jake didn't even notice it.

The longer Emma and Jake were together, the less she believed him. Emma had spoken with Big Joe herself and learned that much of the story Jake had told her was untrue. Jake's sister, Cheryl, was good friends with Joe since Cheryl and Jake had both known Joe since they were kids. Cheryl told Emma her version of the truth.

"Emma, Jake is a liar. You can't trust anything he says, especially when he's using," she drawled in her native South Carolina accent. "He also makes up the past to suit him."

"So, was he or wasn't he molested by his gym teacher?" Emma tried to confirm some of the many stories.

"What? That's ridiculous. Our older brother, Chris, the one who killed himself? I'm sure Jake told you about him. That, by the way, is true. But Chris was the one molested by his gym coach. What did Jake tell you, Emma? My God. He has no shame!"

"He told me it was a murder/suicide. Is that true?" Emma asked.

"Yeah, that's true. Chris never got over the rape by his coach, and Chris was also an addict. He just snapped when he was twenty-one and killed his girlfriend and then turned the gun on himself. He couldn't be with a woman without feeling the shame of the rape, I guess. But Jake was only about seven when that happened. I was seventeen. I'm sure it had an effect on Jake, but he's using it to blame others for his problems. That's a typical personality trait of an addict. But no, he was never raped," Cheryl revealed.

"You know what I believe, Cheryl? He blames you for starting him on drugs. Then he created a traumatic childhood to justify his addiction. So the death of his father, your mother's overindulgence, the rape, and the death of your brother all play a part in his little drama. After all, that would make his addiction the fault of others, rather than himself. It would be the fault of his horrible childhood. It feeds on itself. But the truth is, he had a blessed childhood. He was coddled and loved. But with a wonderful childhood, he can't rationalize the appalling past he needs to create so he can emotionally block it out by using drugs," Emma explained.

"Wow, you really are as smart as Jake said you are. I think that's a good explanation. It makes perfect sense," Cheryl replied. "Oh, the kids are fighting. I gotta go," and that ended every phone conversation with Cheryl.

Emma maintained a friendship with Cheryl despite Cheryl's own problems, her past effect on Jake, and her nutcase of a husband, for two reasons. The most important reason was she was the best source for information about Jake. Jake would confide in Cheryl before he'd tell Emma, and she could get more of the truth about Jake from Cheryl. The other reason was Cheryl's connection to the Jewish community. Her children went to the private Jewish school with several of Emma's other friends' kids. As little as she trusted Cheryl, Emma was obliged to befriend her.

The memories of these conversations echoed in her head as

she and Jake drove home from his probation appointments in complete silence. How did he manage to be drug tested by these people? Emma just couldn't get that question out of her head. She knew he had used drugs, and yet he was being tested. How was he getting away with it? She knew if she asked him, he would lie. To hell with it, she thought. She'd just ask him and wait for his response.

"Jake," she tried to get his attention as they neared her house.

"What?" he grumbled.

"How do you get away with getting drug tested every month when you're still using drugs?" she asked him.

"Oh, for Christ's sake! That's what you've been brooding about?" he answered testily.

"Oh, right. I've been brooding. You haven't said a word since we left downtown and you're the one staring out the window. Anyway, can you answer the question…honestly?"

"Fine. Cocaine only stays in your system for three days. I just have to stay clean for the three days before I go in and my piss comes back clean. Does that answer your burning question?"

"Yep. Thanks for sharing," she poked back.

"Look, I'm sorry, honey. It just puts me in a bad mood to go there. It reminds me of everything stupid I've done. Okay? Now can we go home, play some pool, have a great dinner. I'll make chicken and pasta, and you can make your salad. Then later, we'll make love. Is that all right, baby?" he said sweetly.

"Sure, Jake. That sounds great."

After a nice dinner, a good movie, and better sex, Emma sat

up in bed while Jake watched the History Channel.

"Honey," he said softly, "let's get a puppy together. We're not getting married until next spring, so we can't start thinking about children yet, even though I really want children with you. I want a beautiful little girl who looks just like you. But I'd like to get a puppy together. One that's ours. I mean, I love Tasha. You know I do. But she's yours. I'd like a dog that's ours," he told her.

"Oh, that would be great! I've always thought Tasha needed a pal to play with when I'm not home or when I'm busy. Let's go to the Humane Society tomorrow and see what's there," she agreed.

"Fantastic. Good night, honey."

Tuesday morning they had their coffee, Jake ate a breakfast of two hotdogs with nothing on them, which was his idea of breakfast and turned Emma's stomach. Once they were dressed, they headed out for the Humane Society. Emma had actually thought about this idea before and had already filled out the applications. So if they found a dog they liked, they could bring it right home. Of course they argued about each choice. Jake picked a big, dumb, typically good ole boy hound dog. Emma nixed this immediately.

"It's a male and it's stupid. And he only likes you," she told him. Of course, male and stupid was redundant to Emma at this point. Was there any other kind?

"All right, all right," Jake put the dog back into its kennel. "Your turn."

Emma picked a sweet female Terrier-mix mutt that had a slight limp. She thought it was so cute and would be harder to place. Her heart went out to her.

"How about her?" Emma pointed. "She looks cute. Once she's cleaned up, I think she'll be adorable."

"Oh, sure! The one with the gimp! We'll just call her Gimpy," he muttered. Emma still insisted on taking the dog to the playroom. Emma fell in love with her, but Jake was caustic and negative.

"Fine, fine," Emma said with disgust. "Just put her to sleep because she's got a little limp. Just because it's my money and my house, don't let me persuade you."

"I'm sorry, honey. You're right. It's your choice. If you want the gimpy dog, that's fine with me," he told her.

"Forget it. Let's look at the other dogs and then we'll leave. Clearly we're not going to agree on anything." They walked through the shelter until they found a husky puppy, female and under a year old. "How about that one?" Emma asked.

"Oh, yeah! She's beautiful! Let me get someone to open the cage." When he returned, they took the husky out back to the play area. She was sweet, affectionate, and submissive. Emma didn't want an aggressive dog for her kindhearted Tasha. Emma and Jake seemed to actually agree.

"She's good dog," the worker at the shelter told them. "She was really depressed for the first couple of weeks because she had a litter of puppies, and when she was found, the puppies were all gone. She was totally traumatized. But now she's doing great. She's been spayed, she's housebroken, and already semi-trained," Emma and Jake were told.

"She's seems really sweet," Emma looked at Jake. "We'll take her."

And with that, Jasmine became a new member of the family. Emma's older golden retriever, Tasha, was happy to have a dog to play with, but Jake did nothing but complain. Jasmine, the new husky, was not housebroken. She had several accidents in the house. Emma saw this as normal puppy behavior and was willing to train her. But Jake's negativity never stopped. The dog tried to sleep on the bed with Tasha and Emma and Jake.

"There's too much fur. It's all making me sneeze. She's a monster," he bitched and groaned all evening.

"She's young, Jake. She needs training," Emma tried.

"No. I'm taking her back first thing in the morning. I can't stand it. The noise, the chaos, the fur. My fault, but I can't deal with it."

"Fine, Jake. Do what you want. Take her back in the morning," Emma huffed. And he wanted children, Emma thought. Yeah, that'll work.

Wednesday morning Miss Ellie came to clean the house. She saw the puppy and just said, "Oh Lord! No!"

"Don't worry, Miss Ellie. Jake is taking the dog back to the shelter this morning."

By ten o'clock, they were both gone. Jake called on his cell phone and told Emma that Jasmine had taken off down the street. He chased her down and put her in the truck to take her back to the animal shelter. He was gone until afternoon. Doing what, she didn't know. But that wasn't unusual on Wednesdays. He wanted to be out of Ellie's way.

At two o'clock, Ellie called Emma back to her office. She was holding the John Hardy pouch in her hand. It had a big, wet bite mark taken out of it. And it was empty.

"I just found this while I was cleaning, Miss Emma. It was on the floor over there," she pointed to the corner of the throw rug in the office.

"What about what was in it?" Emma asked.

"I didn't find nothin' in it." Together they tore the room and then the house upside down to find the two pendants. They were definitely gone. Emma quickly went online and closed out the two listings on eBay. With her luck, someone would do a "Buy it Now," and there would be nothing to buy. Then she called Jake.

"Where the hell are you?" she asked coldly.

"I'm at the Bed Depot talking to Big Joe and Kirk. What's wrong?" he asked defensively. He knew he should be looking for clients, but after only two weeks, he was getting discouraged and needed camaraderie.

"It looks like the dog ate my jewelry," she told him. "Do you know anything about it?"

"I'll be right home. No, I don't know what you're talking about." When he returned home, Emma relayed the story as she knew it. He continually denied any knowledge. The bag looked torn into and was still wet.

"We should call the animal shelter and have them check to see if she shit them out," he suggested.

"Yeah, I guess we'd better. It could really make her sick." Now Emma was solely concerned for the welfare of the dog. She called the Humane Society, and they assured her they would check. They would also get an x-ray to see if the jewelry was stuck inside her.

When Emma called her insurance agent, Paul couldn't stop laughing.

"I'm sorry, Emma. But your dog ate your homework? And I thought I'd heard it all!"

"Yeah, I know it sounds nuts, but I have the picture of the

bag, and it's definitely a dog bite."

"Okay, but remember, your jewelry is scheduled, so you'll have to call them. I'm sure they'll take care of you," he said. "I'll remember this one, though. I thought the robbery sounded odd, but this is one for the books," he laughed.

"I know, I know," Emma laughed with him but cringed inside. She called her jewelry insurance company and made the claim. Four thousand dollars was the total theft. But her jewelry insurance only replaced lost or stolen items. So she was going to have to buy more jewelry rather than sell what she had, which was the opposite of what she wanted. She wanted the cash.

Within two weeks, she had the money transferred to Levy Jewelers downtown and went shopping yet again. A week after that, her jewelry insurance company cancelled her policy.

"Jake, I know you had something to do with this. Now I have no insurance on my jewelry. Thanks," she patted his arm.

"Emma, I swear I had nothing to do with it," he said convincingly.

"Isn't it just coincidental that the two pieces come up missing during the one day we have a new puppy in the house? And that you immediately decide you don't want that beautiful dog. Destroy the evidence, as it were," she concluded.

"I know it sounds fishy, but it's the truth," he repeated. "I didn't even know that stuff was in your office."

"Okay, honey. Whatever you say." Emma conceded because she knew there was no way to prove anything. There was no one to ask, no one to check his story. Since he didn't always pawn her personal property, there was nothing she could do. She believed that sometimes he took things directly to his drug dealer to exchange for drugs.   There was no way to be sure of anything where Jake was concerned.

Chapter Nine

Emma and Jake finally sat down to have a long talk about Big Joe, going back and forth about his influence on Jake. How much of Jake's story was true was yet to be told, but at the time, Emma believed it. She already knew that although Jake had agreed to sever the relationship with Joe, Jake had been sneaking phone calls to him every day and seeing him when he was able. She also already knew that he was still doing mattress deliveries for him. Emma couldn't understand Jake's deep emotional draw to Joe. Jake actually turned off the television for the conversation—a monumental task for Jake. The television was always on when Jake was home. He sat across from Emma on the love seat, while Emma remained sitting cross-legged on the sofa. She listened intently to Jake's story.

"Joe is like a father to me, Emma. I lost my father when I was three years old, and since I was best friends with Joe's son, he became my surrogate father. He's such a sweet man. But what no one knows is that he's gay. After all, he was married and had two children. Who would think it? But he only hires cute young men to do the deliveries and…let's just say, he's enjoyed them for years. Some of the guys have lived with him so he'd have company. I was one of them," Jake began.

"When I started doing drugs, Joe helped me. He talked to me. He tried to get me to stop, but later he bought cocaine for me. He thought if he was in control of my using and bought small amounts, he could wean me off it. But it came at a price.

I, um," Jake stuttered and looked down in shame. "He, um. Okay…" Jake took a deep breath and let the words fall. "If I let him go down on me, he would buy cocaine for me," Jake confessed.

Emma was sure she looked stunned, but she tried to keep her composure. There was certainly an effeminate side to Jake, but she knew he wasn't gay. Or at least she didn't think he was.

"Did you ever…" Emma started.

"No! He begged me to once, but I just couldn't. I love pussy, not dick!" he defended angrily. "And it didn't last long."

"No wonder I thought he was a bad influence on you. Doesn't it bother you to even look him in the face after that?"

"I'm ashamed of a lot of things, Emma. That's one of them. But Joe is like a father to me now. I love him in that way, only. He's the only man I can really talk to anymore," Jake continued. "He's really a good guy. You should get to know him. He knows me better than anyone. As well as Mom and Cheryl know me. I've known him my whole life."

"And I can just forget that you had sex with him?" she asked.

"We didn't have sex, Emma. He blew me. There's a big difference. I could just close my eyes and pretend it wasn't a man. Baby, when an addict wants his drugs, he'll do just about anything. There is no brain. When I'm clean, he's just a great friend I can talk to. He knows all about you and how much in love with you I am," Jake rationalized.

"All right, Jake. I'll talk to him," Emma agreed. She had actually always liked Joe. He had been so nice to her in the store, and she needed an ally who could help her sort out the lies from the truth. She would never confront him about his sexual orientation because she couldn't be sure Jake's stories were true, but she could get some insight into Jake's addiction issues.

Since Jake still wasn't closing any deals with his business, he continued to do deliveries for Joe. When Emma was sure Jake was making a mattress delivery, she went to see Big Joe herself. She went to the store and sat companionably across the desk from him. He really was large, hence the name. He must have weighed four hundred pounds but was happy and jolly.

Emma looked around the store before she sat down across from Joe. She wanted to be sure he had the time to talk. Knowing Joe, he would take the time to talk even if he was swamped with customers, but Emma didn't really want an audience. The store was empty, so she sat in the comfortable chair at Joe's desk in the middle of the store.

"Hi there, Emma!" he said enthusiastically. "How are things going?"

"Hi, Joe. Do you have time for a little talk?" Emma asked politely.

"Of course, sugar. I always have time for you."

"I just wanted to talk. I know how close you and Jake are and I thought I should get to understand him better—and you'd be the best source." He leaned back in his chair and smiled as if reminiscing about an old friend.

"He's really got a huge heart, and Jake really loves you. He's told me everything. How great the sex is, how smart you are. He doesn't feel he deserves you. I told him you're the best thing that ever happened to him. I just hope he doesn't screw it up," he explained.

"Do you think he's capable of stopping the drugs? Everything negative in our relationship revolves around his addiction. The lies, the cruelty, the selfishness. If it weren't for his need for cocaine, you'd be right. He has a big heart and a caring soul," Emma agreed.

"I think if anyone can help him through it, you can. There's nothing better for a man than a good woman. And Emma, you're the best."

"Thanks, Joe. I just hope I'm up to the challenge. I know I have a savior complex and I really believe Jake is worth saving," Emma confided.

"Well, honey, if you ever need to talk, you just call me; any time, day or night. I'm there for you. Jake is like a son to me, so you'll be my daughter-in-law. So whatever I can do to help you, I will," Joe held Emma's hand and squeezed.

"Thanks, Joe. You don't know how much I need that."

From that day on, Emma talked to Joe at least once a day and usually several times a day. They discussed any issues that arose. Usually those issues concerned Jake, but sometimes she just needed to vent. They agreed that when Jake had deliveries, Joe would contact the client and be sure Jake wasn't tipped.

"It's that tip money—the cash in his pocket—that may be causing trouble," Emma had mentioned during one of their conversations. "And all his checks should be made out to me," they agreed. "That way I get some of my bills paid, and he doesn't have the ability to get off track."

"I'll make sure of it," Joe assured Emma.

So, together, Emma and Joe became a team—a sort of tag team to keep Jake away from drugs. Jake was fine with this decision. He knew he needed external protection from himself, and the fact that the protection was coming from two of the people he loved the most made him feel nurtured. While he wasn't getting any protection from his mother who was still coddling him, he was being helped by Joe and Emma. He still saw his mother nearly every day in the nursing home. Regardless of his trespasses both in the past and currently, she continued to give him unconditional love. With her, he was back in the womb where he wanted to be, pampered and spoiled.

Emma tried to impart her own strong values to Jake. Yes, she would cover her bases by putting a protective ring around him with Joe, but she would not continue to spoil him the way his mother did. Between their hours of fun and games, Emma calmly and patiently preached to him.

"Honey, you know you have control over your self-indulgence," she began with love. "You have a good brain. You just need to learn how to use it. You've been spoiled your whole life. Your mother did your thinking for you. The only way you're going to extricate yourself from these demons—the drugs, the lying, the stealing—is to believe you can. The only way to believe you can is to use your brain instead of your feelings," she began.

"I used to have a good mind, Emma. I really did. I ran that restaurant perfectly. I did all the books, the hiring and firing, the prep. The drugs just fucked up my mind. And I blame the restaurant for the drugs. I was so stressed at the end. And with the restaurant right in the middle of Garden City, it was easier to do drugs than not. I just know I can get back to be the

Me I know is inside me. The man I know I can be," he proclaimed. "And you're the only one who can help me do it."

"Jake, you need to make a choice. Use your mind or take the easy path of indulgence. If you use your brain, you'll become a man. If you just keep indulging your every whim, you'll stay a child. Your choice."

"Can you teach me?" he sounded solemn.

"Of course I can. I've been trying. Can you learn?" she rebutted.

"I can try."

"Well, first you have to have faith in the power of your mind. That your mind is the most powerful tool you have. When you want—just want—you need to tell yourself that's all it is. You can't do everything you want. You have to think about the consequences of your desires. You may want to shoot someone because they were mean. But you don't because you consider the consequences and realize that the result will be arrest and electrocution. It's the same concept with everything in life. For example, when you want that third helping of spaghetti, you need to use your brain and ask yourself if you're really hungry—determine the consequences. Would that be so hard? If you overeat just because you want, you'll be burping and farting all night. You won't want sex, you'll be miserable, and you'll make me equally miserable. You're disgusting to watch eat because you shovel all the food in your mouth so fast. Do you understand the metaphor?" Emma paused to ask, wondering if he even knew the meaning of the word metaphor.

"Look, I'm gonna eat when I want and what I want!" he defended. "I'm a guy. I'm gonna burp and fart. Live with it."

"No, I don't have to live with it. You can leave if you can't learn how to be an adult," Emma said, her frustration beginning to show. She didn't want to lose him. Her ego was so satisfied by being seen with this gorgeous hunk of man, and Emma enjoyed the idea of being a part of a couple. She hadn't had that companionship in such a long time, and it was the first time she had been in a real relationship. But ego and loneliness aside, he could bring her to a level of anger she had never known was possible. "You're hopeless. You say you want to be better, but you just can't learn a goddamned thing," and Emma stomped out of the great room. "I'm taking a bath. I'd really love it if you were gone when I get out."

She slammed the bedroom door so hard, it rattled the china. She didn't know whether she wanted to scream or cry. Jake was just mentally dense, and it was driving Emma crazy. She calmed down enough to get into a hot bath. Emma kept telling herself she was a member of Mensa. She was Doctor Emma Weiss, PhD, an intelligent woman who prided herself not only on having brains but more on putting that mind to good use. And this situation was testing her ability. He just has to have more brains than the turnip he appears to have, she told herself as she took deep breaths of the lavender aromatherapy.

Suddenly the door flew open. No knock, just pushed open.

"What the fuck do you want?" she asked, obviously not over the anger part of her emotions.

"I'm sorry," Jake said as he closed the lid and sat himself on the toilet to look at her.

"For what? For being stupid? Or for just being stubborn?" Emma asked as she shaved her legs and tried desperately to pretend he wasn't there.

"Both. Everything. Look, honey. I just have a hard time being told what to do. My mother could never control me, and I never had the discipline of a father," he rationalized.

"You know, Jake. I really don't give a shit what your childhood was like. You're an adult. You're thirty years old and you act like a spoiled ten-year-old. Either grow up or get out."

"Please don't say that, darlin'. I love you and I couldn't live without you. Give me a chance. I'll really try to learn from you," he said calmly.

"You don't try anything. You just indulge. If you put forth even a little effort, you could accomplish anything. I believe in you or you wouldn't be here. But you're just so lazy. Remember the concept of giant killer? If you don't get that ingrained into you, you'll never survive."

"I know, darlin'. And I can. I just know I can. I'll eat slower, so I know when I'm full."

"Oh, Jake. Bless your heart," she muttered now in Southern fashion. This was the Southern way of saying "you're a schmuck," without really saying it. "You just haven't got a clue, do you?" He probably didn't know what a metaphor was, she thought with a deep sigh.

"Whaddaya mean?"

"Jake, eating is just a symptom. It's your overall attitude. Once you start anything, you can't stop. When you start eating, you can't stop. When you start drinking, you can't stop. When you start doing coke, you can't stop. You just have no self-control. Except where sex is concerned, which is just my luck. You have perfect control over that," she muttered as she got out of the tub. "I shouldn't be able to stand here naked without some reaction from you. You can't understand how that hurts. You indulge in every other whim but that one."

Emma toweled herself off and untied her long, golden hair from the clip atop her head. After donning a pink cashmere robe, she began to brush her hair. Then she smoothed moisturizer on her porcelain face and long neck.

"You see, Jake. This should be turning you on. And if it did, knowing your lack of control, you should be attacking me. But you don't. Maybe you really do like men more than women," she reproached.

"Baby, you know I love you and find you attractive. I couldn't make love to you at all if I didn't. I'm just not made that way. I have to care about someone to have sex with them. I just can't get it up on demand."

"I'm not demanding anything. But you're thirty years old. You should be ready most of the time and thinking about it even more often. But you don't. You overindulge in every other desire, just not sex. Is it the drugs?" Emma asked.

"Yeah. It takes a while for the drugs to get completely out of my system. It's really messed with my sex drive. But the longer I'm clean, the easier it gets."

"It just really hurts me," Emma confessed. "Here I am, a reasonably attractive woman, naked in front of the man I have sex with and nothing. It's humiliating."

"Oh, baby. Don't feel that way. You are so sexy and so beautiful. You just deserve better than me. I'm just not a normal man. Did I tell you a psychic once said I wasn't of this world? I think I'm really an alien or something."

"Honey, you're definitely human. You just need to use your brain," Emma told him.

"I know, I know. And I know you can show me how. You're the smartest person I've ever known. How do you do it?"

"I told you sitting on the sofa. It's just mind over matter. Think before you act. You just do. You don't think about consequences, and honey, you're going to be forced to do that sooner or later whether you want to or not." Emma certainly didn't realize how much that one statement would foreshadow the coming months. It was just an obvious fact to her.

"You need to see things through to their conclusion. If you get into your truck and start driving toward Garden City, you know what the results will be, but you just avoid looking at them. You need to stop and pull over. Get out of the truck and think. Just take ten minutes to consider what will happen after you arrive in Garden City. Then what will happen after you score the drugs. Not just think about doing the drugs but follow it through to its logical conclusion. What will be the consequences after you get that momentary high? If you try that, you might not continue the drive to Garden City," she patiently explained.

"That's a great idea. And I could call you if I'm really stuck, right?"

"Of course. I'd never be angry with you for telling me you want to do drugs. I would be proud of you. I understand the desire. It's when you act on it that I'll be supremely pissed off," Emma assured him.

"Then that's a plan. You can be my sponsor. If I'm thinking about using, I'll try the pull over thing, and if it doesn't work, I'll call you," he said happily.

"Great, honey. I'm glad we got all this out. Maybe things

will change."

"They will. I promise, baby. Now what do you say to a game of Scene-it?" Jake replied. "Then we can come in here and make love."

"Sounds good," Emma sighed. How had he done this? she thought. How had he taken a volatile situation—one in which she was ready to throw him out in the street—and changed it back into a happy couple completing their evening? Was he just manipulative, or was he genuinely trying to be a better person? Emma only knew for certain that she wanted to believe it was true.

Chapter Ten

Jake didn't keep the promises he made to Emma. He didn't call her when he had a craving because if he called, she would stop him from doing what he wanted to do; use cocaine. She spoke with Joe daily, who was always supportive. But stupidity was becoming the watchword of Jake Stanton. He was coming up with some doozies, and Emma was finally starting to see them for the lies they were, although she couldn't prove any of them. As absurd as the dog ate her jewelry had been, and as hard as he tried to convince her that he was telling the truth, Emma didn't believe a word of his story. But it was difficult to condemn him when he swore his innocence so vehemently.

Some were such absurd lies that only a moron would believe them, and Emma was becoming more and more angry that Jake was trying them out on her, as though he thought she were such a moron. One evening in March, he apologized profusely.

"I broke your camera last night," he said full of contrition. "I was in your office and was looking for a picture on it, and I dropped it. I'm so sorry, Emma."

When she went into her office the next morning while he was showering, she noticed that not only was her digital camera gone, but so was the USB cable that connected it to her computer and so were the spare batteries. Yeah, sure, she thought. If it was broken, he wouldn't have needed all the attachments to it. But it wasn't expensive, and it wasn't worth the horrendous fight that would ensue, so she let it go. His stories were far-fetched but just plausible enough to have difficulty proving them to be the lies they were.

Then Emma noticed her gun missing. Emma had always kept a .22 caliber Beretta in her night stand for protection, and she knew how to use it. Her father had taken her to gun ranges for target practice her whole life. She hadn't noticed it was missing because the holster was there. Any time she looked in the drawer, she saw the holster and assumed the gun was in it. There was no telling when the gun itself had gone missing. Again, she confronted Jake.

"It must have been during the robbery," he replied. "It's against my probation to even be in a house with a gun, let alone take one," he had convinced her. So she went to the nearest gun store and bought a new Beretta .32 caliber Tomcat. She bought the spare clip and hollow point bullets and returned it to the original holster in her beside drawer.

Emma was paying his probation officers routinely, so it was quite a jolt when Jake's probation officer called at the house.

"Jake Stanton, please. This is Mrs. Johnson," an official voice said over the phone. Emma looked at the caller ID and saw it was from Chatham County.

"I'm sorry. He's not here right now. Can I help you? I'm his fiancée," she responded hesitantly.

"He hasn't shown up for probation, which means he has two choices; either outpatient counseling or inpatient counseling. His choice. But he must begin one or the other immediately."

"Can you recommend an outpatient counselor?" Emma asked.

"There are several in the Yellow Pages. Just look under

Drug Counseling. They must be certified, and whoever he chooses must forward the paperwork directly to me. If he fulfills the four weeks, then his probation will be reinstated," Mrs. Johnson told her.

Emma told Jake about the phone call as soon as he got home, and they found an outpatient counselor around the corner from her house. She accompanied him for the first session to be sure he went and to be sure the cash went to the counselor and not into Jake's pocket. John Caldorini was a patient, sweet man, and he knew about drug addiction firsthand. He himself was a recovered addict, having been clean for twenty years. So again, Emma shelled out the sixty-five dollars per session to keep Jake on the straight and narrow. He was forced to go twice a week for four weeks. After the second session, she let him go alone. Why she trusted him, she couldn't say. She demanded a receipt each time he went, and he managed to show her one—most of the time. She knew he was drug tested every time he saw John, so that reassured her. She didn't know at the time that Cheryl was giving him her own urine for his tests. But Emma didn't learn the truth until too late.

The lies just continued, and though she saw them for what they were, she overlooked them. She wanted to trust him because if she didn't, she couldn't save him. Although she still maintained her friendships, she did more complaining about Jake than the mooning over him she had done in the beginning of the relationship. She spoke with Kathy Stein, her closest friend, and told her the truth.

Tall and slender with almost a man's short haircut, Kathy was always there for Emma. Even with her ongoing divorce saga, her job as an ICU trauma nurse, and two small children to raise, Kathy still managed to make time for Emma. Whether by phone or coming over when her soon-to-be-ex had the kids, Kathy was there for her.

"What's going on, honey?" she asked in her Alabama twang.

"He's lying so much, but I can't really catch him. I think he's still doing drugs," Emma cried on Kathy's shoulder. "Cheryl says he is but I just can't believe that." Kathy and Cheryl were friends, mostly because their children all went to the private Jewish school together. The kids spent time together, so the mothers saw each other all the time.

"Well, Cheryl isn't the best source," Kathy helped. "She has her own problems with her husband. He's a drug addict. You knew that, right?"

"Yeah, Jake told me. I know his mother is from a prominent Jewish family here in Savannah. And I know that Cheryl's husband, Aaron, tried to kill Jake once. He threw a brick through his windshield, barely missing Jake's face."

"Aaron is on the methadone program to get off heroin," Kathy confided. "And methadone is almost worse than heroin. It makes you really crazy. And everyone in the Jewish community knows he was arrested in Garden City. Gee, I wonder what he was doing there!"

"Same thing Jake goes there for, I would assume. Drugs. But what was he arrested for?" Emma asked.

"Well," she began dramatically, "he was waiting in line at a fast food restaurant, and the woman in front of him wasn't moving fast enough. He reached into his glove box, took out the loaded gun that was in there, and walked up to the car and aimed the gun at the woman's head!"

"Oh, my God! I mean, I certainly believe it of Aaron."

Emma gasped in amazement.

"Oh, it gets better. He tried to back up, and since he was in line, he couldn't. So he just smashed into the car behind him. Well, he was arrested on the spot." Kathy said positively.

"I just don't understand why Cheryl is still with him. I've heard she was also very into drugs herself. So I don't know that I'd take everything she says completely to heart. Then Emma added, "But all these lies Jake keeps telling. He's covering up something." "Has he ever been violent with you?" Kathy asked, concerned.

"No! Of course not. He'd never hurt me. You've seen the way he is with your kids. He wouldn't hurt anyone, except maybe Aaron. Jake doesn't really have any temper; verbally maybe, but not physically. He'd never hit a woman," Emma assured Kathy.

"Okay, sweetie, I'm just checking." Kathy reached for Emma's hand and squeezed it reassuringly. "I don't know what he's up to. I know he loves you and he's adorable. But if he's an addict and he's back using cocaine, honey, he is major trouble. Do any of his dealers know where you live?" she tightened her grip.

"No. I'm sure Jake would never put me in harm's way like that. I think most of his dealers are in Garden City." Emma told Kathy. Emma had completely forgotten about Jake's truck being delivered to her house when he had loaned it to the drug dealer.

"Garden City? Oy gavalt (oh, my gosh in Yiddish)! That's a cesspool!"

"Well, that's where his restaurant was, so I have to believe that's where most of his still connections are."

"Wait. Which restaurant?" Kathy asked.

"Dr. J's Barbecue," Emma told her.

"Oh, my! That was the best barbecue place in Savannah! Everyone knows it. I even ate there. That was before I started keeping kosher, of course. Actually, I think Cheryl mentioned it to me."

"Yeah, everywhere we go, someone knows him from there. It seemed to have a great reputation. It's too bad he had to close it," Emma said.

"Why did it close? God, it was so popular! It was always packed."

"Kath, I don't know. Not really. I've heard so many versions of the story, I don't know what the truth is. I've heard his mother's version, Cheryl's version, and Jake's version. So I guess somewhere in there is the truth. Jake says the restaurant caused him to burn out, and that's why he got so hooked on drugs. Then Cheryl took it over and ran it into the ground. His mother says it was financial problems. Cheryl claims Jake embezzled so much money from the restaurant, she couldn't afford to stay open. I have no idea where the truth really lies."

"It sounds like you're in a real mess. What are you going to do, Emma? I really like Jake, don't get me wrong, but if this is at all true, you could be in a lot of trouble."

"I know, Kathy, I know." The sparkle from her engagement ring caught her eye and her heart. "But I really love him. You've seen his charming side. He's hard to resist. Not to mention that gorgeous face of his," Emma tried to laugh.

"And don't forget that great ass," Kathy added.

"How could I? Ooh, and those shoulders get me every time."

"Yep. Definitely fuckable. No doubt about it. But Em, sex isn't everything. It's most things, I'll grant you, but not everything."

"After three years without it, it seems like everything," Emma admitted.

"Three years? Shit, honey. No wonder you're so stuck on Mr. Gorgeous. I don't think I've ever gone three weeks without sex. I can't even imagine three years!" Kathy nearly stuttered.

"When I was in Florida, I was so wrapped up with work and sailing and my dad, I just didn't have the time or energy to date. And during my first year here, I never met a soul. I couldn't believe none of my friends here knew anyone they could introduce me to. So no dates equals no sex." Emma sighed.

"Honey, you're a beautiful, smart woman. Any man would be lucky to find you," Kathy said with love.

"Thanks, sweetie. But none have found me. Except Jake. And that was an accident."

"Do you think Jake will really convert so you can get married?" Kathy asked.

"He says he will, but I sure don't see him doing anything about it. There was a one-day class with Rabbi Belzer at Mikvah Israel downtown. I mean, Jeez! He could have done the whole conversion in one day. He would have to go to Friday night services every week for a year, but the class was only one day! Not too much to ask. And Rabbi Belzer only does that once a year. He didn't go. If he really wanted to, he would have," Emma explained.

"Well, he probably will. He just needs to stay clean. Do you know the signs of cocaine use? Have you ever done it?" Kathy asked.

"No, I never have. I smoked some pot in high school, but I never even tried cocaine. Putting something up my nose was just a turnoff. You?"

"Yeah, I've tried it. It's a major rush—for about fifteen minutes. Then the low is gut-wrenching. That's why people get so addicted. They want to stay on that high—which is really great—without the low. From a clinical standpoint, I've seen my share of overdoses in the ER. It's not pretty. Addicts are just destined to either death or prison. I'm not saying that's Jake's future, but if he doesn't get off his ass and realize what he's doing, it could be."

"Everyone keeps telling me I'm the best thing that ever happened to Jake and that he's not that far gone. Cheryl, his mother, Joe—they all believe he can become the good man that they've seen glimpses of now and again. And that I'm the one who can guide him. I just know I can save him, Kathy. I've seen that side of him, too. The man who wants children and stability. He wants a good job that will sustain both of us and will live happily ever after together," Emma blinked back the tears that were starting to form.

"Where is he now?" Kathy asked.

"Who knows? He's supposed to be looking for a job and attending AA meetings. Hell, he leaves first thing in the morning for the seven-thirty meeting. Then sometimes he comes home to eat and then goes back out job hunting. Today he didn't even come home to eat. He calls to check and tell me where he is. I helped him with a great resume, so he's trying every restaurant in town."

"Speak of the devil," Kathy said when she heard the squeak of the wrought iron gate open and the lock on the door turn.

"Yep. Speak of the devil and he appears." Jake walked in, all smiles. He gave Kathy a big hug.

"Hi, Kathy!" He was so sweet. "How are the kids?" And hello to you, angel." He bent over to kiss Emma.

"Hey, Jake. The kids are good. They can't wait to see Uncle Jake," Kathy smiled back at him.

"Bring them by, Kathy. You know I love playing with them," he said.

"Maybe Sunday I'll bring them. Well, I'd better be going. You two have fun," she winked at Emma.

"We will," Emma laughed. Jake had sat down next to her and put his arm around her. He had his hand on her leg and gently squeezed.

Kathy left and Jake led Emma immediately into the bedroom, where he began stripping off his clothes. Emma was shocked. Spontaneity was not a common event with Jake.

"You just look so sexy, Emma," Jake said. She was wearing low-rise jeans, a white tank top, and a cut up burgundy sweatshirt with the Flintstones on it. The neckline was cut so it fell off her shoulders, and the bottom was cut so it left her midriff bare but for the line of white from her tank top. "You know that outfit turns me on," he added. "God, and you smell so good," he bent down and kissed her neck. She wore her usual fragrance. It was a spicy, ginger fragrance from Origins. Emma was environmentally conscious and was a member of PETA. She wouldn't use any products that tested on animals. When she found Origins years before, she was thrilled.

Whatever anger or frustration Emma felt due to his lies flew out the window as he undressed her. He turned out the bright overhead light and turned on the warming floor lamp so he could see her clearly. He dragged her jeans down, and Emma pulled the sweatshirt over her head. As he kissed her and began taking the kiss deeper, Emma forgot everything. He dragged her tank off her shoulders with his teeth and began nibbling his way down her body. She pulled the top off, and he began playing with the straps of her bra.

As he worked his way down her body, she caressed his broad shoulders and even found the small tattoo on his upper arm sexy. Emma didn't like tattoos as a rule, but on those broad, strong shoulders, it was impossible not to be turned on by the single, small tattoo. She looked into the bright green of his eyes and ran her fingers through his curly hair. She nipped lightly at his earlobe and she could feel the small shudder that emanated from him.

As his mouth got busy, working its way down her slender body, Emma also shuddered. He had a mouth that could work miracles. And he knew just how long to work his mouth on her inner thighs and the depth of her to push her right to the edge but never over; just enough to make her completely ready for him. When he entered her, he just slipped gently inside. Their rhythm together was perfect. They almost always climaxed together.

When they were finished, Emma always wanted to snuggle with him for a few minutes to enjoy the emotion of the moment. But Jake popped out of bed so fast, it was impossible. He immediately went into the bathroom to clean up and began getting dressed. And he was always starving afterward. Regardless of the time, he was ready for a meal. Jake's insecurity was also consistent. He never stopped asking if the sex was all right for Emma. She was getting used to it. The reassurance was constant.

He started dinner, snacking the whole time he was cooking. While he was making spaghetti and meatballs, he ate two plain hot dogs. Emma made a salad for herself, since Jake didn't know how to make a salad because he refused to eat one.

They took their meals into the great room, turned on the quiz show Cash Cab on the Discovery Channel, and decided what movie they would watch afterward. The decision was usually a comedy—Monty Python and Kevin Smith were their favorites. Emma listened to Jake burp and fart, as real men will do (life according to Jake, which irritated the shit out of her.) They took a break to play a few games of pool and then played Scene It. Although Emma almost always won, they still had fun playing. But Jake would start jumping up and down and running around the room trying to remember an answer. It was like playing with a five-year-old.

Jake's emotions were usually all over the place. He would tease Emma in cruel ways. He reminded her of a little boy who dunked the pigtail of a little girl in inkwell—that was Jake. And as he taunted Emma by finding a tiny hair on her chin and trying to pull it out with his fingernails, he would tell her he only teased those he loved. Sure, Emma thought, just like a spoiled child would do.

"You're driving me crazy," she would say when his mood was so erratic, she would just fall into her own mood of frustration.

"Not a far drive," he would snicker, thinking he was funny. But with everything Emma had done for him, given him, and put up with, she was damned if she would be talked to with so little respect. So she smiled and looked him in the eye.

"Fuck you," she said, smile still pasted on her face. Then she turned around and walked away.

"Honey, don't take me so seriously. I don't mean anything by it. If I didn't love you, I wouldn't tease. I always talked to Mom that way," he rationalized.

"Sweetheart," she said with venom in her eyes. "I'm not your mother. She had to love you. I don't." And she went into the bathroom, where he couldn't follow her.

Other times, they would be standing in the kitchen, and Jake would grab Emma by her waist from behind and begin to hump her. She took it to mean that he was feeling—amorous. She turned to him and gently grabbed his cute ass.

"Well, hello," she would say and stand on her tiptoes to kiss him. She could feel him getting hard, and yet he would do nothing about it. He would just continue cooking or eating and resist the spontaneous moment.

Emma was totally confounded by these nearly daily occurrences. In the grocery, he would grab her butt and whisper, "Let's do it in the car. You're so sexy." But by the time they got home, he would be distracted and do nothing about his sexual urges. Emma could not understand Jake. If he had an urge for drugs, he acted on it without a thought of the consequences or the betrayal of stealing from Emma to obtain them. But he rarely acted upon his sexual urges. This was a complete mystery to her.

Jake satisfied all of his own desires immediately. If he was hungry, he ate. It didn't matter that Emma had planned a dinner at six o'clock and he was hungry at four o'clock. If he wanted a beer, he just took one. If he wanted a nap rather than look for a job or do a chore, he couldn't resist it. He satisfied himself with no thought to the negative consequences. Yet he could have an erection hard enough to hang an anchor from, and that he would resist. Why?

Emma just couldn't understand how Jake's mind worked. He was so self-indulgent about everything in his life. But this one indulgence that would have helped cement his relationship with Emma and have only positive consequences, he would not gratify.

Chapter Eleven

By the end of March, Emma knew of three jobs Jake had taken and lost. He kept claiming he was burnt out of the restaurant business, having managed and worked his own restaurant for ten years. He needed a rest, and this was the first real vacation he had in those ten long years. His own consulting business had never gotten off the ground, and Emma was sure it was because after his first two rejections, he probably never went into another restaurant. Of course, he continued to lie about going out looking for clients so he could be out on his own and get into trouble. But no money was coming in, and thousands were going out.

Between his two pack a day smoking habit, the gas-guzzling old truck of his, and his bottomless pit of a stomach, his lifestyle alone was breaking Emma. Add to that, his cell phone bill, insurance for his truck (which was now Emma's pride and joy), monthly payments on two storage units, and both of his monthly probation payments, Emma's expenses were skyrocketing. That didn't count the amount he stole from her that she had to replace. Her inheritance was flying through her hands. She had already overspent on renovations to her house, but she believed that had been an investment. Emma had bought the house for far less than its value, and she was sure she would make a profit on it, were she to sell. But it had still taken a chunk out of her funds. Jake was an expense that was just getting out of control.

In early April, Emma was invited to Kathy's house for a birthday party. Kathy was not one to be alone, and she had started dating. It had started out as a friendship, since the new boyfriend, Cal, was not Jewish. Kathy continually told Emma that she could never be serious about him even though he was a wonderful father to his two children who were the same ages as Kathy's. They went boating together with the kids and had kept it rather light, especially during the vicious divorce Kathy was enduring. She didn't want to take any chances. But they began a weekday rendezvous on Wednesdays, and soon they were a couple.

When Emma told Jake about the party, he hemmed and hawed. He felt uncomfortable around large groups unless he had chemical help. He agreed to go as long as he could have a couple of beers. Foolishly, Emma acquiesced for selfish reasons. She wanted Jake with her. She would have a handsome man on her arm and not be the only single woman at the party.

Emma left her long blond hair loose but curled it, flowing endlessly down her back. The springtime weather in Savannah was lovely, so she wore a white eyelet tank top that was reminiscent of a corset and low-rise, tight jeans, and her favorite black leather belt with a huge rhinestone buckle. She wore black cowboy-style suede boots to complete the outfit. She added only navy blue mascara to accentuate her large, soulful eyes, peach blush to her high cheekbones, and peach lip gloss to enhance her already full lips. She was ready to go, once she put on her jewelry. She had splurged long before Jake and bought a silver Tiffany heart charm, and she always wore her large clear quartz necklace on a thirty-inch silver chain. Clear quartz was said to give strength, and Emma liked to cover all her bases.

Jake looked equally handsome in linen (which of course, Emma had bought for him.) A loose white linen V-neck shirt and tan linen slacks. His dark curly hair nearly touched the collar of his shirt and with the way the shirt was cut, the little curly dark chest hair he had was visible. He fussed over what he wore, how his hair looked, did his shoes go with the outfit. He was more concerned about his appearance than Emma was, and she had to continually reassure him.

They left the house together, Jake driving Emma's Lexus SUV, to go the few blocks to Kathy's house. Emma, as was her nature, immediately began helping Kathy in the kitchen. Cal hadn't arrived yet, and Kathy was still preparing. After giving Jake a hug and then a tight hug to Emma, Emma's closest friend confided her fears.

"Em, I'm so nervous. Cal's parents brought over this casserole thing that's soooo traif (non-kosher)! I mean, pork hot dogs and cheese and God knows what else! Oy gavalt! But it's Cal's favorite, so they brought it. I don't know what to do with it," she confessed.

"That's why I brought all my Arthur Court serving pieces, honey. I've had plenty of traif in them so it doesn't bother me. We'll just put it in the Pyrex Arthur Court, and I'll take it with me to wash at home. Don't worry about a thing," Emma rubbed Kathy's back.

"You're the best, Em. That's why I love you. Can I leave some of this to you? Just use your judgment about the traif stuff. I still have to take a quick shower so I can look even a quarter as gorgeous as you do!"

"Honey, go! I'll take care of everything," Emma pushed.

After Kathy left the kitchen, Emma glanced at Jake. He had already grabbed a beer and was heading outside for a smoke.

"Uh, Jake," she stopped him. "You wanna give me a hand in here?"

"Of course, baby," he said, and turned around to make himself useful.

As the party filled with people, Jake drank his second and then his third beer. He was certainly charming—for a while. Then he found Emma and Kathy in the kitchen alone.

"So, ladies," he began. "When are we all going skinny-dipping in Emma's pool?"

Emma was shocked. Where had that come from? The alcohol? But he didn't stop there. "Doesn't that sound fun, Kathy? No one can see anything back there. We could just lie out in the sun as God intended."

Emma looked at Kathy to see if she was as shocked as she was by this unusual outburst, but she didn't seem to be. Maybe Kathy had enough wine in her to soften the silliness of the conversation. Or maybe she was just more kinky than Emma.

Emma glared at Jake. "What's the matter with you?" she asked him.

"Nothin'. Why?" he drawled.

"Forget it," Emma muttered and she walked out of the kitchen to mingle.

Not fifteen minutes later, after they had only been at the party for an hour or so, Jake walked up to Emma and told her he was leaving and would pick her back up when she was ready.

"What! Where are you going?" Emma gasped.

"I just need to get away from the crowds. You know I'm claustrophobic. I'm just going to go home and veg for a while.

When you want me to pick you up, just call me."

"Fine. Whatever," Emma said in disgust. And out walked her fiancé.

Emma stayed and tried to have a good time with people she didn't know, but it was gnawing at her that she had been abandoned and had no idea where he was really going. Finally, at nine thirty, Emma had enough of the drunken people and wanted to go home herself. She told Kathy she'd come by the next day to pick up her Arthur Court serving pieces and help with the clean up. She picked up her cell phone to call Jake at home. No answer. She called his cell phone. When he answered, she became really pissed off.

"Where the hell are you?" she asked. "I thought you wanted to go home."

"Cheryl called and said she and the kids were going to Wal-Mart, so I went with them. Are you ready to leave?" he answered almost absently.

"So being with me and staying by my side was too many people, but being in a huge department store full of people was okay? God, you're an asshole. Yes, I wanted to come home to be with you. Obviously, you don't give a shit about me—or my car. Where is it?"

"Jesus, honey! Your car is in your garage. I'm in Cheryl's. We're almost at the house, so I should be there in fifteen or twenty minutes. I thought you'd want to stay later…"

"Just shut up and come get me," she cut him off in midsentence and hung up the phone.

Jake's selfishness and self-absorption were driving Emma crazy. She waited outside and finally drank a beer of her own. She lighted a cigarette and waited for her car to pull up. When it did, she opened her own door, her hands loaded with some of her serving pieces. Jake tried to run around to help her, but she was too fast. She put the bag in the back and slid into the passenger's seat, slamming the door behind her. Then she turned completely quiet. A bad sign. A very bad sign.

"Please talk to me, honey," Jake implored. He seemed fairly calm, but Emma could never tell when Jake had used cocaine. Not until it was far too late.

"About what?" Emma asked rhetorically. "About why you're such a selfish shit or try to ask if you used and are just lying about Cheryl? Which, exactly, would you like to talk about?"

"Uh, neither?" he tried to make light of the situation.

"Fine. Then just shut up and take me home."

"Honey, why does everything have to be a fight? What did I do?" Jake asked with innocence dripping from him.

"Okay, are you just stupid or are you such a compulsive liar, you don't know what the truth is?"

"Don't call me stupid," he said laughing, quoting one of their favorite movies A Fish Called Wanda.

"Yeah, yeah. And I've worn dresses with higher IQs than you," she answered, continuing the quote from the movie. "But you are so clueless; you don't even know what's wrong. You're a selfish bastard. You couldn't stay with me at my best friend's house for a small party. I didn't know anyone either. It would have been nice to have my fiancé by my side! We could have had fun together. But no, you only thought about yourself. You are so self-absorbed," she screamed. "I've so had it."

"Baby, don't say that. I just saw my sister and my niece and nephew for a little while. Is that such a crime? I never get to see them because of her asshole husband. This was a way I could see my family. You were having fun, and I was so uncomfortable. Then Cheryl called and asked me to join her and the kids," he explained.

"And you didn't go to Garden City first—in my car—and use?" she demanded.

"No, baby. Of course not," he sounded so sincere. "You look terrific, you know," he added. "Let's go inside and make love." Jake was becoming a better liar. At least he knew how to deceive her with a bit of panache.

Emma and Jake went into the house, let Tasha outside for her evening constitutional, and then went into the bedroom. Jake drew his shirt over his head, and as always, Emma melted. Seeing those shoulders, strong and broad, always brought her to her knees. He looked over at her to see her begin stripping down to her lace bra and panties. Jake rarely undressed her, which he didn't understand would turn her on. She lay on the bed, black lace bra and matching black lace thong.

"Wow, you really are sexy," Jake managed.

"Back at you," she smiled. He didn't kiss her mouth; he just began ravaging her body. Finally she initiated the kissing, since he was so good at it. Her thumb followed the little dent in his chin. As she looked into his bright green eyes, she sighed. She was already excited, and he'd barely done anything.

He drew down her bra and began caressing her breasts. His mouth moved south as he pulled off her panties. As his mouth did wonderful things to her body, she was fully excited. Then he looked at her. She knew that look. He raised the full length of his body up, and she saw his disgust. He was limp as a noodle. He began to wiggle his penis with his hands, almost daring it to harden.

"Fuck! Could you just...I don't know. Do something." he snarled. "Touch it."

"Jake, if all that didn't turn you on, then just forget it. Just go away, please," she pleaded and she turned her head away from him. She couldn't stop the tears from falling.

"Oh thanks. That makes me feel better. Turn on the tears," he blathered.

"Jake, I don't turn them on. I'm not one of your Scarlett O'Hara Southern belles that plays games with crying. I can't help it. I'm just in physical pain and emotionally humiliated. Please go away," she said into her pillow.

"Fine. I'll go sleep on the sofa."

"No, please don't. Sleep in the guest room. Then you won't hear me, and I won't even know you're here," she pleaded.

"Whatever," he said as he grabbed his pillow and walked away.

Emma's tears turned into sobs once Jake had left the room. She couldn't sleep. She quietly walked down to the wet bar in the great room and poured herself a snifter of Grand Marnier, sobbing as she walked. She didn't want Jake to see her since she didn't want him to know where she'd hidden the good liquor. So she snuck back into her bedroom and turned on the television, sipping her drink, sobbing.

When he opened the door, Emma was surprised. She thought he would just go into the guest bedroom on the other side of the house and brood.

"What do you want?" she cried.

"Please don't cry, baby. I can't take it when you cry."

"Then don't make me cry," she replied between sobs.

"Don't you think I'm just as humiliated as you are? I don't exactly feel like much of a man right now," he told her.

"That's your problem. You did use tonight, didn't you? That's why you can't get it up. What happened? You had a couple of beers at the party, and that was just enough to muddle your brain, so you decided to go out and do coke. Did Cheryl give you enough cash to score?" she retorted angrily.

"Yes. That's exactly what happened. I'm so sorry. It won't happen again. I'll go back to the AA meetings. I can't lose you and I don't want this life. I'll find a good job and help out at home. I really want a better life, Emma," he tried.

"This is your last chance, Jake. Do you understand? The very last chance. You do coke one more time, and I don't care where you go, as long as it's away from this house and away from me. Are you getting this? I know tonight is the wrong time to confront you because you're wasted, but I hope it's sinking in," Emma told him.

"Yeah. It's sinking in. I'm going to bed and sleep this off. I'll be fine by tomorrow and we'll deal with it. I won't do this again. I promise. Good night, baby." And he slunk off to bed.

When Emma received her Comcast Cable bill the next week, she noticed it was higher than normal. She looked at the back and nearly shrieked out loud, even though she was alone. But she picked up the phone immediately and dialed Jake's cell phone.

"Hi, baby," he said warmly.

"Don't even try. There's fifty dollars-worth of pornography on this bill. The date is the night you couldn't get it up with me and I was crying into a glass of Grand Marnier. How could you? You couldn't have sex with me, so you not only jerked off all night alone, which is even more humiliating to me, but you didn't even consider the cost! Sixteen dollars a pop to get your rocks off by yourself! You asshole!" now she was shrieking.

"I'll be home in a few minutes so we can talk. I'm at Joe's just hanging out and shooting the shit," he tried to hang up.

"Talk about what? At least they're girl on girl and not man on man," she yelled at him. "Teenage girls! What, I'm too old for you?"

"It's not like that, Emma. Can we just talk? I'll be home in a minute." He hung up the phone.

Emma was steaming angry when he returned. She tried to calm herself but nothing worked. She had dropped all but one of the pay channel stations to lower her monthly expenses, so she was missing all the great movies on HBO, Showtime, and Cinemax. Then Jake just runs the bill right back up with this smut. Emma had never even watched a porno movie. But Jake seemed as addicted to them as he was to drugs.

When he walked in the door, Emma sat with the bill in her hand. Her hands were shaking, she was so angry. He tried to kiss her hello, but she turned away from him.

"Let's hear your bullshit, Jake," she taunted. "I'm just sure you've got a good one."

"Emma, honey, don't. The reason I wanted to talk about it here was because it's not like you think. I wasn't even aware that I did it. I swear I don't remember even ordering them. And I couldn't jerk off. I guess I was trying to prove to myself that I could get it up and I couldn't. Not with you, not by myself, not with porn."

"Is that supposed to make me feel better? While I was in bed—alone and crying—you were in my guest room watching girls and trying to get off? Doesn't work, pal. You're a piece of shit."

"Yeah, I am," now Jake sat on the love seat across from Emma and lowered his head in shame. The tears ran down his cheeks, and he wiped them with his sleeve. "Can I have a tissue?" Emma passed a tissue over to him, and he blew his nose. "I am a piece of shit, and you deserve so much better than me. I'll leave. I have nowhere to go but I'll leave."

"Well, you can't leave. You'll go directly to jail. You haven't been to see John Caldorini, have you? He called today, asking where you've been." John had told her (which he wasn't supposed to confide) that he was writing a letter to Jake's probation officer telling her that Jake had reneged on their arrangement. Emma relayed the information to Jake.

"Either he goes into inpatient rehabilitation or he goes back to jail, Emma. Those are his choices," John had told her just that day.

She looked over at Jake, and he was sobbing. It was pathetic. All of his kindness and heart shone brightly, but the guilt and shame far overpowered whatever goodness was left within him.

"I can't go back to jail, Emma. I just can't. I've got to go into rehab. Can you...will you...help me?" he cried. "I'm so miserable. The guilt over what I've done to you is eating me up. I know what I've done, and I know I don't deserve anything from you, but you're all I have. Mom doesn't have the money. Cheryl certainly doesn't, and Aaron wouldn't let her if she did."

"What about Joe? Would he help out financially?" Emma asked.

"No. I've hurt him too many times. He'll talk to me all day long, but he's sworn he'd give me no more money," he replied.

"Well, one way or another, you're going into rehab, Jake. That's the bottom line. I can't take this lying anymore. I can't take the humiliation."

"It's my last chance in life, Emma. If I screw it up, that's the end for me," Jake cried into his sleeve.

Chapter Twelve

The last week in March was spent researching both locally and online for a drug rehab facility for Jake. Emma and Jake searched for one that was affordable, close, and had a good reputation. She spoke with Narcotics Anonymous, John Caldorini (his inpatient drug counselor), his sister Cheryl (who had also been in drug rehab), and researched online. It became a full-time job. Either the drug rehab facilities were obscenely expensive, were located in Mexico, or were all women. Finding a male facility that was reasonably close to Savannah and priced so Emma could afford it was becoming difficult. Finally, they were referred through referral after referral, to a facility in South Carolina.

It was located pretty much in the middle of nowhere, which was perfect. No escape. That aspect of their facility was part of their allure and their success. Once an addict was dropped off, there was literally no way to escape because no cars were allowed on the premises. The compound was miles from civilization. They cooked all their own meals and ate well, according to the head counselor. They received state funding, so the price to the individual was reasonable.

Emma approached Jake with the information. The facility had faxed a copy of their brochure to her, so she showed it to Jake.

"They'll take you and I can afford it. It's the last penny you'll ever get out of me, but if it works, it will be worth it,"

Emma told him.

"I understand, baby. You've done more for me than anyone. I don't deserve you."

"No, you don't. But if I can save you and the drug rehab works, I will have been put on this earth for a reason. I will have saved one life. And that will be worth it," Emma replied.

She got the facility on the phone, and they said there were no open beds at the moment but to keep calling back. Beds opened up every day. So every day, Emma called.

With the decision made and remaining in a waiting pattern, the phone rang. It was Joe's business partner, Kirk.

"Big Joe's in the hospital," Kirk told Emma.

"Oh my God! What is it?" Emma asked urgently. She mouthed to Jake that Joe was in the hospital and that Kirk was on the phone.

"Give me the phone," Jake asked Emma. She handed him the phone.

"Hi, Kirk. It's Jake. What happened?" Jake asked.

"He had a heart attack. They don't know if he'll make it," Kirk stammered.

"We'll be right there. What room number?" Jake asked. Kirk told him, and together, Jake and Emma went to the hospital. They stopped in the lobby, and Emma bought flowers to bring up to Joe. As soon as they got to the room, Emma kissed Joe on the cheek.

"Hey, you. How are you feeling?" she asked. Jake was in utter shock and could barely manage a word to his father figure.

"Oh, looking at your pretty face helps," Joe told her with a smile. "I'll be fine. Don't you worry yourself about me."

"So, Joe. Any hot nurses to sponge bathe you?" Jake

managed. He just couldn't take it seriously. It hurt too much. He paced the room and couldn't look Joe in the eye.

"Yeah, boy. Always that around. You be good, Jake. And don't you lose this beautiful lady. Don't you fuck it up. You hear me, boy?" he drawled.

"I won't. In fact, I'm going into drug rehab. So everything's going to be fine. Okay Joe? Don't worry about me. You just worry about getting yourself up and running that store," Jake told him.

"I'll do that. Y'all go home and have some fun. Don't worry about me, okay? I'll be just fine. I'm tired, though. So I'm gonna catch myself a little nap, and you two go do what you do. Gimme a kiss, gorgeous," Joe said to Emma. She quickly knelt down to his bed and kissed his cheek and squeezed his hand.

"If you need anything at all, Joe, you call me. Okay?" Emma said with an affectionate smile.

"I will. You just take care of this one," he replied, pointing at Jake. Jake lightly punched Joe's arm.

"I love you, man. You know that," Jake said to Joe as they left.

"I love you guys, too. Both of you."

As Emma and Jake walked down the stark corridors, Emma tried to console Jake. He wouldn't have any of it.

"I'll be fine," he kept saying. He just couldn't cope with the vast emotions going on in his head. Emma could only imagine what he was going through. He had lost his own father when he was three, and now there was the distinct possibility that he could lose another father.

The following day was Friday, and Emma called the drug

rehab facility. They had a bed for Jake on Monday. So they began packing and getting Jake ready for his four weeks in nowhere South Carolina. They bought him enough cigarettes and candy to sustain him. They packed a duffle of what he would need, which was mostly shorts and underwear; his leather jacket and jeans for the cooler evenings and plenty of insect repellant. He knew his bags would be checked, so Emma didn't worry about drugs or even Tylenol. They would confiscate anything they found.

"I need to go see Mom, "Jake told Emma. "This is going to be very tough on her. God, I hate to be away from her for four weeks. Will you go see her while I'm gone?"

"Of course. I'll keep her posted on how you're doing and just keep her company. And I'll bring her the treats she likes. Fresh fruit or Doritos. You go. Before it gets too late to see her," Emma said compassionately.

Jake was gone for hours. She knew where he went. Two days before drug rehabilitation and he was using drugs. What an idiot, she thought. She also realized there would be no sex for their last weekend together—maybe their last time together at all. Emma was unsure whether or not she would take him back when he got out and hoped he realized it, too. He probably didn't.

At one o'clock in the morning, he finally returned. He knew she'd be asleep, so he tried to sneak into the guest room. But she wasn't. She was sitting on the sofa—waiting.

"You really are stupid, aren't you?" she said. He just went to the mini-fridge in the wet bar and took a beer.

"Jesus! You scared me. I thought you'd be asleep," he stammered.

"What did you steal to get the money?" she asked.

"Good night, Emma. We're gonna have to deal with this in the morning," he walked away from her.

She slept on the sofa, too upset to even move. The phone woke her at eight thirty on Saturday morning. It was Kirk.

"Hey, Kirk. How's Joe doing?" she managed sleepily.

"He's doing fine. They think he'll make it. But the store was broken into last night. The back door was broken, and there are three mattresses missing."

"Oh my God! Was anyone there or hurt?" she asked, knowing part of what must have happened.

"No. No one was there. We have a camera in the back and we just saw a couple of black guys on it."

"I'll tell Jake. He'll want to know. Keep me informed about Joe, okay? And give him my love," Emma hung up the phone. She immediately went into the guest bedroom and rousted Jake.

"What?" he muttered.

"How could you? You gave the keys to Joe's store to your drug dealers for the money while Joe is in the hospital fighting for his life? Jesus, Jake. You really are a piece of shit," and she turned around, slammed the door, and went into her bathroom to brush her teeth. She grabbed a robe, let Tasha outside, and started the coffee maker. While the coffee was brewing, she fed the dog and ruffled her soft fur. Jake stumbled into the kitchen wearing only his pajama pants. Once again, he was crying.

"You don't deserve the love of anyone, Jake. Just go back to bed and sleep it off. Our last weekend together—maybe ever—and you have to use coke to be sure we don't have sex before you leave. Then you betray the only man who has ever cared about you. You've already betrayed your mother more than anyone has a right to. When you get out of rehab, I really don't think I want you back here. Unless there's a major change, which I don't believe," Emma poured her coffee, added cream and sugar, and walked away.

Jake just went back to sleep. He couldn't handle emotions at all. And he knew Emma was right. He slept for another four hours. Emma did her USA Today crossword puzzle from Friday and sipped her coffee. She got dressed and turned on the television. She needed some mind-numbing activity. All Emma could think about was Jake should be packing and getting organized, but he was just sleeping. There was a Saturday marathon of the television show Monk, which was one of her favorites. Perfect.

Jake finally wandered into the great room and sat on the sofa on the opposite end from Emma. He had nuked a cup of coffee and was half-asleep when the doorbell rang.

"I got it." Emma gave Jake a dirty look. "Don't bother yourself." When Emma opened the door, it was Kirk. He had been to her house before but not often, so it was unusual, and Emma had a bad feeling.

"Hey, guys," he said, obviously putting on a cheerful act.

"You want some coffee, Kirk?" Emma asked politely, and when he shook his head, she asked him to sit down. Kirk sat on the love seat and looked directly at Jake.

"We lost Joe," he said stiffly to Jake. Jake was still a bit under the influence, but she could see his reaction. He was fighting the tears. "He just…slipped away. We thought he was doing better. The blood tests looked good. Then he was just gone."

"Oh, Kirk. He'll be so missed by everyone. He had such a big heart. That's why it couldn't sustain him. It was just too big," Emma said sweetly. "Jake, are you all right?" she asked him.

"No. Yes. I'm—oh, God!" He dropped his head into his hands.

"You know he loved you like a son," Kirk told Jake. "Unfortunately, he knew about the break-in last night. Carl called him and told him."

"The guy who works out of his office? Why would he do that while Joe is in the hospital?" Emma demanded. "That's so wrong."

"Yeah, I agree," Kirk responded. "But he did. I wish Joe hadn't known about it if he was going to—"

"Some people are just insensitive," Emma said.

"I don't think he meant it that way. I think he was just calling to see how Joe was, and when Joe asked what was going on, you know, since I've been with him most of the time, he just told the truth," Kirk explained. "Anyway, I think the funeral will be on Tuesday. It'll take a couple of days to get his family down here and things set up. I just thought y'all should know, and I was driving by here."

"Oh, God," Jake muttered softly. "I won't be here." Emma looked at him for the okay to tell Kirk.

"Kirk, Jake is going into drug rehab on Monday. He'll be there for four weeks. I think that would have made Joe really happy," Emma told him.

"Absolutely. I'll be praying for you, Jake. And Joe would much rather see you in rehab getting your shit together than at his funeral. I know that for sure," Kirk told Jake.

"Yeah," Jake finally looked up. "It would have made him happy. I just can't bear not being at his funeral. I could go up to rehab a couple of days later," he tried.

"No. You can't. We've waited over a week to get this bed, and you can't wait any longer." What Emma wanted to say was she wouldn't let him stay with her another week after what he had done the previous night, but she couldn't embarrass him in front of Kirk that way. She also couldn't explain that his probation officer wouldn't allow it.

"I know I can't," and with that, Jake shut up. As he saw Kirk stand to leave, Jake stood up. Jake went to Kirk and wrapped his long arms around the smaller young man. Kirk was only a year or two younger than Jake, but because of the height difference, he seemed much younger. Jake hugged Kirk with both solace and farewell. "You know how much I'll miss Joe," he said quietly.

"Of course I do," Kirk said to him. "You take care of yourself, Jake. Be good." Emma got up and gave Kirk a hug, as well.

"Let me know, Kirk. I'll be there for both of us. You take care, too. I know you, Kirk. You'll shoulder the whole burden yourself. Let people help you," she urged.

"Thanks, Emma." He hugged her back and left.

When they were alone, Emma became concerned about Jake. He just told her he wanted to go back to bed. He slept the remainder of the day. She was sure part of his exhaustion was from his drug use, but most of it was from guilt and sorrow. Jake was terrible at dealing with his feelings. He was just overwhelmed by emotions. He wasn't sure what to do with them. Consequently, Jake generally just escaped them—one way or another. Either he used drugs or alcohol or television or, in this case, sleep. He would do anything to dull the wild emotions that seemed to attack him.

Emma had tried to convince Jake to write in a journal to get his feelings out and look at them. He told her it was a great idea, but he wouldn't do it. She tried to talk out his feelings with him. He said it hurt his head to think too much. In that way, Emma and Jake were opposites. Emma had been taught all her life to cope with reality. Her father had preached like a religious sermon that whether we want to see our real feelings or not, they exist. Reality is there, like it or not. So watching Jake escape so obviously from the reality of life around him was totally against Emma's upbringing.

As Emma dealt with what was going on around her, Jake slept. She called Cheryl, who was just as close to Joe as was Jake.

"Hi, Cheryl. Honey, are you all right?" Emma asked warmly.

"Oh, Em. I just can't believe it. God! How's Jake taking it?" she asked immediately.

"He isn't. He apparently told his drug dealer pals how to break into Joe's store last night, and they stole three mattresses to pay for Jake to get wasted. Two days before he goes into drug rehab and the day before Joe passes," Emma relayed.

"That part is typical, Emma. The part about him using two days before rehab. He's done it every time. But what he did to Joe? I've got to talk to him," Cheryl told her.

"I just hope that Carl called the police. I know Joe wouldn't call them because he would know that Jake had a part in it. But Carl wouldn't have known, so I hope he did," Emma said.

"I do, too. Jake just can't keep getting away with this," his sister admitted.

"Can we go to the funeral together, Cheryl? It would be a lot easier for me," Emma asked.

"Of course. Well, Aaron is going, and that won't be pleasant for you, but I'll sit between you. Anyway, we'll talk about that later. Right now I want to talk to Jake," she demanded.

"Okay, but he's asleep. He's just running away from it all," and Emma walked the cordless phone into his bedroom. "Here, Jake," she tossed the phone at him. "It's your sister." With that, Emma walked out of the guest bedroom and returned to the sofa and the Monk television show marathon. Okay, even Emma had her breaking point. Even she needed a bit of escapism.

When Jake finally emerged from his depressive, comatose state, he was famished. It wasn't until five o'clock that he wandered out of his room, and he hadn't eaten since lunch the day before. He suggested pasta with sausage, and Emma was in no mood to argue.

"Fine, whatever." Make whatever you want, she thought. You're going to overeat and burp and fart no matter what you make. But be sure to make what you want to eat. I'll be rid of you in twenty-four hours, so do your worst. She said none of this. What for? It had all been said and had gone in one of Jake's ears with nothing in the middle to stop it from coming out the other ear.

As Emma expected, they didn't make love that night. They slept in separate rooms, Jake morose and emotionally empty. By Sunday, Jake started accepting reality and starting packing a bit, though he still tried to con his way out of going, using any excuse possible. Joe's funeral, he wasn't ready, he would miss her. Anything. But Emma's answer was always the same.

"Fine, then go to prison. Jake, you don't have a choice. John already sent the letter to your probation officer, and you either get clean or go to prison."

"You could talk to him. You could convince him to give me another chance," he pleaded.

"No. I couldn't and I won't. You fucked up, Jake. For a change! I won't get you out of it. If you don't go, then just leave here and go somewhere else. But I won't keep supporting this habit or you," she said firmly.

"I know you're right and I'm going to really make it work this time," he promised. "I love you and I need you. I'm really determined this time. Because this is the first time I've had someone to come home to."

"Let's hope so. Because if you don't make it work, you won't have someone to come home to," she said flatly.

"I know, baby. But for Joe, for Mom, and for you, I'm going to come out clean and stay that way forever." Emma sensed at that moment, he really meant it. He might not mean it once he was clean in rehab and needed the high again, but at this moment in time, he was sincere.

They spent Sunday packing, preparing for the trip, and playing. Jake made big, juicy steaks on the grill and his favorite Pasta-Roni, while Emma had her steak with a salad she made. They did make love Sunday night, and it was up to par. They'd had better, but it was warm and loving. And they did sleep together that night before his departure.

Chapter Thirteen

Monday morning, April fifth, was overflowing with anxiety for both Emma and Jake. Fortunately, Emma was able to cope with hers. Unfortunately, Jake wasn't. Emma turned on her efficiency mode, checking Jake's bags for everything necessary. Jake just sat on the love seat—television on—eating and sulking. He had promised to accomplish several goals before he would be gone for a month. He had done none of them. He assured Emma that her fountain would be cleaned out, the bird feeder would be filled, his areas of the house would be tidy, the grass would be mowed, the weeds tended, and flowers watered properly. He did nothing but brood -- and continually tried the con.

"Can't I just go for two weeks?" he was still begging, as late as during the packing of the car. "Then I won't miss your birthday. Isn't it bad enough I have to be in rehab for Joe's funeral and for my birthday, but I don't want to miss yours," he tried.

"Oh, please! Like you give a shit about my birthday! You're just terrified that you'll actually have to give up cocaine. That's all you care about," Emma insisted.

"Baby, that's not true. I love you. I feel so guilty about what I've done to you. All the lying and stealing—I just can't live with myself," he blubbered.

"Good," was Emma's only reaction. "Are you ready to go?"

"Yeah." And with that, Jake carried his duffle bag to the car and got comfortable in the passenger's seat. He said nearly nothing during the four-hour trip to the drug rehab center in South Carolina. He would give occasional directions but little else. It was a very long drive in silence. With one exception. Emma's cell phone rang, startling both of them.

"Hello?" Emma didn't recognize the caller ID number.

"Hi, Jake. It's Aaron," Cheryl's husband started and didn't give Emma enough time to tell him he wasn't talking to Jake. When she heard the rest of his speech, Emma knew Aaron was well aware whom was on the other end of the phone. "I just wanted to wish you good luck. I really hope it works this time. You fucking piece of shit. I hope they never let you out and you end up the same way you always do. Does Emma know that you were the one who committed that robbery? That you let niggers into her house to ransack her personal stuff?" and he hung up.

"Oh, my God!" Emma stammered. "That was Aaron."

"Shit. What did he say?" Jake asked angrily. Emma relayed, word for word, what Cheryl's husband had said to her.

"Why didn't he call your phone if he was trying to talk to you? Wait. He got my number from Cheryl, and he wanted to be sure I got the message. What an asshole! How does she put up with him? Why does she put up with him?"

"I'm calling Cheryl. It's bad enough he said those lies but to call you and do this. Jesus! What a prick!" and Jake dialed Cheryl's cell phone number. She actually answered, which was unusual. Cheryl generally had both kids in the car and didn't answer her phone. Jake told her what Aaron had said. After a beat, Emma listened to try to hear a response. She could hear a loud voice on the other end, obviously a very angry Cheryl.

Jake quickly passed his phone to Emma, who got an apology from Cheryl.

"Cheryl, I don't want your apology. I want Aaron's. He had no right to do that to me. He's a piece of shit, and I want an apology from him," Emma stated plainly. "Just keep him away from me." She handed the phone back to Jake. From her side, Emma could only hear Jake's responses, which sounded like he was defending Emma. She could tell that Cheryl had changed the subject to rehab and was wishing Jake good luck.

"I will, Cheryl. I'll make it work this time. I know I can," Emma heard. Then, "I love you, too. I'll call when I can, and you can get the address from Emma." Jake hung up the phone.

"I'm really sorry for that, baby. Aaron is just crazy. He's probably off his methadone and he just loses it," Jake told Emma.

"I don't care what his excuse is. He had no right to talk to me that way. I've never done anything to that man. And even if he's that pissed off at you, I didn't do it."

"You're right. Of course, you're right. Just stay away from him, okay? He's really got a screw loose. You know he tried to kill me. I want you to be safe, baby. That's all. Just avoid him, okay?" Jake said tenderly.

"You don't have to tell me twice! I wouldn't get anywhere near him. Cheryl just better keep him away from me at the funeral. She said she would sit between us. Shit, why is he going anyway? He didn't know Joe."

"He's probably just going to keep an eye on Cheryl. He gets nuts when she's out of his sight for more than ten minutes. Remember the Christmas party? He wouldn't let her come to your house, and when she snuck out with one of the kids, he called her every five minutes. She couldn't even stay long enough to get a plate of food. That's Aaron. He's a paranoid asshole," Jake reminded Emma.

"Yeah, I forgot about that. Let's just hope he stays out of my way. I swear, Jake, if he crossed the street in front of me I'd hit the gas. Oops, officer! I thought I was hitting the brakes, but I was so startled, I must have hit the gas instead," she laughed.

"I know how you feel but think about the kids. What would Cheryl do?" he defended.

"She'd be better off without him. Did you know Kathy said those marks on Cheryl's neck looked like they were caused by someone trying to strangle her? Aaron did that. You know he did. Anyway, Aaron's not crossing the street in front of my car any time soon, so don't worry." They rode the remainder of the drive in silence.

They stopped at a drive-through fast-food restaurant on the way, Jake stuffing himself, as usual, with more than he really wanted to eat. So Emma was treated, also as usual, to the lovely sound effects that filled the car. Burping along, they made it to the middle of South Carolina and the wilderness where the cabins of drug rehabilitation center lay. The dirt road to the site was at least a mile long. When they finally approached the signs that read "God," "Peace," "Serenity" every twenty feet, they knew they were getting close. Then the cabins were finally visible.

They first went into the cabin that read "Office." Jake picked up his duffle bag and followed Emma inside.

"Hello. I'm here to drop off Jake Stanton," Emma told the kind-looking woman at the desk.

"Yes, we've been expecting you. His bed is ready. I just

need you to both fill out these forms; you as his sponsor and Jake. As forms were passed over the desk, Emma and Jake began filling them in and signing them. Emma handed the woman the check made out to the organization for the first two weeks. The second payment would be mailed before the two weeks were over.

Oddly, Jake's duffle bag was not even checked, which made Emma wary. But they got the tour of the facility and were introduced to the head counselor, Dr. Jeff. Dr. Jeff sat both Emma and Jake down on comfortable, though clearly secondhand, sofas. He began asking Jake questions.

"What is your drug of choice?" Jeff asked, as he wrote the answers on his admittance form.

"Cocaine," Jake answered without looking at Emma.

"Snort or smoke?"

"Both." This time Jake glanced at Emma somberly.

"When did you last use?"

"Yesterday." Jake couldn't look at Emma. She knew he was thinking that she looked too beautiful and innocent and out of place here.

"Shit," she muttered, low enough for him to hear.

"Are you here by choice or by court order?" Jeff continued the questions.

"Choice," Jake said and finally opened up a bit. "I don't want this life anymore. I have this beautiful woman who is the best thing that ever happened to me. I don't want to lose her, and the drugs are taking over my life."

"Have you ever been in rehab before?" Jeff asked.

"Yes. Four or five times. But I never had someone to come home to," Jake answered.

"Uh huh," Jeff muttered. "All right then. Let's take the tour and show you your cabin. I'll introduce you to the other guys and show you how the program works. Emma, you can say your good-byes now. Jake's in my hands now. Oh, and Jake? No cell phones."

Jake handed Emma his cell phone and walked her to her car. He hugged her tightly and kissed her passionately.

"I'm really bad at good-byes." With tears in his eyes, Jake just opened Emma's car door and walked away.

"Good luck," Emma said to his back and watched the man she had once thought was the love of her life disappear in long strides.

Emma's trip home felt interminable. She cried most of the way, though she wasn't sure why. She examined her feelings, as was her way. Were these tears of pain or relief? She would have a month to distance herself from her feelings and try to look at her life more rationally. Emma tried to believe that her tears were because she already missed Jake, but she knew that wasn't true. She was sad that the relationship she had once felt so sure was true love, that Jake was her soul mate, had turned so sour. For a whole month, she could take her jewelry out of her safe and actually wear whatever she liked. She could keep cash on her with no fear of it disappearing. She could keep her credit cards accessible, though she was sure her statements would come in with more fraud on them. Emma breathed a sigh of relief that she could live a normal life, without fear for the following month. She also had to admit she also looked forward to a good night's sleep.

Since Jake had moved into her house or more specifically, since they had become a couple, more nights than not, one of them ended up sleeping on the sofa. Either Emma couldn't take the snoring, screaming, and middle-of-the-night whacks by his sharp elbows or knees and slipped downstairs to sleep; or Jake had used drugs, come in too late, or was just ornery enough that Emma didn't want him in her bed. With Jake gone, Emma had her whole bed to herself and could finally share it with the one she really loved: her beloved Tasha.

Tasha had actually been one of the many fights between Jake and Emma. He acted all day as though he loved Emma's golden retriever, Tasha. But at night, when it was quiet and Jake was self-absorbed, he would complain. He complained about the fur on his side of the bed, complained about Tasha shaking herself (as all dogs do) and the slight jingle made by her rabies tag with each shake, and he would complain about her breath. He would call her up onto the bed and rub her belly, and the moment she got in the way, he physically kicked her off.

"Hey! Don't kick my dog!" Emma would fuss. "She's an old lady with arthritis. Besides, that's her spot. She's been sleeping there for ten years. You've only had that spot for a few months."

It would be a pleasure for both her and Tasha to have their bed back again. No snoring, no wild screams—just quiet. Even the house would be peaceful. But as Emma drove home, she realized she would miss the play and certainly miss the sex. She would miss Jake's helpfulness. He usually made dinner and cleaned up afterward. He always refilled her iced tea and brought her anything she wanted from elsewhere in the house. But there would definitely be a calm that would permeate her world with Jake out of it.

At five-thirty, Emma finally arrived at home. She was exhausted but looked forward to seeing Tasha and being in a quiet house again. She looked around for the peace and saw remnants of Jake everywhere. Just looking at the television brought back thoughts of laughing with Jake. She hugged Tasha instead and let her outside. She waited for the happy face at the back door that said Tasha had done her business and wanted back in. Emma gave her dog a treat and gave her dinner. Then Emma thought about her own dinner.

With a bowl of soup and a salad, Emma took her dinner down to the great room to eat. She poured herself a glass of wine—a luxury she had been forced to deny herself with an addict in the house. When Jake was there, if Emma opened a bottle of wine, it would be gone within hours. Jake couldn't bear to see an open bottle and not finish it. Emma, on the other hand, could have an open bottle of wine around for weeks before emptying it. Now Emma could indulge herself in a single glass. It tasted tart and fresh on her tongue. She turned on the television, and despite herself, watched Cash Cab. It had been Jake who introduced her to the show, mostly because she didn't normally watch the Discovery Channel. That was Jake's favorite, along with the History Channel, or as her mother called it the Holocaust Channel. Emma preferred lighter entertainment when the television was turned on, especially before bed. Otherwise, she liked to read.

In all the months with Jake, she had never seen him read a book. He had the TV on all the time. When they went to bed, the timer on the TV had to be set before Jake could go to sleep. He also demanded that it be the History Channel, which annoyed Emma. She couldn't believe he could listen to such horrors before sleep. But he kept it very low, so she adjusted. With him gone, she could resume her normal behavior of reading before sleep.

She answered most of the questions on Cash Cab while she enjoyed her light supper, then Emma began to cry. She realized that despite all their fights and everything Jake had done to her, she missed him. She was lonely. But was it Jake or just a person she missed? Or was she really crying because of all she had been through? She left her dinner half-eaten and curled up in a ball on the sofa. With tears streaming down her face, she sipped her wine and still wished Jake were there. She hated herself for feeling that way. It made her realize how weak she was, and through her tears, she prayed for strength.

After her first solid night's sleep in months, Emma awoke to a quiet house. Then she remembered Joe's funeral was at ten thirty. She drank her coffee, did her crossword puzzle, and watched a bit of The Today Show. Then she called Cheryl.

"Hey, you doing all right?" Emma asked Cheryl.

"Yeah, running late as usual," Cheryl replied in her usual frantic manner. "I'll have to meet you there, Emma. You know where the funeral home is, right?"

"It's on Hodgsen Memorial, right? Just past Stephenson," Emma asked.

"Yep. I'll be there as soon as I can. How's Jake doing?" she added.

"I don't know. You talked to him yesterday. I don't think they're allowed any outside calls, so I haven't heard from him today. Maybe they'll let him call tonight," Emma answered.

"Probably. That's how it was before. Anyway, I gotta run. Get the kids ready for school and get myself dressed. I'll see you in a bit and we'll talk later," and Cheryl hung up.

Emma put on a simple black dress with strappy sandals, as the weather was heating up. She took a wrap with her just in case the mortuary was cold. She pulled her long hair back in a black satin bow. It would be a difficult day for Emma. Not only would she personally miss her daily conversations with Joe and his kind, healing tone but because she had to represent Jake at the funeral.

When she arrived at the mortuary, there were pictures of Joe set up on easels that represented all the stages of his life. There was no casket, as Emma realized Joe had opted for cremation. Kirk was ever-present and trying desperately to maintain a level of masculine calm. He hugged Emma and asked her to sign the condolence book for both she and Jake. He introduced her to Joe's son, Carson, who had been Jake's best friend for many years. Of course, what ended their friendship was what ended all of Jake's relationships. Drugs. Carson just couldn't tolerate any more of it. But when he met Emma, he acted as though Jake had been the greatest friend of his life.

"Where's Jake?" Carson asked as he looked around.

"He's in drug rehab, Carson. It's where he should be," she answered solemnly.

"Good for him. I hope it works. He's such a good guy, and Dad kept telling me that you were so good for him. He deserves a shot at life." Carson tried to smile.

"He wanted me to give you his love and to tell you how much he wanted to be here. He really misses you. And I know he'll miss your dad," Emma smiled.

"You give him my best, you hear? You tell Jake we're all pulling for him," Carson hugged Emma and went into the sanctuary.

Emma heard those words repeated time after time from everyone at the service—other than Aaron. Cheryl purposely sat next to Emma with her husband on her other side to separate them. Aaron was the only person in the room who refused to speak to Emma. He averted his eyes every time they might possibly meet Emma's. He wouldn't apologize and he wouldn't even say hello to her. He was also dressed like a bum. He showed up at a funeral wearing a Hawaiian shirt, shorts, sandals, and dark glasses. Not only was he a piece of shit but he had no class, Emma thought. Cheryl held Emma's hand tightly throughout the service.

Emma listened to the eulogy from Kirk, who told humorous anecdotes about Joe's business savvy. How Joe kept a big old calculator on his desk that didn't work. When a customer would ask the price of a mattress, Joe would start punching in number after number after number with his chubby fingers. Since the calculator was nonfunctioning, it was just a game to him. He just acted like he needed to add numbers to get the best price, while he knew all along exactly how much the bottom line price was on every item in his store.

Emma smiled because that just sounded so like Joe. He was funny, kind, and generous to a fault. Even while he had been sick, he had listened to Emma's tears and given her advice. She felt guilty for the short time she had believed Joe to be a negative influence on Jake. She was beginning to understand that Jake would blame anyone and everyone for his own problems. But she would learn more.

Kirk invited everyone to lunch at a local barbeque restaurant after the funeral. Emma and Cheryl joined them, sitting together talking mostly about Jake.

"Are you going to take him back when he leaves?" Cheryl asked quietly.

"It really depends on him. If he comes out clean and gets a job, then probably. I'll know from his letters and talking to him. I'll also go up and see him before he leaves. I'll see what I see," was all Emma could commit herself to at this early point.

"He really does love you, you know. He's doing this for you this time. In the past, he hasn't really had a choice. He's gone into rehab to avoid jail or because he was forced. This is the first time he's gone voluntarily," Cheryl told her. "But you should know he's going to beg to come out early. He'll believe he's already cured. The first two weeks are the worst, Emma. He'll plead. He'll use guilt. He'll use everything at his disposal to talk you into coming to take him away. Then, if he makes it through the whole program, he'll come out a ball of fire. Ready to tackle the world. He's totally full of himself because he's clean. Be prepared and don't let him get away with anything. All it takes is one small slip to have him spiraling back down."

"We'll talk more while he's gone. I'll need all the help I can get. That's if I let him back at all. You have no idea how much damage he has done," Emma replied.

"Oh, yes I do. Jake tells me everything. I know what he's done. And you don't even know all of it. He feels so guilty. He knows he screwed things up with you. It's just that when the drugs take over, he doesn't think."

"Yeah, I know. I've been trying to teach him how to think.

He just won't. But that's a conversation for another day," Emma laughed.

They got up, paid their respective tabs for their awful pulled pork sandwiches, and hugged each other. Emma just wanted to go home. She'd had enough of death, addiction, and planning for Jake's return—which might not even happen. She wanted the peace and harmony of her world. Her logical, rational, reasonable world.

Chapter Fourteen

Emma returned from Joe's funeral and quickly changed clothes. She poured herself some cold water and plopped onto the sofa. She thought about Jake and how he must be agonizing about missing the funeral of his father figure. Not wanting to dwell on Jake, Emma turned on her laptop computer to check her e-mails. She was jolted by an e-mail from Jake. He had only been away for twenty-four hours. What could he possibly want? And how did he get access to a computer? She opened the e-mail.

"These people are horrible, Emma. You've got to get me out of here," he wrote and continued on in that vein for a full page. All he wrote was his complaints. Not one word about missing Emma or trying to fulfill his responsibility to get clean. He showed no contrition or shame about what he had done to her or that he had used coke the day before he left. Had Jake not found a way to e-mail Emma less than twenty-four hours after entering rehab, she might have had some hope. But he couldn't make it one day without trying to leave. Emma decided to phone Cheryl for advice.

"Honey, what did you expect?" Cheryl said immediately. "He used Sunday, so he's still high from that and in a horrible frame of mind. He's barely coming down and has to look forward to four weeks of staying clean. Right this minute he knows he can't do it. He's gonna make up any excuse he can to get out."

"Yeah, I get that. How should I reply to this e-mail?"

"Emma, he's gonna be thinkin' like this for the first two weeks. He's been in rehab before, and he knows how miserable it's gonna be," Cheryl explained. "Honey, no matter what you do, no matter what he complains about, do not fall for it. He can't come out one day early."

"Thanks, Cheryl. I'll e-mail him back and tell him to forget it." Which she did immediately. Emma wrote an e-mail that left him absolutely no way out.

While Jake was in rehab, Emma was suddenly forced to endure the monthly probation office errands by herself with total distaste. Even though his probation had been suspended until he got out of inpatient counseling, he still had to pay his probation fees. Since Emma was the only one who would pay them, she had to go on his behalf. Emma went first to the city probation office on Habersham Street.

Emma went up to the reinforced glass window and told the woman she was there to pay Jake's probation fee. She was directed to sit in the waiting area until his probation officer came to get her. She looked around at the people waiting and found a plastic chair on the far side of the room where she wouldn't have to sit next to anyone. After what felt like the longest fifteen minutes she'd ever spent, the locked door opened, and a pretty young woman with a big smile came to get her. Emma followed her through a locked door and down a narrow hallway. They finally arrived at her office, where Emma was asked to have a seat across from the young woman who never introduced herself.

"So, tell me, Miss. Why isn't Jake here, and who are you?" she asked with a big smile.

"My name is Emma Weiss. I'm Jake's fiancée. Jake is in rehab," Emma told her, returning the smile.

"How's he doing?"

"He seems to be doing really well," Emma lied.

"We all like Jake around here and hope he gets his act together," the nameless woman elaborated. "I need you to sign this paper, saying that you were here for him because he's fulfilling his obligation with inpatient rehab."

"Of course," Emma said and signed the paper. "Is that all?"

"Yes, that's it. You give my best to Jake," the nameless young woman said. And with that, Emma was free to leave. Well, that was easy, Emma thought. She had never met his actual probation officer because he no longer worked there and they were still waiting for a replacement. The young woman, it turned out, was an assistant. It would be months before a new probation officer was assigned to Jake Stanton.

Emma walked quickly to her car, and then proceeded to the dreaded county probation office. She found a place to park and took a deep, cleansing breath before she walked across the muck that seemed to symbolize what lay beyond the door. She was right to be frightened. The waiting area was jammed with people who were obviously criminals. They were eying her purse, her watch, and her breasts. She found a chair—again, plastic—and clung to her purse with white knuckles until Jake's name was called.

Once again, the door was locked, but this time it was solid reinforced steel. A middle-aged black woman ushered Emma back to her office. Emma sat in a tiny room across from her.

"Hello," the woman said politely. "My name is Thelma Grant. I've been Jake's probation officer for more years than I'd like to remember," she laughed.

"I'm the fiancée, Emma Weiss," Emma shook the woman's hand.

"So you're the lucky one? How's his mama? She's a wonderful woman," Mrs. Grant asked.

"About the same. She had a major stroke, so she's in a nursing home. But she still has her sense of humor," Emma told her.

"Yeah, she'd need that with Jake as a son. He's really a good boy. He just has a problem. I hope he's getting the help he needs," Mrs. Grant said, genuinely concerned.

"I hope so, too," Emma agreed. "He's in a good rehab facility in the middle of nowhere in South Carolina. I can only hope it works this time."

"We all hope so. I've already gotten all the information from John Caldorini. We are all pulling for Jake. He comes from a fine family. Well, Ms. Weiss, good luck to you." Mrs. Grant stood up, ending the conversation. Emma didn't think it was wise to correct her on her title. Referring to herself as "Doctor" here would not look right. She rose and shook hands with Mrs. Grant, who escorted Emma through the locked door and into the freedom beyond.

While Jake was away, Emma had time. Time let the events of the past months move from her subconscious into her consciousness mind. She had already received a book she ordered entitled It's Not Okay to Be a Cannibal. It described addicts as becoming cannibals when they are using their drug of choice. It opened Emma's eyes to a world she had never known. As she read the anecdotes of addicts and their demons, she grabbed her highlighting pen. She began turning key phrases that related to Jake into bright yellow. Most of the book became fluorescent yellow. It depressed Emma no end to read so many words that described Jake so precisely. It described the compulsive lying, the selfishness, and how the person you think you know disappears when he becomes a cannibal.

The hours alone also gave her time to let her anger fester. She began to wonder if he ever really loved her or if he was even capable of loving anything other than cocaine. That was his true and undying love. Was he even able to love another person? Emma believed the only way a person could love another person was to love oneself first. Jake would never be able to achieve that unless he could stay clean and become a man instead of a spoiled child. Until then, he would never be able to love a person.

Emma began to analyze the relationship Jake had with his mother. She saw that even the love he claimed for his mother was more guilt and shame to cover up his years of resentment rather than love. He had his own guilt for the stealing, lying, and cheating he had done to her during his entire life. Then that guilt had turned into shame—deep feelings of shame for all he had done to his mother and the resentment he felt for Mimi's forgiving his every mistreatment of her. Every child wants discipline, even if he doesn't realize it. Jake knew in his heart that he needed discipline and needed his mother to lay down the law.

While she was alone, Emma became very close friends with

Steve. It had started when her laptop computer acted strangely, so she'd called Dana to get his number. Steve came over to fix her computer, and she began to see the depth of his character. Steve was kind and generous with his heart and was non-judgmental in his attitude. This was one person in Emma's life who she could truly trust. He understood her troubles and was not only sympathetic but empathetic. They began talking in depth about Jake.

"Honey," Steve told her, "I moved out of my parents' house when I was eighteen. I needed to be a big boy. Has Jake ever been on his own? No! Hello? What's wrong with this picture? He slept with his mommy until he was ten and still hasn't been on his own. He needs to feel like a man."

"Steve, she forgave him for everything he did. She should have said 'enough' when he was eighteen. She should have thrown him out and disowned him," Emma said angrily. "Okay, so she's his mother. But even a mother has to know when to say enough."

"Exactly. His mom spoiled him rotten by putting up with his shit for so many years. But, honey, that doesn't mean he won't get through rehab and be able to stay clean. He seemed committed to his rehabilitation. So it's possible. Keep me posted, okay? I love you, sweetie. You deserve the best, and we'll have to see if Jake can manage to be that for you."

"Thanks, Steve. I love you, too. And thanks for not pushing too hard on me. It's tough, you know?"

"Yeah, I do. Love is blind—and usually deaf and dumb. You'll know when you've had enough. Don't let anyone force you to do something you're not ready for. I've met Jake and he is certainly adorable and he truly has a good heart. I can feel it.

His aura is so white and clean. So I can understand why it's a difficult decision for you. I hate him for what he's done to you because I care about you but I also know you love him and it's all in your head as to when you've had enough. I love you either way, sweetie." And Steve left with a big hug for Emma and promised to be there for her. She wished he wasn't gay, but then, so did Steve. They would have made the perfect couple. They would laugh and say if only she were a man or he were straight, they'd be perfect. They loved each other for their souls.

Emma talked with many of her friends to regain her sanity. She felt proud of Jake for checking himself into rehab and assumed her friends would agree with her pride. Some did, but others were disappointments. Jenny was Emma's biggest disappointment. They had been close friends, and she had been one of Emma's real confidantes. Jenny, the manager of Emma's bank, and Kathy were the two women Emma would call close friends. But with Jake in rehab, Jenny turned cruel and unyielding.

"You deserve so much better than Jake, darlin'," she drawled in her Southern accent. "He's a piece of shit and he'll never change. You're a classy, smart, beautiful woman. What are you doing with him?" she nagged when Emma sat in Jenny's office one day. "You should be with a rich accountant who can take care of you."

"You don't understand. I don't want a rich accountant," Emma countered angrily. "I don't want boring and content. Those are your needs, Jenny, not mine. I'm a writer. I need a sense of excitement and drama. Maybe not this much drama but the man you're describing would bore me to tears."

"Honey, I just thought more of you than this. This is like another James incident." James was the contractor Emma had originally hired to refurbish her master bathroom and had been a pathological liar. He was handsome and a great con man. And he had taken Emma for five thousand dollars in the end and left the master bathroom undone, leaving Samantha and Ray to finish the job he botched.

"Jenny, that's absolutely not fair. James was a business mistake based on poor judgment, not love," Emma was getting heated and she didn't like it. She left Jenny's office feeling depressed and betrayed by a close friend.

This encounter caused Emma to evaluate her friendships. Her thirtieth birthday was coming up in only three weeks, and because Jake was away, Cheryl and Kathy had decided to do a girls' brunch for Emma. They felt Emma would be more comfortable than having an evening party during which everyone else would be coupled. But as Emma assessed her Savannah friends, she found she had few that remained. Jenny was getting lower on the list because of her hardness about Jake. Kathy was a true friend, although Emma was already feeling she couldn't count on her. Because of Kathy's vicious divorce, her two small children, her new boyfriend, and being so involved with the Temple Sisterhood, Kathy was tough to reach. At least that was the reasoning Emma was given by Kathy.

Emma mentally scanned the remainder of her friends. Cheryl certainly cared both for her brother and for Emma, but she could never be counted on for help. She was always busy with her kids or her husband. And of course, Aaron wouldn't permit any contact between his wife and Emma. Cheryl would still find ways around Aaron's decree, but visits and phone calls were brief. And Emma was skeptical of Cheryl. Somewhere in her subconscious, Emma feared that Cheryl was more involved with Jake's problems than she let on.

Emma knew Jo meant well and cared about her, but once again, with Jake in rehab she disappeared. The same with Jo's friends. They never contacted Emma directly. Maybe Jo had told them too much about Jake—she didn't know. But the lines appeared to have been severed.

Dana, her writing friend from Rosemary's group the Zona Rosas, was also busy with her own life. She was a good friend but couldn't be counted on for support. She was in the middle of a novel, had a full-time business giving massage therapy, taught belly dancing, and was refurbishing her own house that was only blocks away from Emma. Rosemary Daniell was the same. She was a true friend and cared deeply but led such a busy life between speaking engagements out of state, running the Zona Rosa groups, and her own writing, she was rarely even in town, let alone accessible.

Emma found that with Jake in rehab, her best friend was gone because Jake had become her best friend. She was beginning to miss him terribly, despite the fact that he was the actual cause of her drama. After the phone call she received from him a week into his rehab, he had started to sound so clearheaded and alert, and Emma was building hope that he would return a new man. An adult.

During his absence, Emma found her best friends were really her family. She could turn to her cousin in Chicago, Jean, any time for support. She always seemed to say the right words to make Emma feel whole. Her cousins Jean and Lucy both really cared about Emma. They didn't care about what Jake was going through; their only concern was Emma's well-being. She spoke with them often and could bare her soul to them. But the bottom line was Emma's best friend was herself. She wrote, she thought, and she dealt with her problems. That had been Emma's way of life until Jake entered it. She had always been her own best friend.

After a week, she was confused. She had hope, but her anger was getting the better of her. Every time she found another piece of jewelry missing because Jake had pawned it, the anger intensified all over again. Yet she would go to sleep at night crying because the bed seemed so empty and she missed him.

Then the phone calls started. He began to call every day, begging to come home early. He was purely on the con. There was no remorse, no love, and no repentance. He tried to make Emma believe he was cured and didn't want her to spend any more money. He tried preaching about God and tried sarcasm about Emma's perfection. Nothing worked on Emma. It only alienated her from Jake.

At the two-week mark of Jake's rehabilitation, matters got worse for Emma. She received a four-page letter from Jake that had her emotions somewhere between anger and tears. He was cold, cruel, and totally selfish.

He's in the perfect environment, Emma thought. One in which the world revolves around him. He's refusing to deal with anything outside those walls, Jake is concentrating solely on himself and the counselors were facilitating that illusion. Cheryl had warned Emma that this was commonplace in rehabilitation. People had to think about their own demons. But Jake was taking this selfishness to a whole new level. He appeared to be setting up this new, clean life alone. His letter indicated that anything outside the safe walls of the rehab facility was an unnecessary and unwanted distraction —including Emma.

Emma had planned to go to see Jake that weekend. She knew she wouldn't let him back into her life straight out of rehab until she had seen his progress for herself. After the cruelty of his letter and speaking with his counselor, she cancelled her plans. And she wrote him a letter in response. She described in detail her own pain, while he was surrounded by bliss and harmony. He had a support group; she had none. Her words fell on deaf ears.

As she wrote the letter to Jake, it was the first night of Passover, one of the holiest Jewish holidays that was normally spent with family. Emma was alone. And the worst of it was no one cared. She felt totally abandoned by the very people she thought were her friends. This caused Emma to evaluate Savannah, as well. When life was good, Savannah was a close community that stretched its moss-laden oak trees around its people with love. But when bad news or difficulties arise, those same moss-laden oak trees could strangle.

Emma wanted out. Out of Savannah to start a fresh life where no one knew her or knew about her stupid decisions. She was getting far too many "bless your heart" platitudes from those around her. And the translation of that sweet Southern saying was really "you're an idiot." Especially from Mark, her next-door neighbor. He spoke to her in platitudes and with total condescension. Emma had never in her life been thought of in that manner.

After that second week of Jake's rehab, Emma felt she had lost Jake and she was utterly alone. At this late date, Emma was actually blaming herself for losing Jake. "If I had been—something, he wouldn't have gone back to drugs," Emma told herself in the mirror. "He would want to make things right with me so we could be together." She sat on the edge of her bed, crying. His last letter implied that he was looking for any reason to be angry with her so he could leave her. He doesn't need a reason, Emma thought, and broke down and sobbed.

It was Jake's birthday on April 22nd, while he was away. Emma spoke with Cheryl to commiserate about not being with him on his birthday. During that conversation, she caught Cheryl in a big lie. Emma had loaned Cheryl six hundred dollars a couple of months previously—against her better judgment and solely from the guilt Jake waged on her. Cheryl told her that Jake never gave her the whole six hundred dollars. This was a loan that Emma was told she had to give Cheryl because a sheriff was going to arrest her if she didn't get it. All Emma could think was, "And this is my problem because—? How did I end up being the bank for Jake's entire family?" Of course, Cheryl also swore she would return the money within two weeks. Two months later, no money.

According to Cheryl, he brought her cash and yelled at her that five hundred was all she was going to get. So Emma confronted Jake in rehab. He was angry because she was bringing reality into his world of bliss, but he was clean and clear thinking.

"Think, Emma. How could I cash the check written in Cheryl's name? She's lying. She gave me some cash so I could get drugs, but that was her choice. But I gave her the check," he insisted.

"She gave you cash for drugs?" Emma was astounded. She realized that Cheryl was lying about the check, but why? It had to be to cover up the fact that she was actually helping him use drugs.

"Yeah, baby. Cheryl has been using drugs and helping me use drugs for years. Please don't bother me with this stuff anymore. I have too much on my mind here. I gotta go," and he hung up.

Well, that was loving and helpful, Emma thought. But to cover herself, she went to her bank to see the check. It was signed by Cheryl and she cashed it. It was Cheryl who lied, not Jake. The anger engorged her. What bothered Emma more than anything was Cheryl's motive for lying. After the robbery of her purses and jewelry, Emma couldn't help but think that Jake and Cheryl were some sort of con team, acting together. Cheryl backed up Jake's lies, and he backed up hers. Emma's theory was that Cheryl was back using drugs again. Why else would Cheryl be the only person who was so sure when Jake was using? Because they were using together again—just like in the beginning. Of course, she couldn't prove this, but Jake certainly implied that was the case.

And Cheryl was trying awfully hard to keep Emma and Jake together. Maybe they were working together to get their hands on all of Emma's belongings. At the moment, Emma didn't trust either of them. She decided to demand the money from Cheryl the following day. She was even tempted to call Aaron and tell him what his wife was really plotting. But Emma had no grounds for such accusations. It was all supposition.

The following day Emma did get paid by Cheryl. The check was made out to Emma for six hundred dollars. But oddly on the memo line, Cheryl had written "less $75 to Jake." Why? What was her motivation to make Emma angry with Jake? Cheryl was playing both sides of the fence. On the one hand, she pushed Emma to take Jake back when he was released from rehab. But on the other hand, she seemed to push equally hard to make Emma distrust Jake. Emma was totally confused.

Emma was getting to an emotional breaking point of wanting to leave everything in Savannah behind. She looked at her future if she stayed in Savannah. Did she really want to play babysitter to Jake, watching her ass at every turn? After he was released, she would have to deal with Narcotics Anonymous, resume hiding her jewelry, and do random drug tests on him. She worried that she would have to spend the rest of her life waiting for the other shoe to drop. Emma had been told by countless people that addicts remain addicts. It may take a week, a month, or years, but eventually they return to their addiction. If that were true, Emma feared being married and having children and then—wham! The cocaine demon would reemerge. The thought scared the hell out of her.

As the time passed and Jake remained clean and sober in rehab, Emma evaluated the situation. On his Sunday conjugal visitation day, she would make her decision. It would be a little over a week before his release date, and Emma would have a decent idea of how life would play out. She would be supportive to get him through rehab, and she would keep the part of her that wanted to kill him repressed. As she planned her overnight trip, she made a reservation at a motel that was about twenty minutes from the compound. Emma knew she couldn't make it there, see Jake, and make it back to Savannah in one day. Besides, if they were going to have sex, they certainly couldn't do it at the rehab facility. They would need an air-conditioned room and a bed. He was also adamant that she bring Tasha with her. So she made those plans. Then she began to plan her approach with Jake. She would keep quiet as much as possible and listen. She would let him do the talking and see what he had to say. She wouldn't upset him by flinging accusations and guilt at him. There was nothing to be gained by that. After all, he would have one more week of rehab after their visit. He would need to be focused if there was any hope for him at all.

Chapter Fifteen

With hours to go before Emma went to see Jake at the rehab camp, he was still trying to escape early. He actually had the audacious gall to tell Emma to set up an appointment with a psychiatrist when he got out. He didn't ask if she was willing to pay the two hundred dollars per hour for his visit; he demanded it. He realized he needed medication to get his head stable, and whether he was right or wrong, Emma was angry at his assumptions. He also began calling her his fiancée again. More assumptions. Jake thought it might be best for both he and Emma that he stay in a hotel when he got out. Even more assumptions. Who did he think was going to pay for the hotel?

All Emma could think, with only hours before she left to see him, was that he was taking her completely and totally for granted. When she spoke with him the previous night, he professed his undying love—for Tasha. He missed Emma's dog terribly. Her soft coat, even her bad breath. But not once did he mention how much he missed Emma; he assumed she knew. He assumed she knew how much he loved her. He assumed he was welcome back in her life. He assumed she forgave him. Emma left for South Carolina the following morning with a chip on her shoulder and a list of what not to do when she saw him: don't talk too much, don't make him feel guilty, don't give him a hard time, be supportive. She chanted that mantra all the way to bumfuck South Carolina, with every breath in her wanting the relationship to end when she arrived.

Emma finally pulled up the gravel road to the log cabin compound. Jake was standing in front of the office waiting for her. Or was he waiting for Tasha? She had brought her dog because she wasn't going to put her in a kennel for one night and because Jake had wanted her to bring the dog with her. She felt as though he wanted to see the dog more than he wanted to see her.

Jake was wearing a baseball cap, sunglasses, and shorts with sandals. Emma almost didn't recognize him. He hadn't shaved, and he looked like he had just rolled out of bed. Emma wondered why he cared so little about how he looked when this was such an important impression he needed to make. Maybe he didn't realize the import of this meeting. To Emma this was do or die for Jake. This one day and its outcome would make her decision as to whether or not she would take him back. Was he clueless or was he so full of himself that he thought it didn't matter? But the moment he saw her, he pulled her into his arms and kissed her. Then he gave Tasha a big hug and kiss.

"Hi," he said.

"Hi," was all Emma could come up with. She was a writer, had a PhD in Psychology, and was a member of Mensa, yet she couldn't think of more than that one word.

"Uh, can we leave?" Jake said. The cloud of discomfort between them was palpable. Emma could barely bring a smile to her lips.

"Sure. I got a hotel about twenty minutes away. Are you hungry? We could stop at the hotel to drop off Tasha and then grab a bite to eat," Emma finally found her voice.

"That sounds fine," Jake said. It was odd for him to be so

serious. He wasn't playful and didn't joke; he was acting like an adult.

She let Jake drive since he hadn't driven in three weeks. He even drove differently, she quickly noticed. He drove slowly and cautiously; quite unlike Jake. He usually drove like a sixteen-year-old who had recently gotten his license—fast and reckless. But this was a new Jake. They pulled up to the motel, and he quickly helped her with her bag and Tasha. He took the key from her and opened the door. They entered the motel room, leaving the dog and Emma's overnight case in the room. The tension was still palpable. With all that had transpired between Emma and Jake, they couldn't seem to find any words.

They decided to go directly to lunch, which for Jake meant only one word: pizza. There was a Pizza Hut down the street from the motel, so that was their destination. As they drove through the quaint town, they made small talk about how charming it was. When they finally sat down to eat, Emma had little appetite due to the flip-flops her stomach was doing from nerves. They both chose the all-you-can-eat buffet. Emma loaded her plate with salad and one small piece of pizza. Jake loaded his plate with pasta, pizza, and bread.

While they ate, Jake began to talk. Emma was shocked at the serious manner with which Jake conducted himself. He ate slowly and didn't overeat. Emma had sworn she wouldn't do much talking and do plenty of listening, though Jake didn't know that. He looked puzzled at her quiet demeanor. But he managed to initiate conversation.

"I want you to know how different I am, honey. I know I wanted to leave, but this is the best rehab facility I've ever been in. Dr. Jeff really knows his shit," he started. "He sees right through the lies and stomps on them."

"I'm glad it's working," Emma said quietly.

"It really is. I feel like a man and like I'll never do drugs again. I'm so happy being clean, Emma. I don't ever want to feel like that loser ever again."

"And your steps? Have you gotten to the making amends?" she asked reluctantly.

"I'm not there yet, baby, but I'm getting there. I know I'm miserable knowing what I've done to you. And to Mom. I can barely live with myself for the guilt," Jake told her. "I know being sorry doesn't come close but I really am. I swear to you, Emma, when I get home I'm going to find a great job and pay you back. Every penny I've cost you or stolen from you. You'll get the money first."

"Thanks for that," she said.

"Emma, are you all right? You seem so quiet. So—I don't know—withdrawn. Do you not want me back?"

"Well, Jake, that's why I'm here. To make that decision. I'm nervous because so much is riding on today. I don't know yet," she answered honestly.

"Thank you for being so honest. At least I understand why you're acting like you are. And I can understand that. I mean, I hope you'll take me back because I want to make a life with you. I love you, Emma. That's the truth. But if you don't, I'll understand. I've been so cruel to you. I wouldn't blame you for not taking me back."

Jake's honesty was getting to Emma. His entire attitude impressed her. He was actually dealing with life, coping with reality, and he was calm. This was the Jake Emma had fallen in love with in the beginning. But she was skeptical. He was a great liar, and the trust issue was still at stake.

"I don't know if I'll ever be able to trust you again," Emma confessed. "You've done so much damage. I just don't know."

"I know I can regain your trust. Once you see that I can stay clean and sober, you'll see."

"I hope so, Jake."

"Can we go, baby? You look so sexy and beautiful. I really want to make love to you," he said candidly.

"Sure," Emma replied and finally a genuine smile came to her face. It was the first smile she had managed since seeing Jake standing at the compound. He got behind the wheel of her car and cautiously drove back to the motel. He held her hand and brought it to his lips; a romantic gesture that caught Emma by surprise. She wasn't used to such acts of love from Jake. She couldn't help but wonder what it meant. Was he really a changed man?

When they arrived at the motel, Jake took Emma's hand, and they strode hand in hand to the door. He opened it, gathered her in his arms, and carried her to the king-sized bed. He gently set her down and put the Do Not Disturb sign on the door. He carefully nudged Tasha off the bed, when in the past he would have shoved her off. He turned down the lights but left the bedside lamps on. He kissed her passionately.

"God, I've missed you," he murmured. And then he went to work on her neck. He nuzzled and kissed her neck. Then he slowly removed her white tank top. He gently stroked the top of her breasts that filled her lace bra. "Mmmm. I forgot how beautiful your breasts were."

This was new to Emma. He usually rushed through the sex

act like it was a chore. And he never complimented her. "Wow" was all Emma could get her brain to manage. Jake didn't stop; he slowly and methodically drove her crazy. When he finally removed his own T-shirt, she nearly climaxed. He was tan from working outside at rehab. She ran her hands over his broad shoulders and kissed his chest.

Jake slowly removed Emma's bra and stroked her breasts. He ran his mouth from her mouth down to her belly, kissing every part of her. This was definitely a new Jake. He didn't think of himself first; he thought only of Emma's gratification. He continued down her body, removing his shorts and her jeans. He didn't have his usual insecurity. He completely pleasured Emma in every way possible. And for the first time in many weeks, he wasn't the Two Minute Man. He endured until Emma orgasmed over and over again. When he finally came, he didn't jump out of bed. He actually held her and stroked her hair.

"Honey, all I can say is, oh my God!" Emma said with a husky voice.

"Yeah. I never knew it could be this great," Jake replied somewhat out of breath. Then he stood up and went to the bathroom to clean up. Emma ran a hand through her hair, which was a tangled mass. She rummaged around and finally found her panties and bra. As she put them on, Jake emerged from the bathroom wearing his boxer briefs. He looked like he should be on the cover of GQ Magazine. Tall and lean, muscular and tan. His curly brown hair had grown longer and tumbled damply around his chiseled face.

"Baby, I want to do that forever. No more drugs for me. If this is what sex is like with the woman I love when I'm clean, I want more!" Jake laughed.

"I'll second that!" Emma agreed. She sat on the edge of the bed in only her pale blue lace bra and matching lace thong. She could see the greed in Jake's brilliant green eyes. Odd, she thought. His eyes seemed a brighter green without drugs. She tugged on her jeans and her pale blue lace-edged tank top. "I guess you have to go back, huh?"

Jake looked at the clock, and it surprisingly read four thirty. His face dropped instantly.

"Yeah, I guess I do. We're only allowed four or five hours. Shit," he muttered. They sat on the side of the bed together, his arm around her and her cheek resting on his chest. "I'm scared, Emma. Every other time I've left rehab, I've felt totally full of myself; like I could conquer the world. But this time, I'm scared."

"What are you afraid of?" Emma asked.

"The real world. Triggers. Anything that will make me even consider using. Honey, I'm scared to death."

"That's probably a good thing, Jake. Fear will keep you clean. You may be too afraid to wander into the wrong part of town or talk to the wrong people. It could be helpful," Emma told him with total honesty. Of course, Emma was always honest. At that moment, she had forgotten that Jake was not.

Their ride back to the rehab center was the exact opposite of the drive from there. They laughed and joked, they held hands, and they were clearly a couple again. Emma was taken in by his sincerity and the amazing sex. She believed from the depths of her soul that Jake was cured. That he was whole again.

And that he would never use drugs again.

When they arrived back at the rehab compound, Emma spoke with the head counselor, Jeff, both with Jake present and privately. Jeff was, of course, hopeful when Jake was present, yet he was still very direct in telling her in front of Jake that he could not be trusted. He wished them both good luck and added that Jake had a long way to go toward sobriety. Privately, he told Emma not to believe a word Jake said.

"Ma'am, he's a pro. He knows how to manipulate everyone around him. He's a likeable guy and we all enjoy his company here, but that is part of his addiction. Listen, I hope he makes it. Most of our patients stay clean with the type of program we run, but Jake is a tough customer. I believe he loves you, but his love of cocaine is deeper. He still has another week here, and I certainly hope he'll make it," Jeff told Emma bluntly.

"So do I. I think I'm less naive than I was when we met, and I hope I can see the signs this time. After spending time with him today, I've really seen a change in him. He seems more comfortable in his own skin, if that makes any sense to you," Emma told Jeff privately.

"Yeah, I get that," he replied. "He's clean, at least for now. So that makes a big difference. He'll seem calmer, more mature. That's who he is without the drugs. The question is, will he stay that way? I have my doubts, Emma."

"It will be easier for him since I'm not a trigger, right? I mean, I've never even tried cocaine, and I'm not much of a drinker. So at least I'm a positive in his life," Emma asked him hopefully.

"Absolutely, Emma. That will be a plus for Jake. Having a home to go home to that doesn't tempt him will help. Well, I've got other patients, and I'll talk to you again next week when you pick him up," Jeff pushed up from his chair and shook her hand.

When she left the office, Jake was leaning against her SUV smoking a cigarette. He flicked it away as she walked toward him.

"Jeff is so full of shit, you know," Jake said defensively. "He doesn't know it all. I know how I feel and what's going on inside me. I know I love you and I know we have a future together. And I know I'm scared to death to leave this place. I don't want to take any chances with my sobriety. I've learned so much, Emma."

"I hope so, honey," Emma said.

"I want you to know, Emma, that I don't need you. I want you. I want to make things up to you. You'll have better," he told her. "I'm going to get a great job, and that will help keep me out of trouble. And you -- you're my strength. I only regret one thing right now, baby."

"What's that?"

"That I didn't make love to you again while you were here. God, I'm so horny. I wish we'd made love like that one more time," Jake smiled.

"Well, honey, you'll have plenty of time to think about it, and then when you get out, you can make it up to me. We'll have three weeks at home before we leave for Chicago," she smiled.

"Oh, that's right! I can't wait! I get to see Jean and Lucy. You know I love your family," he said enthusiastically.

"Yeah, and my mother!" she reminded him.

"Don't you worry your pretty head about that. I'm great with mothers," he tried to reassure her.

"Not my mother. She's tough. And she's not stupid.

Anyway, we'll talk about it when you get out. Just work hard this week, okay?"

"I will. I love you, Em," he said and crushed his mouth to hers. He kissed her good-bye and then remembered her thirtieth birthday was the following week and he would miss it. He had turned thirty-one in rehab, and she would be turning thirty while he was in rehab. "Happy birthday, darlin'," he added.

"Thanks. I wish you could be there, but you're better off here. I only hope Cheryl doesn't screw things up."

"That's a strong possibility. She's so unorganized," he said. "It'll be a miracle if she pulls it off. Anyway, drive carefully. I'll talk to you soon."

And with that as the best good-bye she was going to get, Emma got into her car and drove back to the motel. It was six o'clock, so Emma had to get back to walk Tasha and feed her. Then she would worry about her own dinner. When she opened the door to the motel, the happy face of her golden retriever met her.

"Hi, fur face," Emma said happily and received licks of love in return. She attached the leash to Tasha's pink collar and took her for a nice walk. The evening was still warm from the heat of the day. It was the end of April, and it already felt like summer. The gnats were out in force, so as soon as Tasha had done her business, Emma was anxious for the air-conditioning of the room. She gave Tasha her treat and her dinner and then plopped onto the mess of a bed. Emma still had a smile on her face from the activity that had made such a mess out of the bed. But she couldn't stand it. She got up and straightened the sheets, tucking in the bottom so she could sleep on it later.

Emma found she was famished since she had little to eat for lunch. She found a little café near the motel, where she quietly ate a steak and baked potato dinner. Emma brought her journal with her so she could get her feelings on paper. That was her way of coping with life. Make lists, take notes, and write in her journal. Emma believed that once an idea or concern was on paper, it was off her mind and would cease to drive her crazy. So while she waited for her meal, she got all her deepest thoughts on paper. When she was done purging herself, she felt better. Her meal tasted better for the emotional purging. She slept well that night and woke up early with plenty of energy for her trip home.

Emma was happy to be home, but after her visit with Jake, the house seemed so empty. She couldn't wait until he came home. She believed his fear would keep him clean. Emma made sure to visit Mimi Stanton the following day.

"Oh, Mimi," Emma sat on Jake's mother's bed in the nursing home and told her about her visit. "You'd be so proud of Jake."

"Yeah?" she said with a big smile on her face. Emma was always awestricken with Mimi. How could a woman who had three strokes, no mobility in her legs, little mobility left in her hands, and severely impaired speech always look so happy? "How's he doin'?"

"For the first time in his life, he's leaving rehab scared. He's terrified that something will mess with his sobriety," Emma told Jake's mother.

"Oh, that's wonderful," she replied. "Maybe it'll take this time."

"I hope so, Mimi. He's got such a good heart. If he can stay clean, he can do anything," Emma held Mimi's hand and squeezed it.

"He's a good boy. He just needs a kick in the ass sometimes," Mimi laughed.

"Well, hopefully this was the kick he needed. You know if he uses again, it's over between us," Emma confided. "I'll give him this last chance, since he's worked so hard for it. But that's it."

"I know, Emma. I know. I'll always love him because he's my baby. But you've put up with more than you should have. He's lucky to have you."

"Thanks, Mimi. I pray that I'm enough." She said good-bye to Mimi by kissing her soft, smooth cheek. Even with her strokes and whatever medications she was taking, Mimi still had flawless skin. It was milky white, and at seventy-two years old, she barely had a wrinkle. Her huge blue eyes were always bright and full of a mischievous cheer. Her white hair was thick and healthy and, due to Cheryl's hairdressing ability, was always well coifed. Mimi Stanton was still a beautiful woman. Emma cared deeply for this woman, despite the emotional damage she had unintentionally done to Jake. She had a great deal of respect for Mimi. She had started working at sixteen years old and worked three jobs to maintain her family. Through both of her marriages, she had four children and she managed to care for them herself. She lost one child—her eldest son—to suicide. Her oldest daughter still lived in South Carolina, where Mimi's family lived. Then she had Cheryl. It wasn't until her second husband that she had Jake, so he was her baby. Then she lost that husband to a heart attack only three years after Jake was born.

It took pure Southern grit, but Mimi had made a million dollars by investing in property and business. Emma had to respect such a woman. She only wished she could have known Mimi before the strokes so she could carry on a complete conversation and see the depth of her mind.

Chapter Sixteen

During the week Emma waited for Jake to be released from his rehab, she celebrated her thirtieth birthday and lost her best friend. She received her much-anticipated birthday present from her mother—the four carat emerald ring that had been in her family for three generations. But the best gift that Emma received for her birthday arrived via airplane. It was her cousin, Jean, from Chicago.

At the last minute, Jean decided to fly to Savannah with her boyfriend for a long weekend, which coincided quite by chance with Emma's birthday. Emma was thrilled to have them stay with her. They grilled steaks on the barbecue and laughed until their sides hurt. Of course, since Emma's birthday party was planned as a Saturday brunch, Jean was included. Which was lucky because few others showed up, thanks to Cheryl's disorganized mind.

As was typical of Cheryl, she waited until the last minute to do everything. She and Kathy were planning the party together, and there was an absurd blunder, a usual occurrence for Cheryl. Emma learned early in the week that Kathy had made reservations at a ridiculously expensive restaurant. Emma knew that many of her friends, most importantly Jenny, couldn't afford such a luxury. So Emma politely asked Cheryl if it was possible to change it to someplace less expensive. What actually transpired between Cheryl and Kathy, Emma would never know. Emma assumed that Cheryl didn't get around to telling Kathy about the change until the day before the brunch. She also knew Cheryl and figured that Cheryl told Kathy to change the plans rather than, as Emma meant, to ask her if it was possible. Kathy was furious. She had already given the expensive restaurant a large deposit, and she would lose it if the plans were changed. If Kathy had picked up the phone and called Emma to give her this information, Emma would certainly have told her to keep the plans as they were. But Kathy never gave Emma that courtesy. She simply told Cheryl to cancel the whole brunch.

As a result of this lack of communication, Emma had a birthday celebration with four people, and Kathy would never talk to Emma again. It was still a lovely brunch with Jo, Dana, Jean, and Cheryl at Jaycee's Cafe (where Ray had been manager), which was one of Emma's favorite restaurants. Because the organization was all in Cheryl's hands, she didn't call anyone to change the plans until one hour before the brunch. Even Jenny, for whom the change was made, couldn't make it in such short notice since she lived on Whitmarsh Island, which was a good half an hour away. It was terribly depressing for Emma.

Jean cheered Emma up by taking her to her favorite restaurant in Savannah for dinner. Jean and her boyfriend, Rick, took her to The Olde Pink House, a Savannah landmark. And to make it perfect, Emma took pictures of all the ghosts in the beautiful antebellum building. The Olde Pink House is one of the four most haunted buildings in the country, so golden orbs of spirits floated throughout the restaurant and could be caught on film. The food was spectacular as always and the atmosphere elegant. Emma missed Jake terribly that night. He should be sitting at the table sharing in the celebration.

On Sunday, Jean and Rick decided to go to the beach on Tybee Island. Being from Chicago, they needed to see the ocean. While they were gone for the day, it gave Emma time to think. Her savior complex was working overtime, making her sure that Jake would be able to stay clean once he came home. She knew in her heart that he was being totally honest with her when they were together the prior Sunday. She needed to believe him. If she didn't believe him, she couldn't save him. And to her way of thinking, paying for Jake's rehab would be worth every penny if she saved him. She actually felt that if she saved Jake—even if they didn't end up together— – she would have been put on earth for a purpose. She would have saved one life, and for Emma's conscience, that would make her presence on earth worthwhile.

When Jean and Rick returned from Tybee, they had a lovely dinner outside on Emma's patio. They cooked big T-bone steaks on the grill, made a big salad, and baked potatoes. Music played softly in the background, and as the sun set, the fairy lights lightened their hearts. As they ate, they talked a great deal about Jake. Since Emma was supposed to pick him up in two days, she had little time left to get her thoughts in order.

"I really think he's doing great," Emma said primarily to Jean. Rick was nice enough, but he was not exactly Mr. Personality. Jake had actually been the one person who described Rick most accurately. "He's like dry white toast, no butta, no jam," Jake drawled. And Jean laughed raucously when Emma told her Jake's description of her boyfriend—mostly because it was so right. Emma continued talking about Jake. "He's scared to leave rehab, and I think that's a good omen."

"Yeah. That's definitely a positive. If he came out cocky and full of himself, he'd never make it. But if he's scared shitless to use again, he might actually succeed," Jean told her.

"That's what I was thinking. In the past, he's always been forced into rehab, and within two weeks he was using again. He came out, like you said, really arrogant. Ready to conquer the world. He set himself up for failure."

"Honey bunny, I'm just worried about you," Jean said with love. "I saw you two together, and I know you love him. I don't want to see you hurt. You're the one I care about. I mean, don't get me wrong. I think Jake is adorable and sweet. And I believe he loves you. It's just that I know firsthand what addiction can do. I was married to one. He took me for so much, you don't know! I love you and I know you deserve better. You're beautiful and smart and rich. You have everything going for you. Do you hear me, Em? I don't want you hurt."

"I love you, too. So much, Jeannie Ann," Emma reached across and squeezed her hand.

"Gosh, no one called me that but my mom," Jean said tearfully. She had lost her mother, Emma's great-aunt, to cancer only five years ago, and it was still raw.

"I've always called you that, too though," Emma smiled.

"Yeah, but it makes me think of her."

"I know, honey. I know. Well, you wanna help me bring this stuff into the kitchen?" Emma changed the subject. And together, Emma and Jean cleaned up after dinner. They hugged and laughed the whole time. All Emma could think was family was better than any friendship. She had known Jean her whole life, and the love was there through it all.

Tuesday morning, Emma had to leave early to pick up Jake, so Jean left her a note thanking her for everything before she left a couple of hours later for the airport. She cleaned up thoroughly after her and Rick. The drive to South Carolina seemed to fly for Emma. It was the last time she'd have to make this trip.

When she arrived at the rehab compound, Jake was standing with his bags in front of the office. He was tan, lean, and had a big smile on his face.

"We need to do the whole check-out routine. I wish it wasn't such a long drive home till we can be together," he said as he kissed her passionately. They went into the office, signed the release papers, and got the paperwork that Jake had to give his probation officer. During the drive home, Jake drove and they talked about everything; movies, rehab, plans, and the future. He noticed immediately that Emma no longer wore her engagement ring. He thought he noticed it missing when he saw her the previous Sunday but didn't make an issue of it.

"Where's your ring?" he asked.

"I took it off when you went into rehab. It's in the safe. If you decide you really want to marry me, you'll have to ask me again. You'll have to ask me when you're clean and sober and you really mean it," Emma answered.

"I did mean it but I understand. When I ask you again, I will be perfectly clean like I am now," he answered.

They arrived home that evening just in time to walk and feel Tasha. Jake unpacked, mostly to put everything in the washing machine. Since they had stopped at a drive-through for food on the way, they weren't hungry—for food. But they were hungry for each other. Jake couldn't wait to get Emma horizontal and in her own bed. They made love like they had at the motel on that hot April afternoon in South Carolina. And they made love again before they went to sleep.

During the three weeks between Jake's leaving rehab and their trip to Chicago, they made love at least twice a day. Jake worked on a new resume for a better job and put in applications at car dealerships, furniture stores, and large corporations for sales positions. He figured it would take a good deal of time to land such a job, so by putting in the applications before the trip, they might request interviews by the time they returned.

Jake went to the nursing home nearly every day, but he and Emma went together. Mimi was so happy to see Jake doing so well, she was giddy. After all she had gone through to get him to this point herself, she was overwhelmed with his stability, and Jake was in tears. When Emma saw him starting to tear up, she gracefully walked out of the room to give them a moment of privacy. She could hear as she left the room that he was trying to make amends to his mother. He needed it and so did she. Of course, Emma needed that as well.

Jake was staying out of trouble, and he was reading his material from rehab. He was dedicated. He didn't even look at the bar in Emma's house. He was considerate, mature, and kind. It was absolute bliss for Emma. This was a man she wanted to spend her life with. He asked her to marry him again, and this time when she said yes it was with an open heart. He placed the ring back on her finger, and they made love to seal the deal.

The next day, they left for Chicago to meet her mother there. Emma and her mother did this quite often. They would meet in Chicago, where they could see Rose's mother and the rest of the family and Emma and her mother could spend some time together. This would be the first time Jake would meet her mother, and that had Emma nervous. Rose put on an exterior of joviality and fun, but she was quite astute. What unnerved Emma was that her mother would appear to like Jake, but Emma knew that her mother's real feelings could be totally different. Jake had stayed clean, and they were engaged—again. So it was time for Emma's mother to meet her betrothed for herself.

Chicago was, as always, fun. Rose was the kind of woman everyone liked. She was outgoing and funny. She and Jake seemed to hit it off from the moment they met. They went to dinner the first night they were together, which was the day after Emma and Jake arrived. Since they drove from Savannah and Rose flew from Phoenix, they worked out their schedules to be there at dinnertime. They met at Rose's hotel—a different hotel from the one where Emma and Jake stayed, since they smoked and they had Tasha with them. But the hotels were close to each other, so it didn't take long. They met in the lobby bar, where Rose had to have her before-dinner single malt scotch. To Emma's shock, Jake ordered a glass of wine. She knew he was nervous about meeting her mother, but she also knew this was a bad sign. A very bad sign.

They sat together for an hour, schmoozing and laughing over drinks and the nibbles on the table. After Rose's second drink, Jake was still nursing his glass of wine. Emma breathed a sigh of relief at that. They went into the hotel restaurant, where they had a lovely dinner. As far as Emma knew, all was going fine.

When Emma and Jake left to go back to their hotel, she quickly confronted him about the wine.

"Honey, are you sure you should be drinking?"

"Oh baby, one glass of wine isn't going to make me want to do a line," he defended.

"No, but it's a start. You know what Jeff said. One drink is the beginning of a downward spiral," she retorted.

"Honey, let's just make love and stop thinking about this," he said and swept her off her feet. He knew her weakness, and that weakness was his sexuality. With great sex, she forgot about everything else.

The next day they had lunch with Emma's mother, Jean, and Lucy, and they took Emma's grandmother out of the nursing home to join them. They all laughed and joked as one big happy family. Jake didn't have ants in his pants, as he had on the last trip, and everyone noticed. When he finally left the table to go outside for a cigarette, Jean was the first to make mention of the change.

"Wow, Em. Jake looks great! His face has filled out, and he doesn't have schpilkes (Yiddish for antsy) like before! Don't you agree, Aunt Fran?" she looked to her aunt, Emma's grandmother.

"Oh, there's definitely a difference. He seems more mature and stable," she agreed.

"Yeah, he's really doing well," Emma added. "I'm so proud of him."

"You should be, honey. He's got a big hurdle to overcome, and he looks like he's doing it," Emma's mother, Rose, added. "I think he's darling."

That was the way the lunch ended. Emma and Jake did a

little shopping at her favorite new age shop, which was next door to Steinmart, so Rose went into Steinmart to look around. Emma and Jake drove Rose back to her hotel so she could rest and so they could take care of Tasha. They said they would meet with the whole family for dinner at six o'clock, which was two hours away. The moment they got into the room, Jake started taking Emma's clothes off.

"What are you doing?" she asked playfully.

"Come on. They'll never know. Let's do a quickie before dinner," he urged. And they did. More great sex and then a change of clothes for dinner. When they arrived at Emma's favorite Chinese restaurant, PF Chang's—a restaurant they didn't have in Savannah—she had a silly grin on her face when she saw Jean. Emma pulled her aside and lit a cigarette while her mother went to the bar for a drink while she waited for her grandmother and the rest of the family. Jake went inside with Rose, so she had a moment with Jean.

"Oh, my God, Jean! He's like Superman now! He had to do it before we came to dinner!"

"Quit bragging, you bitch!" Jean laughed raucously. "I can't get any because of Rick's back, and you are getting shtupped (Yiddish for having sex) every fucking hour!" Emma merely grinned devilishly.

"Yep!" and she tossed her hair back, laughing.

But as great as the sex was, Jake insisted on a beer while they waited at the bar for everyone to arrive. Then he ordered sake with dinner. He was increasing his alcohol intake. He wasn't drunk and he knew when to stop, but Emma was getting concerned. She covered it up well with everyone at dinner. They all had a great time. Emma loved her family, and Jake was being very polite with them. He called all the women ma'am, which Emma had to explain was Southern manners. Especially to her mother. Rose thought it was an affectation. Emma had to assure her it was not.

"It's just the Southern way," Emma drawled in a perfect Savannah accent. Her mother laughed and accepted it.

"Should he be drinking, sweetie?" Rose quietly asked her daughter.

"He's not an alcoholic, Mom. He gets nervous around a lot of people. But if you noticed, he only had one beer. I think he's okay," she lied. Of course, since her mother could drink Jake under the table, Emma assumed she accepted the lie.

The next two days were about the same. Lots of family. Lots of food. Lots of sex. It was actually a wonderful vacation for Emma. She may have worried about the drinking, but she selfishly loved the result. Jake was a sexual animal, and he was relaxed and patient with his lovemaking. His stamina was greater than it had ever been. How could Emma be dissatisfied?

When they returned home, it stayed the same. Life was fantastic. And it got better the day after their return. That afternoon the phone rang, bringing great news that Emma was sure would be the big red bow on their new life.

"Hello," Emma answered, looking lovingly at her engagement ring and at her fiancé.

"Is Jake Stanton there?" the man answered.

"Hold on, please," and she handed the phone to Jake.

When Jake got off the phone, he started jumping up and

down like a kid.

"I've got an interview at the Mercedes dealership! It's at three o'clock tomorrow." He dressed in a beautiful suit and looked the part. His looks, along with the resume Emma had created that was bound and quite impressive, made the interview successful. The interview went so well in fact, he got a call the following day. "I got the sales job at Mercedes! I start on Monday! I'll be in training for a week, then start actually selling the following week. They said the worst salesman there makes sixty-five thousand a year!"

"Oh, my God! Jake, honey, that's fantastic! Let's celebrate." Emma thought the celebration would be dinner and lovemaking. Instead, Jake kissed her and walked out of the house. He didn't return for hours. She tried calling him, but her calls went to voice mail. When he finally returned, she looked up at him from the sofa.

"Do I need to ask where you've been?" she had fire in her eyes.

"No."

"Hungry, dear?" she asked with syrupy sweetness.

"No."

"You son of a bitch! You celebrated with your mistress instead of with me? How could you?"

"It was a slip. Once I start working, I swear I won't be able to do drugs. I won't jeopardize this job. And you'll get every penny I make."

"Fuck you!" and she poured a double Grand Marnier and stormed out of the room. She slammed her bedroom door so hard, the heavy wooden panels that were held by magnets to cover the front of her jetted tub fell onto the marble floor with a crash. Emma started her bath and decided on a whirlpool to calm her. She poured lavender bath salts into the hot water and lit the candles that surrounded the tub.

Jake came barreling into the bathroom when he heard the crash.

"Are you all right?" he asked with some heat.

"No, Jake. I'm not all right. Just leave me alone. Oh, and if you hadn't noticed, while you were gone I had the cable box removed from the guest room. So you can go sulk and sleep it off, but you won't be able to order any more porn. And every good piece of jewelry I own is in the safe-deposit box at the bank. So don't even think about stealing my jewelry."

"I'm really sorry, baby. I panicked. The job and all," he stammered.

"I don't want to hear your apologies. Just get away from me."

Jake skulked away to the guest room, where Emma thought he would quickly pass out. She got into the tub, turned on the jets, and sobbed. Every penny she had spent on his rehabilitation had been for nothing. He was the most selfish human being she had ever met, and nothing would change. The last weekend they would have together for a good while was ruined by his self-indulgence. Once he started working full-time at the car dealership, he would have to work weekends, but that didn't occur to him when he went out that afternoon to be with the love of his life—cocaine (or crack, she had no clue which he had chosen.)

By the time her fingers began to prune, Emma finally emerged from the tub to dry herself off. Out of habit, she smoothed on body lotion. She used the ginger mousse from

Origins, despite the fact that Jake would not be touching her or taking in her scent. She moisturized her face and put on a tank top and pajama bottoms, all the while sipping her drink. She crawled into bed with the only one in the house she could count on for love. Her beloved Tasha. Emma's golden retriever happily curled up on Jake's side of the bed next to her mistress. At least Tasha devoured Emma with kisses.

Chapter Seventeen

Emma awoke long before Jake did, since he had been high the night before. She began to search her bar for bottles missing, and of course, she found the entire bottle of Triple Sec was missing. Yuck, Emma thought. How could someone drink a whole bottle of Triple Sec straight? It was only used as a mixer to make margaritas or cosmopolitans. She couldn't imagine drinking that sickeningly sweet drink straight. At least it was cheap, she mused. Emma had hidden all of her expensive liquor, so she assumed that was all Jake could find. Of course, she couldn't remember exactly where she had hidden the good stuff, but at least Jake couldn't get a hold of her Grand Marnier or Glen Fiddich.

With coffee in hand, she examined the rest of the house. He had to have stolen something to pawn in order to score drugs, and she was determined to find it. She walked to the back of the house into her office. The television! Her new fifteen-inch television with the built-in DVD was conspicuously missing, along with the remote. She immediately turned to look at the door right next to the office. The guest room. Emma turned the original 1950s crystal handle to open the door. It was locked. She banged on the door with full force. Sleepily, Jake came to the door.

"Why is this door locked?" Emma asked with heat in her voice.

"I didn't realize it was. Wazzup?"

"You pawned my brand new television, you prick!" she yelled.

"Baby, I'm sorry. Just let me get some more sleep and we'll talk," he begged.

"No, Jake. This is my house, my rules." Then she looked at the cherry wood nightstand. There was a glass filled with cigarette butts; the brown water in it turned her stomach.

"And one of the rules is no smoking in the guest room. Remember?" She walked to the nightstand and picked up the glass. She also noticed the cigarette burn in the antique lace that covered it. "Jesus, Jake. You're a fucking slob. You've ruined this lace. It's Victorian. Oh, you wouldn't know what that means, would you? It's a hundred years old!"

"I'll make it up to you. I'll be making plenty of money at Mercedes. You'll get every penny," he tried sleepily.

"I fuckin' better!" and she slammed the door in his face. The weekend went about the same. He hid in the guest room for most of it.

Since Emma was alone for most of the weekend, she had more thinking time than she wanted. Why was she putting up with this? She asked herself that question over and over again. She resolved there were two reasons. One was ego. She loved being seen with this gorgeous hunk of man. It had been so long since she'd been with a man, it was a big ego boost that he was so handsome. The more important reason at this point in their relationship was financial. If she didn't stay with him once he started his job, she'd never get paid back for at least some of the money she'd spent. On their way back from Chicago, they had stopped at the Neiman Marcus outlet store in Atlanta. She bought him a beautiful suit for his interviews. It had been marked fifteen hundred dollars but at the outlet, she had paid three-fifty for it. She had spent a total of eight hundred dollars in clothes for him on that trip. If she kicked him out now, she'd never get a cent back. So she had to put up with him until he started repaying her.

The odd feeling that overwhelmed her was her own suicide. She didn't wish Jake dead; she wished herself dead. Emma's own life felt worthless. She was taking all her anger and frustration out on herself. But she endured.

By Sunday night, Jake was back to acting somewhat normal. They took an evening swim, during which he held Emma most of the time. He caressed her and kissed her, telling her how much he wanted her. He continued telling Emma how much he loved her. They talked about his job the following morning, and he admitted how nervous he was. When they emerged from the pool, she was sure they would make passionate love. Whether it was the drugs or the sheer terror of a real job, he couldn't perform.

He awoke early and dressed in his new suit for his new job. He ate two hot dogs for breakfast. Jake left for work with his paperwork stored in a leather briefcase Emma had lent him. He looked like a real adult.

Jake came home for lunch so he didn't have to spend any money. He quickly nuked some Ramen noodles and crumbled bacon and cheese flavored crackers into the noodles, and then covered them with hot sauce. Whatever, Emma thought. If that's what he wants, at least it's cheap. Then he left to go back to work and did the absolute unthinkable. He did cocaine again that evening. It was a work night, and Emma couldn't fathom how he was going to get up in the morning.

This was, without a doubt, pure stupidity. He was still going to have to talk his way through having a felony conviction on his record to his new boss. He was going to be drug tested the following day. Emma was dumbstruck. Okay, she was a member of Mensa. She had her doctoral degree in Psychology. She knew she had a tremendous mind. But she couldn't understand how anyone could be this outrageously moronic. He had already done eighteen months in prison for drug possession, and he claimed he never wanted to do that again. His description of prison was as a horrible, violent, degrading place. So exactly how high an IQ does one need to figure out that using drugs again is bound to put you back in the same place? Was Jake really this stupid? Obviously, yes.

He asked her for a urine sample to take to work with him. He explained that Cheryl had done it for him several times before going to probation where they drug test. Emma initially told him no. She wasn't going to save his ass due to his own stupidity. Then she reevaluated. If he could keep the job, she'd get paid back. And closing some big sales would do wonders for his self-confidence, which Emma believed would curtail his drug use. So she peed into an old prescription bottle and gave it to him. She felt guilty for the deception, but her greed overpowered her guilt. In retrospect, she wished she had let him get caught. But even as she thought about it, she knew he would just go to Cheryl who would have no qualms about helping him.

"I hope they don't find out you're pregnant," she said as she handed him the bottle.

"Yeah, that would be embarrassing."

"So what do you do with it until they test you?" she asked

with genuine curiosity.

"Put it in the fridge and then the day I take it in, I'll nuke it to room temperature. It's always worked."

"Fine. Whatever," she muttered.

Understanding his attitude when he was coming down from using cocaine, Emma seriously doubted he'd get away with any of the lies he was preparing. Emma had no confidence in him whatsoever. And she determined that if he did lose his job the next day, which was a high probability, she was done with him. If he lost his job, she was sure he would spiral so far downward, there would be no recovery from it. Emma knew she could not pick up the pieces from that disappointment.

Surprisingly, Jake managed to get the job. He conned his way through the felony conviction and through the drug testing. He was still in training, so he was being paid very little. His boss liked him, and he got along well enough with his co-workers. Since the dealership was around the corner from her house, Emma stopped by every so often to see him and break up the boredom of his day. She was introduced to everyone, and her presence in Jake's life gave him some semblance of credibility. After all, he had won the heart of a beautiful, brilliant, successful woman. He couldn't be all bad.

By June, Jake began working full-time in sales. He had done his studying of the brochures on each car in the line and could spout off all the specs. He did role-playing with Emma, trying to sell her a car. He actually went overboard on his sales technique. He was really pushing Emma to buy a new Mercedes. That got her back up, but she knew he needed the experience, so she let him use her for practice.

Jake was also becoming more and more selfish. He had sex with Emma only when he was in the mood. His days off were spent napping and watching television. He wasn't making any sales, and Emma could see he was getting discouraged. He still hadn't brought home a paycheck, but he was still pushing the point that he would and she would get it all. By mid-June Emma was totally disgusted. His selfishness and self-indulgence were becoming major real problems for Emma.

For the two weeks after Jake had left rehab and before they went to Chicago, the relationship had been heavenly. He was clean, neat, caring, and loving. Once he took that first drink in Chicago, he began the downward spiral. Emma knew in her heart that it was happening, but she was so happy that she pretended she didn't notice. Now there was no denying it. Jake couldn't stay clean for more than three days. She knew he would lose his job, and that would be the end of Jake, both to Emma and to himself. He wouldn't be able to cope with such losses. If he lost Emma, he didn't have the stability or the intelligence to deal with life. The same with his job.

Since Jake started his job, he either acted like a child or a puppy, bouncing off the walls with energy, or he was sullen and quiet. There was no more romance, no more interesting conversation, and rarely any sex. He bottled all his emotions inside and then exploded or imploded when he couldn't cope anymore. Emma and Jake slept apart nearly every night, one way or another. Either Jake slunk out to watch television in the great room and would fall asleep on the sofa, or Emma had enough of his screaming and snoring and slept on the sofa. The worst part of this finality was neither Emma nor Jake was doing anything about it.

After one of the worst nights, Emma finally and calmly, asked Jake to leave. She told him she'd had enough and kicked him out yet again. They never actually resolved anything; he just stayed. Because of his new job, Emma gave in. After her demand that he move out, he had all day to ease the tension and win Emma back. He did nothing. Emma knew the easiest con to win her back was to have make-up sex. He never played that ace. He could have wanted to play a game of pool or do something together. He didn't. Oh, he talked about the great make-up sex they would have that night. But when night finally arrived, all Emma was offered was a quick fuck to appease her. No romance, no foreplay. Emma refused. She didn't want to start a fight the night before he had to go to work, so she quietly turned over and began reading a book. After all, everything was now about Jake. His job. His nerves. Emma actually felt a bit of pity. He was losing all that mattered to him by not making an effort to win Emma back. He was so wrapped up in himself, he didn't notice she wasn't wearing her engagement ring. He was pushing her farther and farther away.

As Emma was at the verge of giving up, a new window opened. She finally paid for Jake to go to a psychiatrist, and they went together. She learned two interesting facts that day. The most important was the diagnosis that Jake was bipolar. That made a great deal of sense to Emma. She had seen his mood swings for months and assumed it was due to drugs. But the fact was, he was manic-depressive, and the drugs merely exacerbated the existing illness. He was given medication by the doctor. Unfortunately, they were ten dollars a pill; fortunately, the doctor gave him free samples.

Maybe that would give him the internal stability he needed to keep him clean. If his emotions were all over the place, she could understand his desire for self-medication. Jake's personality was starting to come in focus to Emma. She understood bipolar disorder in part because she had studied it in college but she had seen it up close because she had a secretary who had the same problem. One day she would come to work and tell Emma she was the greatest boss in the world. She would do anything for Emma on that day. The very next day, however, she would come to work hating Emma. She would refuse to do any of her own work, let alone be helpful to Emma. Oddly, this secretary also self-medicated with alcohol and cocaine. Hmm, Emma thought. Interesting. Maybe this was common for manic-depressives. When they're in the manic mode, they use alcohol to calm down. When they're in the depressive mode, they use cocaine to bring them up.

She could certainly see the symptoms in Jake. He had moments in which he was so manic, when he couldn't sit still. Schpilkes, as Jean had described him. Then, like a light switch, he would lie on the sofa and zone out watching television. No energy, no brain function. And there was every emotion in between. He could be cutting and mean one moment, then gentle and caring an hour later. Typical bipolar behavior.

The second bit of information Emma learned from the psychiatrist was mind-boggling. Jake didn't use cocaine for the desired high that most people abuse. He took it for the miserable low that followed. He used cocaine when he was in his manic stage so he could spend the next two days sleeping and being basically unconscious. The alcohol he used to come down off the cocaine kept his brain from going in a thousand different directions, as it did in his manic state. Emma couldn't help but think this was one stupid person. If all he wants is the low, why doesn't he just smoke pot to mellow out? It would be cheaper, less dangerous, and would accomplish exactly what he wanted. But not Jake. He had to take the more dangerous and indirect route to the same destination.

Emma watched Jake carefully, and the first medication he was given made him completely nuts. He went to work and said he was jittery and edgy at first and then started getting drowsy. So what did brilliant Jake do? He took Max-Alerts (the over-the-counter equivalent to cocaine) and a twenty-four ounce beer. Once again, Emma thought, this is one stupid human being. He didn't call the psychiatrist and ask what to do or even call Emma; he just did the exact opposite of what he should do. Then he lied to Emma all afternoon, telling her that he was at work, and arrived home an hour after he should have, based on his schedule.

It got worse. When he finally came home, he didn't eat. He didn't talk. He had been late because he went to Cheryl's house and broke into their garage to steal Aaron's beer. Jake was dead drunk when he got home. Emma was at a breaking point. She was getting more physically ill by the day. She had all but stopped eating; she got no sleep and was quickly losing her spirit. She had no energy. She felt as though she were already dead.

On June 22nd, Jake left for work; and never came home. Emma was worried because she couldn't contact him by phone.

When he finally called at eleven thirty that night, he told her he had been arrested.

"I went to see Mom, and I stopped at the drug store to buy something for her. The CVS right there on DeRenne? (Only a few blocks from her house.) I was minding my own business, and this big black dude came at me. He was trying to sell me drugs, and I only pushed him away." Jake meandered around the story so poorly, Emma knew it was a lie. "Anyway, I was leaving to come home, and I was pulled over. This nice police officer is letting me call you."

"Right," Emma responded sarcastically.

"I had borrowed the lawn equipment from the house, and the nigger stole all of it while I was talking to the store manager."

"Jake, don't you dare use that word in front of me. You want to be a bigoted asshole, don't do it in front of me!"

"I don't have time for this argument, honey. I'm lucky the police even let me make this call. Just please come and bail me out." And he hung up. Emma immediately called Cheryl and told her what happened.

"Oh, God. Emma, I don't know what to say. Go online to the Chatham County Sheriff's Office and find out what the charges are. Keep me posted, Em. I'm so sorry about this," Cheryl said before she hung up.

It took Emma most of the night online and on the phone to find out what happened. By two in the morning, his arrest was finally logged into Chatham County. Shit, Emma thought. He even looks cute in his mug shot! The bastard. Three charges were brought against him. Driving under the influence, possession of a controlled substance, and an open bottle while driving. Emma called the Chatham County Sheriff's Office to find out where he was caught and the particulars.

"Ma'am, we can't divulge the particulars in a case," the officer on duty drawled. "But he was arrested in Garden City. That's where he's in jail and where you'll have to post bail."

"Thank you, officer," Emma said, while in her head she could hear her own screams of "You son of a bitch! I'm going to kill you."

Emma began looking through the Yellow Pages for bail offices and found the one in Garden City. She called them immediately. It was near four in the morning.

"Hello, I need some help," she said sweetly. "I've never done this before, so what is the procedure?"

"Yes, ma'am. First, I need the name of the inmate." Emma told them Jake's full name. "Here he is. His bond is twenty-five hundred dollars. We need two hundred and fifty dollars plus processing fee of thirty-five dollars."

"Okay. I'll be there later this morning," Emma told them. She got directions to their office and hung up the phone. She was surprised that the bail was so little. If the bond had been any more than that, she had determined she wouldn't pay it. She had assumed with his past conviction, the bond would be steep. But for two hundred and fifty dollars, she'd get him out of jail. What she did with him from there, she didn't know. She was working on straight adrenaline at that point.

Emma fell asleep on the sofa for a couple of hours. The mental and emotional exhaustion finally overtook her adrenaline. When she awoke, she let Tasha out, made coffee, and called Cheryl.

"Hey Cheryl. His bail is only two hundred fifty bucks. So,

yeah. I'll bail him out. I may kill him afterwards, but at least he'll be out of jail."

"Thank you, Emma. I know he's a fuck up, but he shouldn't be in jail. I think the reason he wants to be bailed out so fast is because here in Savannah, the law moves real slow. They probably haven't contacted his probation officer yet, or there would be no bail. If he gets out quickly, they won't have time to really throw the book at him," she told Emma.

"Fine. I'll get dressed and go out to Garden City this morning. He's such a fucking liar, Cheryl. He told me he was caught right around the corner from the house, which didn't make any sense. He said he went to see your mother and went to the drugstore to pick something up for her. God, he's such a piece of shit!"

"Yeah, that's my brother. Emma, I love Jake. You know I do. But his lies are so stupid. I talked to Mama and he was never even there yesterday. It's hard to put up with the lies."

"Yep, I know. So how does this bail work? Do they take credit cards, or do I have to bring cash, or what?" Emma asked.

"Oh, they take just about anything. They don't care. All the credit cards, cash, cashier's checks, pennies—doesn't matter."

"Okay. I'm getting my act together here. I didn't get any sleep, as you can imagine. I'd also really like to see him sit there and rot for a while. But I'll get out there as soon as I can," Emma told Jake's sister and hung up.

Chapter Eighteen

Emma slipped on a pair of jeans and a nice T-shirt and for the first time in her life, was heading to a bail bondsman and to a jail. How had she come to this? Emma barely had a traffic ticket. She had never taken drugs. She was clean as a baby's freshly wiped bottom. How had she become involved with probation officers, drug dealers, and jail? It seemed surreal, as if she had been dropped into a strange world that made no sense to her. Her father—thank God—was not on this earth to see it. He would surely have made her suffer for her naiveté. But at this moment in time, it was her life and she had to cope with it.

Before her drive to the dregs of Garden City, Emma stopped first at Mimi's nursing home. Emma felt Jake's mother deserved to know the truth. She dreaded telling her that her baby boy was back in jail, but someone had to tell her, and Emma wanted to be the one. She parked and, as if trying to get it over with, quickly walked back to Mimi Stanton's room.

"Good morning, Mimi," Emma tried desperately to smile when she kissed Mimi's cheek.

"What's wrong?" Mimi saw right through the ruse. This was one smart cookie. You couldn't pull anything over on her, Emma thought as she carefully sat down on the side of Mimi's bed. She took Mimi's hand in hers, hoping that the connection would help.

"Jake's in jail, Mimi. I'm sorry. I'm going to bail him out right now, but I thought you should know," Emma blurted the truth. She saw the tears falling onto Mimi's cheeks. Emma pulled a tissue from the box and handed it to Mimi. With difficulty, Mimi dabbed at her eyes. "Can I do anything else to help you through this?" Emma asked.

"Use that pretty belt of yours and whip his ass," she answered, a wan smile coming to her lips.

"I wish I could. I'm just not capable of physical violence."

"I should have done it years ago. Go, Emma. Go get my baby out of jail. Then bring him here. I'll give him a piece of my mind—what little is left anyway."

"Okay. That I can do. And there's plenty left of your mind." Emma smiled, kissed Mimi good-bye, and started the drive to Garden City. Kathy had been right. Garden City was cesspool. Though it felt farther, she arrived at the bail bond store in fifteen minutes—much quicker than she wished. But when she went inside, she wished she'd never come. She'd never seen anything like it.

The entire store—or whatever they were called—was orange. Not pumpkin or peach but bright, psychedelic orange. Emma felt she had been transported back in time to the 1960s. The carpet was bright orange shag, the chairs had bright orange faux fur, and the walls were painted the same obnoxious orange. It was blinding. Emma had learned through her psychology studies that orange was the favorite color of most inmates in insane asylums. Was she reading into this decor too deeply? Maybe the owner just liked orange. Regardless, she wished she could leave her sunglasses on to shield her from the glare.

Emma walked up to the glass window and saw an elderly woman working.

"Hello," Emma half-called to the woman.

"Be right with you," she heard from behind the tempered glass. Emma waited until the woman came to the window. "What can I do for you?"

"I'm here to post bail for Jake Stanton," Emma told her. The woman went to her computer and pulled some paperwork. She shook her head in disgust.

"You're here for Jake? He's such a sweet boy. What a shame," the woman said.

"You know Jake?" Emma asked rather awestruck.

"Oh, yeah. I know his mama, too. How's she doin'? I hear tell she's in a nursing home. That true?" she drawled.

"Um, yeah. Mrs. Stanton had a stroke and she's in a very nice nursing home in Savannah. She's doing all right. She can't use her legs at all, and her arms don't work very well. Her speech has also been affected by the strokes," Emma told her. "I saw her this morning."

"You should have seen her in her prime. She was a force to be reckoned with. Smart? That lady had smarts. So who are you?" she asked.

"Oh, sorry. I'm Emma Weiss. I was engaged to Jake. I'm his…girlfriend, I guess. After this, I don't know."

"Hah! I understand completely. He's a good boy. Just got himself in too much trouble. Let's see here," she shuffled papers. "Here it is —. Two hundred eighty five dollars. You pay that, then you take it to the jail and they'll process him out. Take yourself a book to read. They process folks into jail real quick, but processing out, well that takes a while." Emma handed her a MasterCard, and the woman returned with the receipt. Emma signed it and signed the form handed to her as the person responsible for Jake.

"Thank you, ma'am," Emma said and left for Garden City Jail.

Emma drove the couple of miles from the Orange Room of the bail bonds office to the stark White Halls of jail. She had never seen a jail before, except of course, in movies. This was not like the movies. This was far too real. She stood in line behind others who were there for the same purpose as she. When she got to the window, she asked what she was supposed to do. There were several serious, cold police officers behind the window.

"Your purse, miss. We have to check it," she was told. They took her black Prada and searched its contents. "Okay. Here you go," he handed Emma's purse back to her.

"Yes, sir. Here's the, uh, paperwork for the bail for Jake Stanton," Emma stuttered and handed him the form she had been given.

"Okay. We'll start processing him. You want to go back to see him while you're waiting?"

"Uh, sure," Emma responded, although she was thinking this was a bad idea. "Where do I go?"

"Through the metal detector, then up to the next level all the way back to Cellblock C. You'll see the signs. Oh, you'll have to leave that purse here with me. Here's a receipt so you can claim it when you come out. Next!" and the officer was on to the next person.

Emma began the walk. Okay, she thought, I can do this. She started up the elevator; that was easy. Then when she reached the second floor, all she saw was stark white.

Everywhere she looked was bright, eye-searing white. The only relief from white was black, block letters and arrows. Cellblock A with a left arrow, Cellblock B and a right arrow, Cellblock C had an arrow straight ahead. Emma followed the white floors and white walls. She could swear they were getting smaller. Emma was not claustrophobic, but the walls seemed to close in on her. After walking through the sea of white for what felt like a mile, she saw the sign for Cellblock C. She looked to the right and saw windows with thick glass. Behind one of the windows was Jake. He was wearing the blue paper jumpsuit of a prisoner. She slowly walked toward the window.

On closer look, Jake was crying. He sat his lanky body down and picked up the phone. Emma picked up her phone and heard the bawling.

"I'm so sorry, Emma. You didn't have to walk all the way back here. But you've got to get me out of here as soon as possible. I can't take another night of this place. I'm so miserable. Just a bunch of niggers around me," he moaned and saw Emma wince at the use of the word she so despised.

"Jake, you're where you deserve to be. You're still, at this late date, thinking only of yourself. No thought at all to what you've done to me. You're right. I deserve better," and with that, Emma dropped the phone, turned around, and walked away. She didn't look back. Emma knew it was cruel. She left Jake to wonder if he would ever see her again. And she meant him to think exactly that. Let him sweat, she thought, as she began the long walk back to the lobby area.

When Emma finally found the door to the lobby area of the jail, she was grateful. She needed a cigarette—and color. Green trees, flowers, anything with pigment. She told the officer where she was going and asked how long before Jake was processed.

"Oh, I couldn't say, ma'am," a young officer told her. "Coupla hours at least." She handed the officer her receipt for her purse, which he released to her.

With that, Emma walked out the double doors and walked toward the wooden gazebo that was clearly the smoking section. She sat with several other people and, as was Emma's way, began talking with them. Since Emma hadn't thought to bring a book, she found it more entertaining to talk to people than to merely sit around and wait. She was curious about the stories other people would tell. It would be far more interesting than any book to Emma. She lit a cigarette and asked the older black woman who was there to pick up her son.

"My boy's in there," she told Emma. "Drugs. Stupid kid. This is my third time here. You here to see your kin?"

"No, my boyfriend. I guess he's my boyfriend. After this, ma'am, I don't know."

"Oh, I'm sure he don't mean no harm. But I know what you're goin' through. Such a pretty young thing, too. You sure you want more of this?" she asked as though reading Emma's mind.

"No. Not sure at all. He swore he would stay clean after I put him in rehab. But they're such liars when they want their drugs, aren't they?" Emma asked the veteran on the subject.

"No doubt about it, sugar. They just can't tell the truth. Because the truth is, they want the drugs. So any truth is better than that," the old woman explained.

"I'm here to pick up my roommate," a young woman spoke up. She looked like she had been through a war. Her makeup was smeared, her hair dirty, and her clothes looked like she'd slept in them. "She got picked up two weeks ago for her fourth DUI, but I couldn't get the money together for her bail until today. Without her money for rent, it's been rough."

"Has this happened before?" Emma asked the woman. As the woman inhaled her cigarette, Emma tried to judge her age. It was difficult. She could have been anywhere between thirty and fifty years old. It was obvious to Emma that this woman had done her share of drugs and done more than her share of drinking. Her face was wrinkled and drawn.

"Not to me," she rasped. "She'd only been living with me for a few months, even though we'd been friends for years. We partied plenty, but I'm smart enough not to drive. She wasn't so smart."

"So she's been in here for two weeks?" Emma was stunned that someone would leave a friend to rot in jail for two weeks.

"Yeah and she's miserable. She was brought in wearing a red bra and panties, so they were confiscated. You ain't allowed to wear anything but whites in jail. So she's spend two weeks wearin' nothing but that paper jumpsuit. She said it's freezing cold back there, too. And the food? Beans and rice. That's it. And that video in the lobby claims they wash clothes every day. Hah! Once a week is all." She inhaled deeply on her cigarette. "I've been waiting over an hour already. Had to miss a day of work for this bullshit."

"I guess they weren't kidding about how long it takes to process people, "Emma answered.

"No, indeed," another young man answered. "Hell, I've been here two hours waitin' on my brother. He's been in for three weeks. I couldn't get the money together any sooner. Old fool! Been caught so many times and just can't stop," he muttered.

"Drugs?" Emma asked him.

"Yeah. He been through rehab, NA. We tried everything, Mama and me. Nothin' works. So what's a pretty thing like you doin' here?" he smiled, showing a gold tooth.

"My boyfriend was picked up last night. DUI, possession, and an open bottle. Probably beer. I'm so angry I could spit!" Emma told the young man.

"I know just how you feel. You feel like they doin' it to you. To spite you. But that ain't the way. They just care 'bout they selves. They don't even think about the pain they causin' their kin," he answered. "You don't mind my askin', where y'all from?"

"Florida," Emma answered. "Fort Lauderdale, to be exact." She wasn't about to answer Chicago. She'd be called a Yankee, which was worse than a criminal.

"I been there," the young man answered. "Pretty place. Lotsa palm trees and sun."

"I've been there, too," the young woman added. "Great bars! Right on the water, too. I had me a good job for a while. Tendin' bar while I looked at the ocean! Nice gig—while it lasted. Then I came home to Georgia."

Emma chatted a while longer and then excused herself to go inside. She wanted a picture in her mind of the waiting area in jail. She sat in a white plastic chair in the front row. She didn't dare squeeze through the fifty people waiting—some falling asleep in their chairs—to the last of the five rows of chairs. Most of the people waiting were African-American, and the ones who were white looked rougher than the African-Americans.

There was a television mounted on the wall facing the waiting family and friends. It showed a video about the jail that was on a continual loop. The video praised the jail for its cleanliness and food. It explained the rules of jail. Emma only winced as she watched it. She noticed she was sitting next to a well-dressed, sophisticated, older black woman. She caught the woman's attention and smiled.

"Is it me, or is that video totally racist?" Emma said quietly to the woman.

"Hmm," the woman looked up at the screen and thought for a moment. "I guess you're right."

"Doesn't it bother you that the video shows every prisoner as being black? I haven't seen one white face on that screen. That's so racist. There are plenty of white people in this jail who've committed crimes," Emma said indignantly.

"Honey, you're right. It shouldn't be that way," she agreed with Emma.

These inequities bothered Emma. She had been raised to believe all men were created equal. That there were good and bad people of every race and creed. She always waited to pass judgment until there was cause. Emma saw every human being as an individual and assumed all people were good until proven otherwise, which is why she became so angry when Jake and Aaron had used the "N" word. That word had never escaped her lips in her life, and she disdained anyone who used it. It was also why she was in the trouble she was in. Her soft heart was destroying her.

Sitting in the jail waiting room, she felt the same. She would not let this change her basic belief structure. She looked around and saw white people who looked tough and beaten and black people who looked kind and distraught. She had nearly two hours to evaluate her surroundings before she finally saw Jake walk out of the door to the left of the counter. He looked tired, beaten, and dirty. She stood up and began to walk toward him. He tried to hug her, but she kept her distance.

"Let's go," she said briskly. He followed her outside and to her car. He climbed into the passenger's side and slumped down in his seat. Emma could see on his face that he had no idea what to say.

"We need to get my truck out of impound," he finally said as they drove away from the jail.

"Where is it? I'm not as intimate with Garden City as you are, so you'll have to give me directions," she answered coolly.

He directed her to the impound facility and to her dismay, the man recognized Jake. He also knew Jake's mother.

"Son, what kind of trouble you gotten into this time?" he asked.

"Same as last time," Jake tried to put on his winning smile, but it didn't work.

"Jake, you got your paperwork from the bail bondsman?"

"Shit. I forgot. We'll go there now and be right back," Jake answered impatiently.

After an hour of running back and forth from the bail bondsman to the garage, Emma finally got Jake's truck out of impound. That was another hundred and fifty dollars out of Emma's pocket. From there, Emma followed Jake home. With this arrest, Jake had lost his license. They had kept his license and all identification at the jail until his hearing in August. So now Jake was driving illegally. He had Emma follow him, both because he knew the directions, and because if she was right behind him there was a lesser chance of a cop getting behind him.

"Emma, I don't know how to thank you," Jake said when they arrived home. "I know I don't deserve you, and you certainly deserve better than me."

"That's all true, Jake. I don't think I'll ever trust you again. I wish you would make some money so you could leave."

"Oh, shit. I've got to call work. I'll make up something about why I wasn't there." Emma passed him the phone, and he shook his head. "No, I have to use my cell phone. I'll tell them there was a death in the family and I had to go to South Carolina. I'll go back tomorrow."

"Fine." When they got home, Emma went to the drawer in the wet bar and handed him the phone. He made the call, and then took a long hot shower. He threw his clothes in the hamper and put on fresh, clean clothes.

"Well, that feels better," he said with a smile. "Emma, I'm never going back there again. I just can't deal with it. The n—people in there (he stopped himself from using the word Emma so hated) are so horrible. If this didn't put the fear of God in me, nothing will. I swear on my life, I will never use drugs or drink alcohol again. I'd rather kill myself than be there again," he began to sob.

"I'll believe that when I see it," Emma muttered. "Come on. We have one place to go before you get too comfortable. We've got to go see your mother."

"Oh, God. She knows?" Jake whined.

"Of course. I saw her this morning. I thought it would be better coming from me than from Cheryl. There would only be a crying jag with Cheryl. I kept things light. But I promised her you would see her when you got out. She needs to know you're safe."

"All right. Let's go," Jake accepted his punishment.

She drove to the nursing home and walked in with Jake. He tried to hold her hand as they walked, but she pulled away. With his long strides, she had to nearly jog to keep up with him. When they reached Mimi's room, Emma walked in first. She walked to Mimi's bed and gave her a kiss on the cheek.

"I brought something for you," Emma smiled. Jake walked into the room and into his mother's arms. Mimi cried as Jake kissed her on the mouth like he always did. He began to sob.

"I'm so sorry, Mom. I know I fucked up," he put his head on her breast. Emma walked out of the room. She couldn't take the scene that was unfolding. She could only think of Mimi and how many times this scene had repeated itself. Would Emma become the next Mimi? Emma shuddered at the thought. Jake seemed to be working as hard as he could to repeat the performance. Emma could easily become penniless and incapacitated from a stroke. Jake was fully able to cause it. When Jake walked out of the room, he was still wiping his eyes.

"What did she say?" Emma asked.

"That I was a piece of shit," he answered, sniveling.

"She's right. She asked me to take my belt and beat your ass. I told her I couldn't do it. I couldn't inflict physical violence, and she looked disappointed. Jake, you claim you love people. Your mother, Joe, me. But what you do to us, it's a miracle anyone even talks to you."

"I know. I swear, Emma, I wish you would beat the shit out of me with your belt. I deserve it. But I can't live without you. I don't want to. Mama just told me I'd better make amends to you or she will beat me. I'm going to do everything I can to do that."

"Good luck," Emma stated with finality.

Chapter Ninteen

After spending one night in jail, Jake was obsessed with never going back to that place. Nothing else seemed to matter to him but finding a way around his dilemma. His first idea was to contact the Georgia Bureau of Investigations, the state equivalent of the FBI. He had worked for them as a snitch in the past, and he thought he could do it again.

Of course, it evaded his brilliant mind that the last time he worked for them he screwed them. They set him up to turn on his dealer, and Jake ended up stealing the drugs for himself. That did not bode well with the dealer or with the GBI. The GBI was furious with him and made sure he got sentenced to nine years. He got out of prison after eighteen months and would be on probation for another seven years. That was only two years ago, so he still had five years left on his probation. What made him think they would help him again, God alone knew. And Emma tried to make that very clear to Jake.

"Jake, not only will they not work with you again because of what you did to them before, but even if they did, you're small potatoes. They would use you and then turn you in. You're a nothing to them. They're not going to help you," she told him.

"But the agent I talked to said he would have the charges dropped if I wear a wire and give them the dealers," he pleaded.

"And you believed them?" she asked with utter awe at his naïveté. "Jesus, Jake."

"Well, what other choice do I have? I'm not going back to

jail. I just can't. I'll kill myself first," he whined.

"Go to court in August. Cheryl already said she'd get you a lawyer. Yeah, you'll do a little time, but at least you'd be safe. Dealing with these GBI guys is going to get you killed. Not to mention going back to the drug dealers," Emma replied. "That's too much temptation for you."

"Let me talk to Cheryl. See what she says." Jake picked up his cell phone and called his sister. Emma could tell from his side of the conversation that Cheryl was giving him the same advice. When he took the phone and walked out of the room to finish the call, Emma knew Cheryl was telling him he was stupid for even thinking of trying this again. When he reentered the room, she could see it on his face.

"She agreed with me, didn't she?" Emma glared at him.

"Yeah, she did. But it's my only hope. That or running. I'd need a driver's license in any event, since they confiscated mine. A birth certificate, too. I know I can get both, but they're probably really expensive. Working with the GBI is my best chance," he decided in his infinite wisdom.

"Please don't do this," Emma pleaded. "It's way too dangerous."

As June came to an end, Jake played both sides. He kept in contact with the GBI, leading them along. Meanwhile, he started asking some of his less scrupulous acquaintances how he could get false identification. He had one especially sleazy friend whom Emma disdained. Jake met with Al several times. Of course, Jake lost his job at Mercedes, and with no driver's license or identification, he couldn't get another job.

One morning Jake asked Emma for a couple of dollars to go to Starbucks for coffee. This certainly seemed odd since there was a pot of coffee in the kitchen.

"Why?" Emma asked.

"I just want to think for a while," he answered.

"So go sit outside with a cup of coffee and think," she replied.

"Emma, please," he demanded.

"Fine, here," and she handed him a five-dollar bill. "Whatever." What she didn't know was that he took her laptop with him and he was planning to research identity theft. He didn't want her to know so she wouldn't be involved. She also wouldn't know for a month that he had stolen her Visa card to be able to go online and buy a fake driver's license. Even when her Visa bill arrived, it didn't exactly refer to fake driver's licenses, so it was tough to find.

He continued his clandestine calls to the GBI, all the while also sneaking around to find ways to obtain fake identification. He asked Emma if he could see her birth certificate. She looked at him with incredulity.

"Jake, my birth certificate is from Illinois. Even if you could duplicate it with your own information, you'd never pass for a Yankee," she expressed deep concern. "But if you want to see it, fine." She went into her closet and closed the door so she could open her safe without him seeing her. She took out her birth certificate and locked the safe behind her. He was standing at the door, shouting out guesses to the combination.

"Very funny," she replied. "Not even close." With every combination of numbers he guessed, she said the same thing. She knew he could never figure out the combination to her safe. She had picked a new number he could never know. She handed him the birth certificate.

"God, it looks so different from mine," he told her. Jake had been born in South Carolina, and his birth certificate was the size of a credit card. It had no information on it compared to Emma's. Emma's had the doctor's signature, the hospital's signature, time of birth, and the races of her parents. It was a full page of pertinent information. Jake's merely had his name, date, and some numbers on it. Easily forged, she thought. But not hers. "Well, this won't work. It's too complicated."

"What did you expect, Jake? Just scan it and change the name? The government is not stupid. It's on special paper and the edges are raised. There's no way you can fake this," she told him.

"Yeah. It was a dumb idea," and he handed it back to her. But he was not finished. Not by a long shot. He knew his own was simple to recreate but it was in terrible condition. He had to think of something. Behind Emma's back, Jake borrowed Cheryl's birth certificate. Since it was also from South Carolina and Cheryl's was in better condition than Jake's, he started hatching ideas. Emma had mentioned scanning it and changing the name and birth date. Maybe it really was that simple. He began plotting.

The end of June brought about Jake's mother's birthday. He made sure to visit her, as did Emma. But he had to be sure it was when Cheryl and Aaron and their kids were not there. It was sad that he could not see his own niece and nephew. He adored them, but seeing them was difficult. Aaron absolutely wouldn't allow it, and since it was Mimi's birthday, Jake was sure Aaron would be with Cheryl at the nursing home. He decided to see his mother the day before her birthday to ensure he wouldn't run into Aaron.

Emma and Jake went into Mimi's room together to wish her a happy birthday. There were balloons in her room from the nurses and aides. After the small talk was over, Jake sat alone with his mother, while Emma walked out into the hall. She knew he was telling her about his plans to either deal with the GBI or run from the law with fake IDs. And she didn't have to be in the room to know that his mother would disapprove of both options.

When he came out, he was concerned about his mother and didn't mention the conversation. He explained to Emma that his mother's stomach was so distended that she looked nine months pregnant. Her doctor was preparing to take her to the hospital on Monday for some tests to find out what was wrong. Emma was worried about Mimi, too. She kept close communication with Cheryl to find out the status of the tests. Jake was consumed with his own goals. He started going to Narcotics Anonymous meetings again and as many Alcoholics Anonymous meetings as he could. A week later, Jake received a phone call at eleven thirty at night. According to him, it was his AA sponsor.

"He wants to go for coffee," Jake told Emma, who was already in bed.

"Are you nuts? Who calls at this time of night?"

"Really. It's only Carl. He wants me to meet him and a couple of friends for coffee," Jake assured her. "You don't believe me? Here," and Jake dialed the phone number and handed her the phone. Whoever was on the other end confirmed Jake's story.

"I really don't give a shit. Go," she said. "What do you care that I have to wait up for you because you don't have the keys to the house—remember?" When he got out of jail, she had confiscated his keys and changed the deactivation code on the alarm. With her alarm system, the only way he could get in or out of the house once she activated the alarm was if she got up and turned it off. Since the keypad was in her bedroom, he couldn't sneak out without it waking her. Or so she believed.

"I'll be back in an hour."

Emma got out of bed and deactivated the alarm so he could leave. She turned on the television in the bedroom and waited. He returned an hour later from wherever he'd been. She didn't know and she didn't think she wanted to know.

The next day Jake once again wanted to go to Starbucks. Since he had no driver's license, Emma knew he would be careful. So she gave him a couple of dollars for coffee and sent him on his way. He called three hours later from Starbucks. He sounded frantic.

"Emma. Your computer was stolen! I went into the bathroom for two minutes, and when I came back it was gone! The manager is trying to look at the security cameras to see if he sees anything. God, I can't believe this is happening!"

"You took my laptop? You fucking piece of shit!" Emma looked next to her on the sofa where she always kept her computer, and it was, indeed, gone. Including the Prada computer case. Emma didn't believe a word of his story. She knew he had pawned it and used the money to buy drugs. She knew he was a moron for trying it but did he really think she was that stupid to buy this pile of bullshit? Obviously, yes. When he came home, it was the usual song and dance. No appetite, shower immediately with no singing, and straight to bed. God, he was pathetic. He'd been out of jail for two weeks and already he'd used. To Emma, it was past humorous.

Emma had made one decision when he came out of jail. She was leaving Savannah. She wasn't sure whether it was to get away from Jake or to get away from the people who had turned on her. She found a real estate broker and listed the house she loved. Emma had lost all of her friends because of Jake. Kathy had written her a scathing e-mail, saying she never wanted to talk to her again and it was all because of Jake. She was afraid for her children because of Jake's connection to drug dealers and there might be a drive-by shooting, among many other cruel remarks. Emma answered the e-mail by telling Kathy she was clearly watching too much CSI on television. She tried to impress upon Kathy that Jake was small-time and no one cared enough about him to kill him but it didn't matter.

Jenny was barely talking to Emma. She was so frustrated with the situation, she didn't know what to say to Emma, so she said nothing. Jenny's claim was she loved Emma too much to watch her ruin her life with Jake. Ultimately, she would lose Jenny's friendship completely due to the mounting lack of respect Jenny felt for Emma.

Emma's neighbors, who had respected and liked Emma, became condescending. Ray and Samantha were getting divorced, and Ray was sliding deeper into alcoholism. He had long since lost his job at Jaycee's Café and would drop by every so often to cry on Emma's shoulder, and bum cigarettes and beer from her. Everything Emma had built in Savannah was crumbling. She wanted out.

Emma knew it was cowardly, that it was a form of running away, but she didn't care. She needed a fresh start herself. Whether Jake got his act together and ultimately joined her or not, she wanted a new life with people who didn't know about Jake. The only friend who had stuck by her was Steve. He gave her unconditional love. It was really too bad he was gay. But he was steady, stable, calm, and remained by her side.

Emma's most important criteria for a new house was downsizing. She was tired of having the fancy house that was too big for her. She was tired of having the house no one wanted to leave. She was tired of being a big shot. This time she wanted to blend in. Nothing ostentatious. And she wanted a house that was cheaper. She began doing her own computer research on her desktop computer until she received the new laptop she ordered. She looked for bedroom communities close to major cities but not in major cities. Emma realized she enjoyed a small-town atmosphere but she needed to be closer to a bigger city. There were stores that Emma missed. She thought of her trips to Chicago and the stores she had to take advantage of because they weren't in Savannah. She didn't want to be in the cold north and didn't want to be in the heat of Florida. Emma had been to Charlotte, North Carolina, and liked the conveniences there, although the city itself held no charm. So she began searching the areas surrounding Charlotte. She found some lovely bedroom communities that were fifteen minutes from Charlotte. And when she checked the prices in those towns, they were ridiculously cheap. She could buy a three-bedroom, two-bath house for one hundred and fifty thousand dollars. That would recoup some of her losses due to Jake and would get her far enough away to accomplish her goal.

Emma made the mistake of telling Jake her plans. Once he knew where she planned to move, he got excited.

"That's perfect, honey. I could live in the house until this one sells and I could fix it up for you. Get a job and then work on the house. I would be out of Savannah with no drug triggers, and I would save you a bundle of money. I could paint and refinish the floors. Lots of things," he told her with enthusiasm.

"We'll see," was all she could muster at that point. "I have to examine the area first and see if I even want to live there."

"That's great. We always do well on trips together. Why don't we plan a trip next week to look at some of the houses?"

"I'll call the agent I've been working with and see if he's available," Emma agreed. She had to admit—Jake was right. They did have a good time when they were out of town. He stayed clean and he was fun. Savannah was the ultimate trigger for Jake's drug use. Having lived in Savannah all his life, there wasn't a corner of the city that didn't remind him of using drugs. If there was any hope for Jake, it would be away from his home territory.

They left for North Carolina Tuesday morning and arrived that afternoon. They were shown the entire area of bedroom communities north of Charlotte by the realtor, and they looked at several houses.

As was typical, Emma fell in love with the landscaping of one house, but the house itself was a dump. Or the house was perfect and had no yard. They walked into one house, and Jake went directly into his manic mode. He was nearly jumping up and down with enthusiasm. Emma felt like slitting his throat. She pulled him aside and scolded him like a mother scolding a five-year-old.

"Jake, calm down! You can't show so much excitement when you're house hunting. It costs money when you do. The agent knows how badly you want it, and they don't negotiate the best price. Besides, I need quiet and calm to look at houses. I have to analyze carefully if my furniture will fit, if there's enough wall space for my artwork, and determine the real condition of the house. You're so excited about this one, for example. But did you notice it doesn't have a separate dining room? Where is my sideboard going to go? Did you notice the master bedroom doesn't have its own bathroom? So, please, Jake. Just calm down."

Jake actually pouted as he walked outside to have a cigarette. Then he heard the two large dogs next door barking incessantly. They were tied to a doghouse, and it was clear they were going to bark like that constantly. He came inside the house and told Emma, "no way!"

"I thought you loved this house, honey," Emma said sweetly.

"Did you hear those dogs? I couldn't live right next door to all that racket. We couldn't even sit outside on the patio," he complained. Emma sighed deeply and told the agent she agreed with him. The house was lovely but too much noise.

By the end of the following day, they had gotten the lay of the land. The three towns they examined were ghost towns. The houses were old, like Emma wanted, but most needed too much repair. There was clearly no financial or social activity, which explained the low prices of the houses. They were referred to an Italian restaurant for dinner that was in a historic downtown area. They went back to their motel, changed clothes, and decided to try it. The realtor was right. The restaurant was fantastic. The food was delicious, the service was excellent, and it was lovely. Emma and Jake talked about the town.

"It's strange, isn't it? Look outside. Three Mercedes, four Lexuses, and two BMWs. Yet it looks like such a dead town. Where is all this money coming from?"

"Yeah, I noticed that, too," Jake agreed. "And these are brand new models," Jake added, referring to the Mercedes. "I saw up on the north side of town, there were some big estates. That must be where they came from."

"Hmm. There must be some big business here somewhere. Or else this is old money," Emma figured.

"I think there used to be a major restaurant wholesaler here. You know, like equipment and stuff. They were national and based here. Then they sold out, but I would guess the owners and upper management made a killing. They had their families here and their big mansions, so they just stayed. That would be my take," Jake explained.

"Then wouldn't there be more activity? More stores for them? I don't know, maybe they drive down to Charlotte."

"Maybe. But it is really nice here, isn't it? It's quiet and small town. I could really live here," Jake smiled.

"Yeah, it is. And the prices are great. It's definitely a possibility," Emma feigned. They finished their dinner—or more accurately, Jake waited for Emma to finish her dinner since he had inhaled his in five minutes. They took a walk around the downtown area, and Emma saw a store that struck her as interesting. They went inside, and to Emma's dismay, she saw a huge case of pipes—not for smoking tobacco. But there were some cute hats and various other accessories. It wasn't until they walked back up to the counter that Jake saw what he wanted.

"Oh my God, Em. You have to buy me a couple of these pills," he laughed. Emma stepped next to him and saw they were pills guaranteed to enlarge the penis.

"You've got to be kidding me," she said and looked up at him.

"No, for real. These things work. Let's try them, Em. And they definitely help with stamina," he winked at her. Since they were only three dollars each, she figured, what the hell. She bought three of them. Jake intensely read the instructions, which was unusual for Jake. Normally, he would read the directions long after he had already used a product. But this was obviously important to him. "It says to take it one to two hours before, so I better take one now." He grabbed the water bottle in the car and took the blue and red pill.

They went back to the motel and found the pill most definitely worked. In fact, they made love three times because he was hard all night. And half of the next day. While they were driving home, she leaned over and gently touched him. Boom! Hard as a rock!

"Cut that out," he cried. "Geez. I can't even get a thought in my head without him getting hard."

"Oh, yeah?" she teased and rubbed very lightly.

"Okay, you're going to have to pull over. Ever fucked in a Lexus?" His green eyes glistened with pure lust.

"All right, all right. I'll stop. We're not doing it in my car. Besides, Tasha has the back. Wait 'til we get home," she laughed. They got home Wednesday afternoon. They had barely gotten the dog and overnight cases in when he yanked her into the bedroom and ripped off her clothes. The pill clearly affected his stamina. By the time he made dinner and they ate, the pill had finally worn off. They went to sleep still laughing about it.

Chapter Twenty

Emma and Jake returned home to Savannah, and Jake awoke at six thirty the next morning. He leaned over and whispered to Emma that he was going to a morning AA meeting. He kissed her good-bye and said, "Oh, your mouth is so warm." She managed a slight smile and started to turn over to go back to sleep. Then remembered she had to get up to turn off the alarm. Jake had been nice enough not to turn on any lights while he dressed, so she stumbled over to the burglar alarm to deactivate it. She crawled back into bed and snuggled with Tasha as she fell back to sleep.

She was awakened an hour later by a loud banging. She couldn't imagine what it was but grabbed a robe and quickly went to the side door where the noise seemed to be coming from. She was right. There was someone at the door. Her side door was one of those beautiful wooden doors with an oval of etched glass in the middle. There was a fist attacking the glass. She thought to grab the phone and peer through the glass to see who was there before opening it. She looked into the face of Aaron. He was banging on the glass so hard, she was sure it would break. But it was the words that accompanied the fist that really scared her.

Aaron was screaming and cursing Emma. Emma never opened the door, though she almost did. But she could tell the face of a madman when she saw it. The cursing was as violent as she had ever heard, and incredulously, it was directed at her.

"Aaron, I'm calling the police," she said as calmly as she could manage.

"Fine, you bitch. Call them," he bellowed.

"What do you want from me? Jake's not even here, so if you're pissed off at him, you're wasting your breath. Did you even notice his truck isn't here?" she asked.

"You cunt! You have no idea what he did. He stole all my lawn equipment last night. So you go ahead call the police," he ranted.

"You're on probation, Aaron, so if I call the police, they'll put you away. And Jake was here last night, and he doesn't have a key to the house. You're crazy, Aaron. Go away," Emma demanded. He finally left, and shakily, Emma called Jake first. She was crying from the combination of fear and anger.

"Jake, your dear sweet brother-in-law was just here. He was screaming and cursing me. He almost broke the glass in the door. What did you do?" she asked between sobs.

"Nothing, baby. I didn't do anything. I'll be right home," he told her.

"I'm calling the police. That nutcase belongs in jail. He's crazy," she said emphatically.

"I know, baby. I know. But please, for me, don't call the police. Think about the kids," he begged.

"I don't give a shit about Cheryl or her kids. Right now, I care about me. This guy is dangerous," she cried.

"Look, I'll be home in five minutes. I was at the AA meeting on Eisenhower, so I'm almost home."

She was so scared, it didn't occur to her that if he had been in an AA meeting, his phone would have been turned off. Nothing occurred to her, to be perfectly frank. She just wanted to file charges against Aaron. But when Jake arrived, it got worse instead of better.

"This is a sign, Emma. I have to leave now. Aaron knows about the arrest, and he's going to send the cops or my probation officer here. You can call the police when I'm gone." With that said, he hugged her tightly to keep her from being so afraid and then began a mad race around the house to get his belongings. "Do you have a spare suitcase?"

"Uh, yeah. In the laundry room on the top shelf," Emma said as she watched Jake scrambling for safety. "Where are you going?"

"I don't know, and you shouldn't know. I'll call you when I land. But Emma, I'll need some money to get out of Savannah. Can you help me? I've got to run. I won't go back to jail. I got the IDs that I'll need, so I should be okay. You don't know where I went, so you can't get in trouble. But I'll need enough for a couple of week's rent and enough food and gas until I get a job. Please, Emma. This is the last time you'll ever have to give me anything," he pleaded.

"All right. Let me get dressed so we can go to the bank. How much will you need?" she asked. Finally, this would be then end, she thought. No more money out the door and he would be gone.

"Six hundred and fifty should be enough. Yeah," she could see him adding numbers in his head, "that should be fine."

"Okay." She checked his bathroom to be sure everything was taken. She checked her bedroom and closet. Anything that wouldn't fit into the suitcase, he was taking garbage bags and hanging clothes in them. Shoes were being thrown into garbage bags as well. He began hauling everything to his truck, moving with the speed of lightning.

Emma threw on whatever was handy. Jeans, T-shirt, sneakers. While Jake was taking his belongings to his truck, Emma let out the dog and fed her. By the time they were both finished, it was nine o'clock. They kissed quickly and met at the bank. She went to the drive-through and cashed the check, and then drove to the other side of the parking lot where he waited for her.

"Here," she said. She saw tears in his eyes, but he couldn't say good-bye. He just kissed her and told her he loved her. Then he was gone.

Jake called Emma only an hour later. He sounded so proud of himself, she couldn't help but smile.

"I made it! All the way through Garden City without stopping for drugs!"

"I'm proud of you, honey. Really, I am. Just keep it up."

"That's my plan," Jake said enthusiastically. "I know I can do it. I needed to be on my own and out of Savannah, with no one to cover my ass for once. I feel really strong, honey."

"That's great, Jake. I have faith in you," she told him. She knew she was lying, but she wanted to believe it so badly, she almost did. "Call me when you land somewhere."

"I will. I've already made arrangements for a room. It's a crappy boarding house, but it's cheap and relatively clean."

"So that's what you were doing on the computer—before you pawned it," she regretted throwing it in his face before it came out of her mouth.

"Thanks for that," he said sarcastically. "Anyway," he shook it off, "yeah. That's what I was doing. One of the things, anyway."

"And getting new identification," she surmised.

"You don't want to know about that," he said somberly. Then changed the subject. "Emma, I miss you so much already. I hope we can see each other soon. I don't think I could stand it if I didn't think I was going to see your pretty face really soon."

"Right now, I'm more interested in your getting work and stability. Once you do and you manage to stay away from drugs, then we'll see," Emma answered evasively.

"Well, at least we can talk, right?"

"Of course," Emma answered but feared that answer. She could only remember his constant phone calls when she was in Chicago. God, she thought, that seemed like forever ago. When she had trusted him to stay in her house alone. She stopped reminiscing and came back to the present. "Call me when you're settled."

"I'll be there in a few hours. I won't be that far. I'll call you later. I love you."

"I'll talk to you later," was Emma's only reply.

Since she had been up since six thirty and it had been an emotionally distraught day, all Emma wanted was to take a nap. But she had to call the police first. She was not going to let Aaron get away with his temper tantrum. And frankly, she was scared to be alone with him living only a few blocks away. Emma called the police, and they were at her house within fifteen minutes. She gave them a complete report, including

Aaron's address and phone number.

"Ma'am, if you were so afraid, why did you wait four hours to call us?" the young officer asked Emma.

"Because I was asked not to call, at first. His wife is a good friend of mine, and I didn't want it to affect her or the children. But I finally decided that my own well-being was more important," Emma answered. Her explanation wasn't good enough for the police, though. They nearly laughed in her face. They wrote the report and quickly left, leading Emma to realize they would do absolutely nothing. She decided it was definitely time for that nap.

Emma curled up on the sofa and slept for two hours. She didn't think she would sleep that long, but she was obviously more exhausted than she realized. She went into the kitchen to make some fresh coffee when the phone rang. It was Cheryl.

"Emma, I'm so sorry about this morning. Aaron was way out of line," she told Emma.

"I don't want your apology, Cheryl. I want his. And I want it today. He had no right to scream and curse at me the way he did. If he was angry with Jake, he should have called Jake. He nearly put his fist through the glass in my door. He was crazy," Emma said angrily.

"I know, Emma. But he won't apologize to you. It's just not in his nature."

"Oh, I'm sure of that. I've already called the police. If he ever steps foot on my property again, I won't wait. I'll have him arrested on the spot. Do you understand?"

"Yes," Cheryl said quickly. "Um, I called for another reason. Mama's in the hospital. I haven't told Jake because I know he's vulnerable right now. But she's not doing well,

Emma. My aunt and uncle have come down from South Carolina to see her. She's got a very bad infection. That's what was making her stomach so distended," Cheryl explained.

"I'll go see her later today," Emma promised. "I don't know what I'm going to tell her about Jake. He's gone, you know. He packed all his stuff and ran. I don't think he's coming back for court next month."

"Oh, shit. This is not good. He'll be running the rest of his life. Even I didn't think he was that stupid," Cheryl said. "I don't know what to tell Mama either. But I do want to talk to the idiot. Does he still have his cell phone?"

"Of course. It's the only way he can keep in contact without letting us know exactly where he is," Emma explained.

"Okay. I still can't believe it. I should. I mean, I've known him his whole life. You'd think I'd be able to second-guess every stupid stunt he's gonna pull. But this takes the cake. Oh, shit! Emma, he asked for my birth certificate, and I still haven't gotten it back. And he got a small package—you know, one of those padded envelopes? It came in yesterday's mail for him. He told me to leave it in the mailbox, and he'd pick it up. When I woke up this morning, it was gone."

"Fake identification is my bet," Emma told her. "I wonder what he stole to pay for it."

"I'm sure you'll find something missing," Cheryl replied.

"Yeah. I will. When are you going to the hospital?" she changed the subject.

"I'm going there now. I want to see Aunt Corrine anyway. I haven't seen her in years."

"Then I'll wait until later this afternoon to go, in case your husband decides to join you," Emma decided.

"He won't go with me, but I understand."

Emma hung up and decided not to contact Jake about any of the goings on. Not about the police, not about his mother. She figured Cheryl would find a way to tell Jake about his mother and even hearing the word "police" would make him nervous. For the time being she would enjoy the solitude and peace. She could take her jewelry out of the safe, she could go to the liquor store and buy some beer and wine, and she could live like a normal person.

She took a tour of her house in silence. Emma wanted to take stock of the condition of her house, now that Jake was gone for good. She started in the guest bathroom—his bathroom. There was a cigarette burn on the shelf and one on the toilet seat. Empty beer cans were in the trash and hidden behind the sink. With a deep sigh, she picked up the trash and planned to paint the shelf. She got a trash bag from the kitchen and dumped it all. Then she went through the medicine cabinet and threw away everything Jake had forgotten.

She continued on to the guest room. She knew about the cigarette burn in the lace, but she noticed there was a DVD in the recorder. She pressed "eject" to see what was in it. Two naked women graced the disc of porn. Terrific, she thought, and kept looking. She looked in the closet, where he had left a box. She brought it to the bed and looked inside. There were dozens of pornographic DVDs in it. She added the one she'd found in the DVD player and systematically broke each one in half. Then Emma looked under the bed. Several more porn DVDs were under the bed. She broke those in half as well and threw the whole lot into the trash bag.

She hadn't yet found what he had pawned to order his fake

identification. It had to be her jewelry. She checked her drawers, knowing that whatever was left out couldn't be expensive. She noticed two pairs of earrings were missing and a sterling silver necklace. He couldn't have gotten much for them. They had been purchased on QVC, so they were not valuable. What could he have taken? Then she figured it out. Her new camera. The one that replaced the one he had stolen earlier. And all the pictures she had taken of the houses she'd seen in North Carolina were still on it. She was annoyed, but it wasn't a terrible expense or anything that couldn't be replaced.

Emma had enough reality for the moment. She took a shower, washed her hair, and got dressed. She would go out for lunch and sit like a human being to eat a meal. She took the book she was currently reading and left the house. Emma chose Clary's Café, a neighborhood coffee shop that boasted excellent food and better service. It was familiar and cozy—exactly what Emma needed. She enjoyed scrambled eggs with lox and onions and iced coffee. She read her book and ate leisurely for a change. Without Jake there to rush her through a meal, it was calming.

When she finished her meal, Emma went to the hospital to see Mimi. It was three o'clock in the afternoon, so she was sure she could spend some time visiting. When she got to Mimi's hospital room, she was told to put on a mask and paper gown to cover her clothing. She went into the room and saw Mimi. Emma had to admit, Mimi didn't look well, and she looked to be in pain.

Emma met Jake's Aunt Corrine and her husband, Tom. They were warm and friendly to her.

"Oh, it's so wonderful to finally meet you. We've heard so

much about you. Why, you're even more beautiful than we imagined," Corrine said.

"Thank you so much. It's nice to meet you, too." Then Emma turned to Mimi. "How are you feeling? Are they treating you well?" For the first time since she'd known her, Mimi didn't smile.

"Nausea," was all Mimi said.

"I'll see to it," Emma smiled and quickly walked to the nurse's station. Like a drill sergeant, Emma demanded immediate results to stop Mimi's nausea. Within five minutes, the nurse entered the room and added Phenergan to Mimi's IV.

"There," Emma held Mimi's hand. "That should help." Tears welled in Mimi's eyes.

"Thank you, Emma. I wish you could be my daughter," she said meekly. "I know my son doesn't deserve you. But I so hoped he would." At that moment, Emma's cell phone rang. It was Jake.

"Hi Jake. Guess where I am?" she said lightly.

"Hi, baby. I have good news. I'm in my new digs, and the man who owns the building, Rob? He gave me a job. Ten dollars an hour to help him maintain all his properties," he said with delight in his voice.

"Oh, that's wonderful. Would you like to tell your mother? I'm in her room with her. And your Aunt Corrine and Uncle Tom are here," she told him.

"Yeah, that would be great." Emma took her phone and held it to Mimi's ear. She saw the tears flow down her cheeks. She prayed they were tears of happiness. Then she heard Mimi tell Jake how proud she was of him. Thank God, they were tears of pride. When she took the phone back, she walked away from the bed and asked Jake what he had said.

"I told her I'm clean, I'm on my own, and am finally a man. I told her about the job and my own place. She said she was proud of me." Emma could hear the tears in his voice. He had told Emma countless times that when his mother died, he was sure she would pass her strength on to him. Emma really hoped that was true.

"She is, Jake. She's very proud of you for getting out on your own and staying clean. So am I. Do you want to say hello to Corrine?"

"No, not now. I can't. Call me when you leave, okay?"

"Sure. Bye, honey," she said with a smile. Then she turned back to Mimi. "Are you okay?"

Mimi was dabbing her eyes with a tissue. "Yeah. I'm okay."

Emma stayed for a little while and kept Mimi company, as well as talked with Corrine and Tom. They seemed to be good people. "Nice country folk" would be her description. After she left, she called Jake back. He asked about his mother, and she answered with as much information as she had.

"She has a very bad infection, and she's on massive doses of antibiotics. That's why her stomach was so distended—bloated—when you saw her. Her stomach is filled with an infection. I had to put on a mask to get into the room. But they're taking really good care of her. I'll keep you posted, okay. Don't worry. You just work hard and stay clean. Concentrate on yourself, Jake. That's what she wants," Emma told him.

"I know you're right. Mom only wants me to be clean and grow up. I'm doing both of those. That's all I can do," he answered. She knew it was hitting him hard, but he wasn't about to deal with those emotions.

Early the next morning Cheryl called. Emma didn't even have to ask. She could hear it in her voice.

"Mama's gone," she said through sobs.

"Oh, honey, I'm so sorry. Thank God I saw her last night. When?" Emma asked.

"About three o'clock this morning."

"The funeral?"

"I don't know yet. Not until next week probably. I've got to talk to all the aunts and uncles. They'll be coming from all over, so I'm not sure. I'll let you know."

"Can I help with anything? Make any calls for you?" Emma asked.

"Yeah, you know, you can. Call my uncle Dan and get him to call the rest of Mama's sisters and then give me their numbers. He stays in close contact with them all. Thanks, Emma." Cheryl gave Emma Dan's phone number and then added, "I'll call Jake and tell him."

"Are you sure?" Emma asked. She knew calling Jake would be the toughest phone call.

"Yeah. If you can take care of the rest of the family, I'll take care of Jake. I hope he can handle it," Cheryl said tearfully.

"Not well, I'd say. He'll hold it all in, but it's going to destroy him. You know, he believes that he's going to get all your mother's strength now that she's gone. He's told me that for months. I pray to God he's right. He's going to need that strength," Emma told her.

"Yeah, he is. Either this is going to send him over the edge and he'll do coke tonight, or he'll stay clean forever for Mama. You never know which way he'll swing," she answered.

"Hang in there. If there is anything I can do, let me know. Okay, sweetie?"

"Thanks, Emma. You're the best," and Cheryl hung up the phone.

Chapter Twenty-One

Emma waited for Jake to phone her since she wanted to be sure Cheryl talked to him first. When he called that afternoon, he sounded not crestfallen from his mother's death but terribly distant. He wouldn't broach the subject. Finally Emma couldn't keep avoiding the pink elephant in the room.

"Honey, I'm so sorry about your mom." With that simple statement, he broke down but pulled himself back quickly.

"I don't think it's really sunk in. I wish I could have been there. Seen her."

"Jake, you saw her more than anyone. She knew how much you loved her," Emma desperately tried to reach his heart.

"I know. But—" he couldn't finish the thought.

"But what, Jake?"

"I don't know. I guess I feel so guilty about everything I did to her. I don't know if I'll ever be able to forgive myself."

"Jake, remember the last words she said to you. She was proud of you. You're clean, you're working, and you're on your own. Her last thoughts were pride. Maybe that's what she was waiting for. She had been ill for so long. Don't you find it strange that within hours of you pulling your life together, she passed?"

"Maybe you're right, Emma. I hope so." Emma could hear his voice begin to crack. "I'll call you later." He hung up.

Emma knew this would be a hard blow to Jake. Her only concern was how he would deal with it. She was sure he wouldn't cope with his mother's death as she would. He wasn't capable of the depth of feeling or depth of thought. He did call back later, sounding exhausted.

"I've been thinking and thinking. I don't know if I should go to the funeral," Jake told her, but the way he said it, it seemed more of a question. "I think Savannah is dangerous for me. And my sobriety is the most important thing in my life now. If for nothing else, for Mom."

"And it's dangerous for you because of Aaron. He's out to get you. There's no doubt he would call the police. Maybe out of respect for your mother he wouldn't do it right then and there, but he would make trouble," Emma added.

"Yeah, I know you're right. It's just...it's just, so tough to not be there."

"Jake, everyone will understand. You have to do what's best for you. Your sobriety is your top priority, and your mother would be the first to agree. If she thought that by coming to Savannah there was any chance you might use, she wouldn't want you to come. Especially not for her funeral," Emma soothed.

"But will I be able to live with myself if I don't go?"

"That's up to you. It's all in your mind. Either way, I'll support you. If you come, I'll be by your side. If you don't, I'll go on your behalf and for you. Your family will understand. I'll make them understand."

"Okay. If I write something, will you read it for me?"

"You don't even have to ask. Of course I will. Can you get access to a computer?"

"Um, yeah. The one in Rob's office. They don't use it that much, so I can write it on there and e-mail it to you."

"When do you start work for him?" Emma asked.

"Tomorrow," Jake answered.

"Are you sure you're ready?"

"I've got to get busy. It's the only thing that will keep me sane."

"Okay, honey. The funeral is still up in the air. Cheryl doesn't know when or where it will be at the moment. I talked to your uncle Dan and got the phone numbers of the other aunts and uncles. He's helping figure out the logistics so Cheryl can make plans."

"Did you get Aunt Pammy's number?"

"Um, let me look at the list." She checked her notebook for the phone numbers. "Yes, it's right here." She gave him the phone numbers he asked for, including his uncle Dan's. "Maybe talking to family will help you deal with this," Emma urged.

"I don't think so. I think it'll make it worse. But talking to Uncle Dan would be good. He's a great guy," Jake said and Emma could hear the smile in his voice.

"Yeah, I thought so, too. He'll be staying with me while he's in town for the funeral. He seems really nice," Emma agreed.

"Just don't fuck him," Jake teased. "He's a really cool dude. You'll like him."

"Oh, for God's sake, Jake! I wouldn't do that," she chided.

"Yeah, well. He's always been the ladies' man."

"Shut up, Jake," she chided. "I'm not going to sleep with your uncle—or anyone."

"I know. I'll talk to you tomorrow," and Jake hung up the phone.

Emma was getting annoyed his abrupt ending of conversations. But it was the least of her worries. As much as she warned Jake about not coming to Savannah to avoid seeing Aaron, Emma didn't much want to see Aaron either. But she had to go to the funeral. For Jake, for Cheryl, and for herself. She had so much love and respect for Mimi and she already missed her; that always cheerful disposition, despite her pain. It was uplifting. And she could always talk to her frankly about Jake. Now Emma had no one to fill that void. Joe was gone. Mimi was gone. Cheryl was the only one who had known Jake all his life and knew all his deep, dark secrets. But her trust level with Cheryl was not high. Emma was still unclear as to Cheryl's real role in Jake's addiction or his problems.

With Cheryl grieving, trying to get the money together for a funeral, and taking care of her two children, the burden of relaying information to all of Jake's family fell on Emma. She spoke with all four of Mimi's sisters and her two brothers, including their spouses. Cheryl hadn't spoken to any of them. After all Emma had been through with Jake, she couldn't help but wonder how she became responsible for his entire family. Emma was almost waiting for Cheryl to ask her for money for her own mother's funeral. Cheryl didn't of course, but it wouldn't have surprised Emma if she had. It wasn't above her wiles to do it.

By the day before the funeral, Emma had received a lovely letter from Jake for her to read on his behalf. She also wrote a poem dedicated to Mimi. She had e-mailed it to Jake for his approval, and when he called her about it, his only response was, "it's fine."

When the day finally arrived for Mimi's funeral, it was arranged to be on Saturday at Aaron's mother's house. Strange, Emma thought. Why would Shirley, who hailed from one of the oldest Jewish families in Savannah, plan a funeral at her house on a Saturday? Jews don't have funerals on the Sabbath. And she further planned Jewish Sabbath food for a bunch of gentiles from South Carolina? It all seemed odd. But she met all of Jake's family, and his uncle, who was a minister, delivered the sermon. Other than immediate family, there were ex-employees of Mimi's who attended. People in the community who respected and loved Mimi Stanton. Then Emma got up to read Jake's letter and she read her own poem.

Tears filled the eyes of nearly everyone at the funeral. Most wanted a copy of the poem, it moved them so much. They gave her their address or e-mail so she could send it to them. That gave Emma the courage to face Aaron's cold stares and total avoidance. He never so much as said hello to her. Cheryl turned to her with tears flowing down her cheeks and enwrapped her in a hug. She whispered in Emma's ear, "That was beautiful. Thank you."

Emma stepped outside with Dan to smoke a cigarette and get some fresh air, though Savannah in July did not offer much relief. The temperature was well into the nineties, and the humidity hung heavily. But they both needed the distance from death, if only for a moment. Emma learned quickly that Mimi had been the favorite sister among all the family.

After everyone picked at the luchen kugel (Jewish noodle pudding) among other Jewish delicacies Shirley had prepared for her gentile guests, Emma and Dan left. He followed her to her house, which was only a dozen blocks away. She showed him to his room and his bathroom and gave him the grand tour. They talked mostly about Jake, and she found she could open up to him in the same way she could to Joe. Dan was an attractive man with a thick moustache and an easy smile. They drank wine and grilled steaks on the barbecue. Emma made salad and baked potatoes. The crux of their conversation over dinner was how moronic Jake would be if he really skipped bail and ran. Jake's Uncle Dan was the first to agree that it would be a stupid move. The closer it got to August, the more nervous Emma got. She still hoped that Jake would show up for his court date and turn himself him. But for that one evening, she and Jake's uncle played pool and had a good time. In the morning they had coffee together, and Dan left to return to South Carolina. He gave Emma a hug and thanked her for her hospitality. They promised to stay in touch. And they did.

When Jake called Emma during a break from work the following day, his first question was expected.

"Did you fuck him?" Jake asked about his uncle.

"Jesus, Jake. Of course not," she responded with obvious exasperation.

"Well, he's a good-looking man. I wouldn't blame you," he added.

"Will you stop it?   I wouldn't do that to you. Especially not with your uncle!"

Emma was more frustrated with Jake's lack of interest about the funeral. His escapism was showing in every aspect of his life. She was becoming more and more aware of why he was a drug addict. He was self-indulgent and he had never learned to deal with life. Emma saw this as a dangerous combination with being bipolar. Take a person who was already suffering from a physiological problem that prohibited emotional stability and throw into the mix having been raised as a spoiled little prince as Jake had been, and there would be an explosive result. She decided to broach the subject herself. She wouldn't allow him to pretend it never happened.

"Jake, the funeral was lovely, and your family is really nice. Your mother was obviously really loved." She could hear the beginning of crying but heard him choke it back.

"Yeah, she was," he said simply. He refused to open up. Emma didn't know if it was her in particular or he had to bottle his feelings inside.

"You know, I miss her too. She was a remarkable woman," Emma tried.

"Look, I have to work. The job is going fucking great. Rob is an amazing man. You know he owns half the fucking town? And when he came here from Canada forty years ago, he had nothing. He really wants to retire, and since he only has daughters, he's grooming me to take over. It could be a fucking awesome opportunity," Jake evaded everything emotional.

"That's terrific, Jake. You'll do well." Emma noticed the change in his demeanor. He sounded more hard and tough. More like a redneck. She assumed he'd started chewing tobacco again, which Emma detested. She didn't say anything about it but took mental note.

"I gotta go," he said abruptly. "I gotta take a shit."

"Thanks for the info, pal," she said with disgust.

"Yeah, yeah. Bye," and he hung up.

Emma didn't know this Rob person, but she could bet that he

was a real good ole boy redneck. Chameleon that he was, Jake was now taking on the persona of his boss. Jake had only worked for Rob for two days, and already Emma knew she didn't like or trust Rob. How could Jake not see it? Of course, she could be wrong. She was—she didn't know how many miles away he was—but she wasn't there; wherever "there" was. But she certainly had some good ideas. She knew damn well it was somewhere in the South. This Rob person was definitely a Southern boy, even if he had been born in Canada. And she knew Jake. He wouldn't go far. He was too insecure.

Jake called back an hour later, full of apologies. Sorry for the way he talked to her, sorry for his hasty end to the conversation. This time, he called full of self-confidence.

"Emma, you'd be so proud of me. I haven't had so much as a beer. I'm working really hard. Rob has me fixing stuff in tenant apartments. I'm learning how to do all kinds of stuff. We even dry-walled this morning. And I fixed a broken garbage disposal. He's showing me all the ropes," Jake said enthusiastically.

"You're right. I am proud of you. So you're staying away from drugs and alcohol?" she asked.

"Are you kidding? Not even a beer and by the time I'm finished, I'm exhausted. A good tired from working hard. I'm really feeling like a man. I'm responsible for myself. I'm working to support myself. Mom would be so proud," he said and then Emma could tell he regretted mentioning it.

"I know she would," she replied simply. Emma could sense he was going to hang up on her in a second.

"Look, honey, I'm having a hard time dealing with this. Give me a little time, okay? It's so—I can't believe she's gone," he said meekly.

"Yeah, it is. But remember, you got all of her strength when she passed. You said you would, and I think you did," she encouraged.

"I feel that way, Emma. I don't even have a craving for drugs. Not even for a beer. I only want to stay clean. It's the most important thing in my life. I don't even think about drugs. And I want to feel this way always. Clear and calm and in control. It's great," he told her.

"Honey, that's so great. And hopefully you can stay that way. I know you can accomplish anything you want if you say clean," Emma said.

"I know I can. If for nothing else, for Mom. In her memory. She deserves that from me," he said with utter conviction. "I can't let her down."

"Hey, that's as good a reason as any," Emma replied. Sure, she was disappointed that he was not staying clean for her—that she was not important enough to motivate him. But she'd take what she could get. If he stayed clean, did it really matter why or for whom? No, she decided. Much as she would have preferred that she was the motivation—that his love for her was enough to make him change his ways, it was enough that he did it. "I'll talk to you later," she told him. This time she was trying to get away. There had been so many calls, she hadn't been able to do anything for herself.

"Okay, baby. I love you," Jake said.

"I'll talk to you tomorrow," Emma tried to drop the hint for him to not call again that day. She was also sure that he noticed how many times he told her he loved and she did not reciprocate with the same words. He hadn't mentioned it, but he had to notice. Didn't he? She hung up the phone.

Emma managed to run a few errands. She went to the grocery and thankfully didn't have to buy junk food. She bought fresh fruit and vegetables. Chicken breast and fish. Then she saw it at the fish counter. Fresh sushi-grade tuna. With Jake gone, she could enjoy her favorite meal without making him squirm. Tuna sashimi, Japanese rice, and Japanese pickles. When she returned home, she happily took out her Japanese rice cooker and started the rice. She filled her teapot to make green tea and then began slicing the tuna into neat slices. She placed the tuna, pickles, and wasabi neatly on her Japanese plate as the rice cooker clicked off, so she filled the rice bowl. She placed it all on a tray and went into the great room to enjoy her meal in peace. She turned on Cash Cab and savored the delicacy in front of her.

There was one more phone call that night for Jake to say good night. Oddly, it was at eight o'clock. He was too exhausted to talk long and was going to sleep. Emma knew that wasn't true. He would sit up and watch television for another two hours at the very least, but he wanted to crawl into a hole. That she did understand. His state of mind was work, eat, and sleep. He purposely left room for nothing else that might jangle his nerves. He didn't want deep conversation about his emotions. He didn't want to see the real world. He wanted to hide from it.

Emma figured that as long as he wasn't using drugs or drinking, it didn't matter how or why. If hiding in his room and watching television would keep him out of trouble, that was fine. It wouldn't be her way, but then, she wasn't an addict. She couldn't get into the mind of an addict. She was just pleased that he was growing up. If he remained on the same track, he might have a life ahead of him. It might even turn into life for them together.

Chapter Twenty-Two

With the heat of July came constant phone calls to Emma from Jake. Every time Emma would get comfortable in her office to write, the phone would ring. Every time Emma would decide to relax and watch a movie, the phone would ring. No matter what Emma tried to do, the phone would interrupt her. Most of the calls were obviously Jake's loneliness. It was heading way past annoying. She tried to persuade Jake to make some friends, more specifically to join Alcoholics Anonymous or Narcotics Anonymous wherever he was. Then he would achieve all of his needs. He would have someplace to go after work instead of vegetating in front of his television, he would make friends and have someone—anyone—else to talk with other than Emma, and it would keep him clean. He refused. He used every excuse to avoid attending the meetings. He was too tired after the physical labor of the day, he didn't like people, and he didn't need NA because he had absolutely no cravings. He claimed he was happier than ever before because he was clean and didn't even think about using drugs. Emma finally let it alone. But since he wouldn't make any new friends, he continued calling Emma so often she couldn't even go to the bathroom without the phone ringing. Finally she asked him to slow down to no more than three times a day. He sounded disappointed but he agreed.

With Jake staying clean and sober, Emma kept hoping he would come to his senses and make his court date late in

August. Although she broached the subject every so often, he always replied the same way. He would never go back to jail. He could make it in the real world with a new persona and identification. He could stay clean as long as he didn't return to Savannah. Emma knew in her heart that he was living in a fantasy. But as long as he stayed clean, she tried to sound supportive.

Late one night, Emma was sitting in bed actually reading a book. This was a pleasure she had not been able to enjoy until Jake had moved out, since he always had the television on in the bedroom before they went to sleep. Finally she could enjoy silence before sleep and, within that silence, a good book. She was involved with the novel, so when she heard a strange noise, it startled her. She checked the alarm system to be sure it was armed and breathed a sigh of relief when she saw the red light on. But she still heard what sounded like footsteps. Before she got out of bed to check the spooky noise, she reached into her nightstand drawer for her new pistol—just in case. It was gone. The eerie sound stopped, but she could almost hear the anger roiling within her. The son of a bitch had stolen her gun! The first had been stolen—according to Jake's story—during the robbery. Now the new one was missing. She picked up the phone by her bedside and actually tried to be calm. It didn't work. She was far too angry to be calm. He answered the phone sleepily.

"Jake, you asshole! You pawned my gun!" she said furiously when he answered. She didn't notice what time it was, nor did she care.

"Emma, calm down. What's going on?" He had clearly been awakened by the phone, and she honestly didn't care.

"I can't believe you would take my only protection! What is wrong with you? Not to mention how fucking stupid it was to take a gun! You're on probation, you're running from the police, and you steal—a gun? You really are an idiot!"

"I did that, like, two months ago," he answered, as though that made it okay.

"What difference does that make? You took my gun—something you're not even supposed to be in the same house with, let alone in your truck—and pawned it. And you left me alone in the house with no protection, with every drug dealer in Savannah knowing where I live. You claim to love me and you would do this to me?" she exploded.

"I'm sorry, baby. Really I am. It was stupid. I wasn't thinking," he tried to pacify her.

"I'm sorry too, Jake. You know I have to call the police and report it missing. If someone uses that gun and kills someone, it's registered to me. That's one more charge against you. You're a fucking moron, Jake. And a heartless one. Oh, and for the record, Mark—next door—saw you making a drug deal in the garage at one o'clock in the morning. He said there was, and I quote, 'a pimpmobile' parked on his property. He saw a big black guy walk into the garage for about five minutes and leave. The people across the street saw the same thing the next night. You're lucky they didn't call the police, which I told them they should have. Of everything you've done to me, Jake, those are two things I cannot and will not ever forgive. Stealing my gun and making drug deals at my house. How could you put me in harm's way like that? And my neighbors! You really are a piece of shit!"

"You're right. I was but I'm not any more. I'm clean and I care about people other than myself. And so you know, I called every drug dealer I knew to tell them I was gone and I was not coming back. So you won't have any problems from them. I'm truly sorry, Emma. I know now how horrible I was, and I'm trying like hell to make amends. I know you don't trust me or believe me, but I swear to you, I'm a changed man. That kind of shit will never happen again."

"Right!" she mocked him.

"I know you don't believe me and it's going to take a long time to earn your trust, but I'm not going to stop trying. I swear, Emma. I'm really sorry, and I understand completely that you have to make a police report. I hold no ill will about it."

"You don't hold any ill will? That's a joke! I'll never forgive you for this shit," she said incredulously.

"That's not what I meant. I mean, I understand. I love you, Emma. I still believe we have a long life together, and I'm going to do everything in my power to make that happen."

"Whatever," she said. "I'll talk to you tomorrow."

The next morning, she called the police and filed the report about the missing gun. The officer who came to her house asked her when it happened. She couldn't give him a definitive answer because she honestly didn't know. But Jake had left the original box the gun came in—probably because he didn't know where it was—so she had all the identification numbers. The officer asked who did it, and she gave him Jake's name. She explained that they had broken up in June and he was gone. It was simple and quick, with not a lot of questions.

Jake's boss, Rob, had initially been his savior. Jake was thrilled with the potential future with Rob and hoped to be managing all of his properties eventually. But after only two weeks, Jake's tone began to change. He was angrier and more frustrated.

"He treats me like a moron," Jake complained. "If I don't do something fast enough, he calls me a fucking idiot. And he's such a prick. Emma, you won't believe what he did. We were fixing the clogged bathtub of this really nice black couple. Rob went into their bathroom and took one of their toothbrushes off the sink and used it to clean out the bathtub drain full of disgusting hair and shit! Then he put the toothbrush back in the cup without telling them! How disgusting is that?"

"Eeow!" was all Emma could say. "Jake, you've got to tell them! You're as anal- retentive as I am, and that is just plain old gross! You have to tell them."

"I couldn't. He was standing right there. But he's such a prick. He does that kind of shit all the time. He has no respect for anyone. He talks to his granddaughters and his wife like shit. And he busts my balls all the time. He says the only thing I'm good for is dummy work. Tomorrow I'm going to start cutting down a tree. Not that I mind the physical labor outside but it's really hurting to have him talk to me the way he does."

"Jake, you shouldn't take it from him. He's not God. He's only your boss. You need to stand up for yourself. If you let him continue, he'll never stop. It's a bad precedent," Emma advised him. Emma wasn't at all surprised by his boss's attitude. Jake could be pretty damned stupid. But even if everything Rob accused him of was true (and it probably was), that didn't give Rob the right to talk to Jake in such a demeaning manner. She couldn't help but have a bit of empathy for Rob. Jake could be frustrating. Emma also knew that Jake's ego couldn't take the continual slamming it was taking. In order for him to feel like a man, he would have to at least try to exert some confidence and stop Rob from his verbal abuse.

"I'm afraid I'll lose the job if I do. But I'll try," Jake acquiesced.

"Good luck," Emma said. Then, on a whim, she added, "Maybe we could get together over the weekend. Meet somewhere."

"Really? I miss you so much, and I need you, Emma. That would be great. I'll look forward to it all week!"

"Okay, you figure out where and I'll be there," she told him.

"Columbia, South Carolina, is a good halfway point," he said vaguely. It's only a couple hours from each of us. Why don't you check on your computer and let me know where to meet."

"Okay. I'll go onto MapQuest and check it out. Which expressway will you be coming from so I can see what's convenient for both of us?"

"I'll be coming from I-77. You'll be coming I-95 to I-26 to Columbia. Just tell me where, and I'll be there!" Jake said with so much enthusiasm, Emma felt guilty. She didn't know why she had decided to see him. Probably because he needed a jolt of self-confidence and she couldn't afford to have him lose this job.

"I'll let you know, okay? I think you could use a little boost," Emma confided.

"You're right, baby. I need you," he agreed.

They met in a small town outside of Columbia, South Carolina. Emma found a motel that took dogs, had smoking rooms, and this one boasted a big jetted tub. That could be fun, Emma thought. Since it was only an extra ten dollars a night, she decided to go for it. Jake arrived first on Friday evening. Emma saw his truck, and he was standing outside their room smoking a cigarette. He had already checked in, so he ran down the steps to help Emma with Tasha and her with her luggage. He pulled Emma into a kiss and held her tightly.

"God, you look terrific, Emma. I've missed you," he said as he grabbed her bags. "You, too, Tasha," as he ruffled the dog's fur. They walked together to the room and it was lovely. They were in the middle of nowhere, but here was this motel with a big Jacuzzi at the side of the bedroom with romantic lighting, and it had a separate living room. There were two televisions, one in the sitting room and one in the bedroom.

"I assume you're starving," Emma turned to Jake.

"Yeah, I could definitely eat. Anything other than Ramen noodles would be great."

"Okay. Let's take care of Tasha and then we'll find someplace. I'm sure they've got a pizza place, which would be your first choice," she laughed.

"You know me too well," he replied. "I'll go walk Tasha. You get your stuff organized, which I know you want to do."

"You know me too well," Emma answered. "Okay. I'll get Tasha's dinner ready and get myself organized. Then we'll call the front desk and ask where there's a place to eat." She took out her cosmetics and touched up her face. She brushed her teeth and then took out her moisturizer and other toiletries to set them in order on the counter. She hung up her clothes and put her underwear in the drawer. She hid her jewelry where Jake couldn't find it. Then she called the front desk. There was a Pizza Hut around the corner. Perfect for Jake, she thought. As Jake came back into the room with the dog, she told him the good news about Pizza Hut.

"Awesome, baby. Then we can come back and make love," he said dreamily.

"Maybe we can take a dip in the Jacuzzi together," she said hopefully.

"Sure," he replied. "That sounds like fun."

They went to dinner where, of course, Jake stuffed himself. When they returned to the room, he was bloated and full. He turned on the television in the bedroom and fell onto the bed.

"Just give me a little time for the food to go down," he told Emma grumpily. She noticed he was scratching his neck, so Emma looked.

"My God, Jake. What is that?" she asked when she saw a lumpy rash on his neck.

"Poison oak, from cutting down that tree. The tree was covered with it. I didn't think it touched me, but I'm starting to itch."

"Well for God's sake, Jake. Don't scratch it. It'll spread. Do you have any calamine lotion?"

"No. I'll be fine. It's no biggie," he told her.

"Okay. Well, if we're not going to have sex, then I'm taking a bath in that fabulous Jacuzzi," she told him.

"By the time you get out, I'll be ready," he claimed. But she didn't trust him. His mood had changed, and Emma didn't like it. He was turning irritable. Emma started the bath water, which took forever to fill, since the tub was so big. As she undressed to get in, Jake began stripping off his own clothes. "I think I'll join you," he said. He put one foot in and pulled it out quickly. "Damn, Emma. It's hot."

"It's supposed to be. It gets better once you get in," she told him while she turned on the jets and laid her head back on the edge. "Oh, it's wonderful! So relaxing."

Jake got in quickly and mirrored Emma's position. He didn't touch her but tried to relax. He agreed with her but got out quickly. "I can't take the heat, baby. You finish up."

He got out, and after toweling off, he lay on the bed watching television. The History Channel, of course.

Emma shaved her legs and sipped from a glass of ice water, while Jake ignored her. When she looked at him, he was scratching his entire body. This was not good. She got out, toweled off, and went over to him. The hot water had worsened his poison oak. His whole body was covered with welts.

"Oh, Jake. You're allergic to poison oak."

"I always have been. When I was a kid, this happened at least once every summer," he told her.

"The why did you get near it if you knew?" she asked. He couldn't be this stupid, she thought. Anyone with half a brain would keep his distance from anything he was allergic to. Not Jake. She learned that not only did he know about the allergy, but when he was cutting down the tree for his boss, he was surrounded by it—and wore a sleeveless shirt while he worked. It took every bit of strength for Emma to summon an ounce of pity for him. "Jake, start by taking two Benadryl," she handed the pills to him. "That should help with the allergy." Emma always carried Benadryl with her because she used it at night to sleep or in an emergency if she needed it. "I'll go to the store and get some calamine lotion. Just stop scratching," she told him.

"I can't. It itches like a motherfucker," he replied testily.

"I know but you're opening the wounds and spreading it all over. You should slap at the itches, but don't scratch." Emma took a deep, cleansing breath and threw on some clothes to go buy the calamine lotion. She bought two bottles and some cotton balls. She returned to the room to find Jake lying on the bed right where she left him. "Here," she handed him the calamine. "This should help." He grabbed the bottles and walked to the bathroom mirror. He began slopping on the pink goo everywhere he could reach. The entire bathroom was becoming pink. As he put it on his body, she washed it off the counter top. He was becoming so irritated, more emotionally than physically—or maybe it was a draw—she couldn't stand being near him.

They never did have sex. Jake curled up on his side of the bed with the television on, trying to sleep. With all of his scratching and cursing, it was difficult for Emma to sleep. Finally, she drifted off but was awakened by him at two in the morning. She opened her eyes, and without her contact lenses in, she saw a blur of Jake sitting on the sofa with his arms crossed in front of him.

"What are you doing?" she asked groggily.

"What the fuck do you think I'm doing?" he yelled at her.

She turned over and tried to go back to sleep. It was difficult because she was so angry. He was being a spoiled brat and impossible to deal with. She wanted to shoot him to put him out of her misery. By seven o'clock, he was cursing so much and reapplying calamine. She got up, turned on her coffee, and threw on clothes to take Tasha for a walk. She came in—totally ignoring Jake—and gave the dog her breakfast. Then Emma quietly and methodically started packing.

"What the fuck are you doing?" Jake yelled.

"I'm leaving. You're being a prick and I don't need this shit," she yelled back at him.

"Fine!" and he threw his stuff into his duffle bag. He walked outside to get some air. Emma stepped outside and surprised herself by screaming at him where everyone could hear her.

"You're a fucking idiot, Jake. You brought this on yourself. You knew you were allergic to poison oak, yet you did everything possible to make it worse. I've had enough of your complaining and nastiness. I'm outta here!"

"Do you have any idea how miserable I am?" he screamed after her.

"Yeah, I do. I've had chicken pox and allergies. But I'm nice to other people because I'd like to have some sympathy. You act like an asshole. You think you'll get any sympathy from me? Not acting like this!" she yelled. By that time the manager walked by. He was a small Korean man who spoke little English.

"Please," the manager said to both Emma and Jake, "be more quiet."

"That's okay, sir," Emma managed to say. "We're leaving."

"Baby, please calm down and come inside," suddenly Jake was acting sweet.

"Fuck you!" she screamed at Jake. The manager winced and Emma didn't care. She desperately wanted to leave. She began taking her bags to the car, slamming the back door. She went back to get Tasha, who was always the last to take into the SUV. Tasha jumped into the back, and Emma burned rubber to leave. She saw Jake get into his truck a moment later. She drove around to the front desk, the tears finally starting. The lady at the desk was kind and considerate of Emma's feelings.

"I'm so sorry," Emma cried. "We're checking out of room twenty-two. I know we had reserved one more night, but I can't take any more," she sobbed.

"Don't you worry about a thing, young lady," the woman said sympathetically. "Did you get some breakfast, darlin'? Maybe a little food would help," the woman crooned.

"Maybe," Emma replied through muffled sobs. She walked over to the buffet and took a sweet roll. "Thanks." With that, Emma signed the credit card slip and left. She drove directly to the expressway, still crying, when her phone rang. "What?" she yelled when she heard the ringer she had programmed for Jake. Emma loved technology. It was so easy to give the people who called her most often their own ringtone. Jake's was Monty Python's "Sit on My Face." Not appropriate in many situations but it made Emma smile. She didn't smile this time.

"I'm sorry, baby. I'm grouchy from this itching," he tried. "I thought maybe you'd turn around and come back. Or maybe you were only going out for breakfast to cool off."

"No, Jake. I'm on I-26 heading as far away from you as I can get," she sputtered.

"Oh, baby," he crooned. "Don't do that. Come back to me. I feel better already."

"Nope. You treat me like this when all I tried to do was

help? Fuck you. When you're completely healed, maybe we'll try again." Emma closed the phone to hang up. The tears started again. She couldn't help it.

Emma knew this incident had nothing to do with drugs. He hadn't used or he wouldn't be able to eat as he did. She had learned the signs. He was a bastard when he was sick or hurting. She had suffered with him through a common cold with him and saw how cruel he could be when he was sick. He thought because his sainted mother put up with his spoiled antics that everyone would. Since this was the first time in his life—at thirty-one years old—that he had been on his own, he would find out quickly that the real world was far different from his mother. He had to learn that no one else would take his crap. Certainly Emma wouldn't. So after one night with him, she was on her way back to Savannah and peace. She heard "Sit on My Face" three times on the way home. She didn't answer the phone.

During the next week, Jake was good about only calling three times a day. But with each call, Emma lost respect for him. Everything she told him to do, he did the opposite. He continued scratching his open wounds, spreading puss over his body. The poison oak started with a small rash on his neck. Now, Jake told her, it was on his face and covered his arms. What did he expect? Emma thought. After two weeks of misery and continuing to work on the same damned tree that was covered with poison oak, Jake finally went to a local doctor who gave him a shot of antibiotic. The wrong shot! He should have gotten a shot of cortisone to get rid of the allergy. Of course, the doctor's visit was charged to her credit card, but at this point, what could she do? She had to hope it would work.

Throughout July, Jake suffered with the poison oak. He did nothing intelligent to stop it and bitched and groaned every day. He would tell Emma it was better, and then tell her he tried some new miracle gel that Rob recommended, which didn't work. What Jake needed was to work inside where he wouldn't perspire, further irritating the rash. Of course, he also needed to keep away from the damned tree that kept re-infecting him. But did he demand any of this from Rob? No. He did everything wrong, all the while begging Emma for another chance.

"Not until you're completely clear. I won't go through that night again."

"I promise, baby. It won't. I was horrible. I know I was," he claimed. But she could hear in his voice he didn't mean it. He blamed her for not being understanding.

"Yeah, you were. We'll try again—at another hotel—when you're okay," she told him.

During that time in July, Emma showed her house several times and was hopeful that it would sell. She began packing some of the superfluous decor. Her house had so much artwork and personal pictures, it was difficult to see the house without being totally distracted by her belongings. She packed all her family pictures, much of her artwork, and as much of her Arthur Court collection as was possible. She certainly wasn't planning any more parties at her house, so most of the Arthur Court serving pieces could get packed. She packed her books, other than those she hadn't read yet. She uncluttered as much as she could. At least it kept her busy. Not only did the house not sell, Emma still didn't know where she wanted to move.

After her visit to North Carolina, she was pretty sure it was not for her. The realtor up there had continued to e-mail her listings, and Emma was not impressed. Either the houses were duplicates of those she had already seen, were too small, or were dumps. She was quickly losing interest. Emma continued to look on realtor.com for houses. She might make one more trip to North Carolina to see a few houses she liked, but she was skeptical. She e-mailed her realtor there and changed the area from Spencer to Salisbury or Kannapolis. There were five houses in those two towns outside Charlotte that Emma wanted to see.

When Emma spoke with Jake at the end of the month, his mood was clearly lifted. He sounded as though the rash was gone and he was feeling fine. She decided to give him another chance since he was staying clean and still hadn't drank so much as a beer, which lifted Emma's own spirits. Maybe he really had gotten his mother's strength when she passed away. Even though he had been miserable with the poison oak, he wasn't getting into trouble. He hadn't asked Emma for any financial assistance, other than for the doctor, so he clearly wasn't using drugs. Making only ten dollars an hour, staying in a flophouse from which nothing valuable could be stolen, and paying for his cigarettes, food, and gas, he couldn't have any money left over to buy drugs. He complained about money and how frugally he lived, but he never asked for more. So Emma agreed to meet him again.

"Baby, I'm so glad. You'll see. We'll have sex three times a day and have fun," he promised. "I'm really fine now. And I can meet you in Salisbury. It's not far," he slipped. He was careful not to tell Emma where he was living, as this would jeopardize her safety and his own. As long as she couldn't tell the police where he was, she wasn't committing a crime and he was safe.

"Okay, Jake. This coming weekend?"

"Perfect. That'll give me the rest of the week to be tip-top. The same motel we stayed at last time we came here?"

"Yeah. I think it was nice. And it was convenient."

"Terrific. I can't wait. And I'll be paid on Friday, so I can take you out to dinner. That Italian restaurant we liked so much. How does that sound?"

"Wow. Really? Are you sure you can afford it?" she asked.

"Yeah, I'll manage. I want to take you out for a change. It would make me feel like a man."

"I'm sure. Okay, I'll make the arrangements." Emma e-mailed her agent and set up Saturday for seeing the houses. She called the motel and made reservations. She was ready for another road trip and prayed that Jake would be the kind, considerate person he was when he was clean. The man that she had loved.

Chapter Twenty-Three

Once again, Emma began a trip to North Carolina. This time she was driving alone and would be meeting Jake there. As she packed in her methodical manner—without Jake around to rush her impatiently, the nerves started sneaking into her. Jake had been clean for over a month, with no assistance from any outside force. She couldn't help but be proud of him. For the first time in his life, he was staying away from drugs through the power of his own conscience and his own strength of will. He was finally self-sufficient, and all he had accomplished he had done on his own. Emma wished he would attend meetings to add to his resolve, but since she wasn't an addict and had never known an addict before Jake, she assumed it was a good omen that he had found the internal fortitude to stay clean on his own.

Emma was nervous about seeing him again. The last encounter had been such a fiasco, she didn't know what to expect this time. But she kept telling herself he was worth the effort. Emma had seen him clean and sober and still felt the pangs of love for that man. Reality had not yet hit her that he had fake identification and was running from the law because technically, until his August court date, he wasn't. She didn't know how he got the fake ID, but she hoped she'd be able to talk him into turning himself in to the police before August. Emma and Cheryl were both trying to convince him of doing exactly that, and Cheryl assured both of them that her lawyer would get him out of doing much actual jail time.

Jake maintained his self-confidence. He told Emma that changing his name would help him change his life. A new identity would give him a whole new persona—a persona that had never used drugs. With the identification he had, he claimed he could get a real social security number and a real driver's license. Once he had that, he could get a great job because he would have no criminal background. Jake was so confident that he could live the rest of his life as a new person and his enthusiasm was so evident, it had initially rubbed off on Emma.

But with Jake living far away, Emma had the time and distance to evaluate the situation more objectively. She doubted he had the smarts or the emotional stability to pull off this scam. Sooner or later he would screw up. Emma knew Jake as well as anyone could know him, so she was sure his mouth would get away from him. Jake rarely thought before he spoke, which Emma supposed, went along with addiction. The whole act before you think type of mentality. She wanted to believe that he could change his name and they could live happily ever, but reality kept creeping in.

So Emma packed and began the drive north. Tasha was in the backseat, curled up happily, and Emma turned her attention to the houses she was about to see. Her instincts were changing. She had liked the area in North Carolina and the fact that she could buy an old house in a small town while still being close enough to a large city to enjoy both. But now that she knew Jake had moved somewhere in the same area, she didn't want to be there. She needed more control over her life than that. If Jake screwed up again, she wanted to be sure that wherever she moved she could leave him behind if need be. But she continued driving north and would give North Carolina the benefit of the doubt. She'd deal with the Jake issue if and when it arose.

After the four and a half hour drive, she arrived at the motel in Salisbury, and once again, Jake was waiting for her. She always saw his ugly old white truck first. Then she noticed his tall, muscular body leaning casually against the building. Then came the killer smile. He crushed out his cigarette and strode on those long legs toward her. He kissed her softly and gathered her bags. Emma took Tasha's leash and led her to the grass while Jake took her heavy luggage into the room.

Even when Emma went out of town for only a weekend, she still brought a lot with her. Not clothes—there was only one small overnight case with two changes of clothes, sleepwear, and underwear. But she brought a separate duffle with her cosmetics and toiletries. Emma always brought a gallon bottle of spring water to make her coffee, for drinking, and for Tasha. Then there was another tote for Tasha. Food, bowls, treats, and toys. Emma never left town without her laptop computer and another tote with her journal, crossword puzzles, and pens. So even for a weekend, Emma had plenty to schlep into a motel room.

Once everything was in the room, Jake showed Emma his clean and clear arms. There were a few scars left from his bout with poison oak, but he looked fabulous to Emma. His once again smooth skin was tanned from working outdoors and his muscles taut.

"You look great, Jake. You seem to be all healed," Emma ran her hand over his arm.

"Thank God! Yeah, I'm fine now. You look gorgeous," he pulled her into a hug. He wasn't going to let this pass. He lowered his mouth to kiss her long neck, and then her shoulders. "Let's try out the bed. See if it's comfortable," he whispered.

"Let's do," she murmured. He took his time with her as he had while he was in rehab. They made passionate love and to Emma's surprise and pleasure, before dinner. As when they clicked so perfectly, they came together. And when they clicked so perfectly, Jake didn't jump out of bed so fast. He actually held her for a few minutes afterward, enjoying the sheer togetherness. "Wow," was all Emma could say.

"Yeah, that was great. And I promise I won't overeat so we can do it again later," he smiled that winning dimpled smile at her. "Speaking of which—are you hungry? My treat at that great Italian restaurant downtown."

"That sounds so wonderful. I can still taste their salad dressing. It was so good!" Emma exclaimed as she got out of bed and got dressed for dinner. She brought a special outfit for the occasion. It was pink linen that was lovely without being fussy. It was part of Flax's Underflax line, so technically it was sleepwear. But it was a lightweight linen dress with spaghetti straps and high slits up the sides. She wore the dress over the matching bedskirt bloomers—pull-on pants with a ruffle at the bottom. Heavy women wore it full, but with Emma's figure, she belted it with a silver and rhinestone leather belt and wore strappy silver sandals with it. She wore Jake's favorite lipstick, which was a shimmery pale pink and his favorite perfume, Origins ginger.

"You look fantastic!" he said immediately. "Ooh, and you smell great."

"Thanks, honey. You look pretty fantastic, too." He was wearing light tan linen slacks with a white linen shirt that had a V-neck to show off a bit of chest. He matched it perfectly with a brown leather belt and brown leather sandals. And Jake always smelled good. Whether he was working in the yard in the Savannah heat or lying next to her in bed, he always smelled great. Jake never wore cologne because both he and Emma were allergy sensitive, so it must have been his deodorant and soap, but boy oh boy, he always smelled fantastic.

They left the room, and Jake drove them to downtown Salisbury for dinner. To her astonishment, Jake actually took a bite of her salad. And his reaction was not the puckered-up face of disgust. He looked as awestricken as Emma when he proclaimed it was good. Maybe he really was changing, Emma thought.

Over dinner, they finally talked about his mother, and though tears welled in his eyes, he was able to talk about her. More surprises for Emma.

"Mom would be so proud of me," he said. "I've been clean for over a month. I didn't even want wine with dinner. And I'm self-sufficient. I'm working my ass off, but it feels good. I'm paying my own way and standing on my own two feet. I know now I should have done this years ago. If I had left Savannah to go to college and stayed away, I probably never would have gotten back into drugs. I'd be a man instead of a grown child."

"You're right, Jake. On all counts. Steve said he moved out at eighteen and never looked back. I mean, he was still close with his parents but he needed to be his own man. You never did move out. Even when you were engaged to Cindy, you both lived with your mother. You've never been on your own.

And yeah, your mother would be proud of you. She is proud of you. I know she's up there looking down on you with that wonderful smile of hers," Emma said with genuine warmth. She saw Jake's eyes start to water, and she excused herself to go to the ladies' room.

Emma looked in the mirror and saw her own eyes start to tear. She missed Mimi, too. Her strength and tenacity, her kindness, and her love. Yes, Emma thought. She knew Mimi loved her. She had felt it with every visit. Mimi had to feel a sense of love for the one woman who could save her son. Emma also knew that Mimi respected her—certainly more than any of her own children. She thought of what a disappointment Cheryl must have been to her. Cheryl had been in prison for drugs and married a crazy addict. Mimi's eldest son had committed murder and suicide. Her eldest daughter was—Emma didn't know where. Emma had to be a breath of fresh air for Mimi, after seeing the trouble her own children had caused. So Emma sat in the ladies' room and silently wept. She touched up her face with a little concealer, reapplied her lipstick, and joined Jake at the table.

"Hi, honey," she said sweetly when she returned. "Miss me?"

"Yeah, I did," and he touched her hand to his mouth. "You did wash your hands, didn't you?" he laughed.

"Of course!" she smiled. "So you want to take a walk or a drive around town before we see houses tomorrow?"

"That would be smart. Let me see the addresses and I'll find them. Then we can get a sneak peak," he answered.

"Okay," and she gave him the listings that she had left in the car. They drove a total of five miles and saw four out of the five houses. One looked very promising. It was a two-story brick house, only blocks from downtown. However, there were two obvious problems. It was behind a tire store, which Emma didn't like. She'd have to build a really high fence around that side of the house. But the neighborhood looked—questionable. The house across the street looked like a crack house. There were several young people hanging out on the steps smoking. What they were smoking, Emma wasn't sure, but she knew she didn't like it. She'd have to wait until daylight so she could talk to some of the neighbors. But the brick house looked amazing.

The other houses they saw were Victorian from the outside, which Emma loved, but couldn't pass judgment until she saw the inside. She and Jake tried to walk the perimeter to peak into the windows and see the backyards, but in the dark, it wasn't easy.

After a night of great sex, the next day they drove up to the north side of town to meet the realtor. They got into his SUV and returned to downtown Salisbury. They looked at all five houses, and Emma was not impressed with any but the brick house behind the tire store. It had been completely upgraded with a new kitchen, new windows, and new air-conditioning. But the upstairs was not air-conditioned. That would be a large expense. When they returned to the office, Emma left her realtor to speak with some air-conditioning experts and get some quotes on air-conditioning the upstairs. When they left the real estate office, Emma and Jake returned to the house. They saw the local mail delivery person on his rounds. Perfect! Emma thought, and approached him to ask what the neighborhood was like.

"It's okay now. We've had some trouble in the past, but the

police patrol the area all the time now, so it's pretty safe," he told her. Reading between the lines, Emma didn't like it.

"What about that house over there?" she asked as pointed at the dump across the street.

"Oh, they're just transients. They come and go," was all he would tell her. Again, reading between the lines, she determined she was right. It was a crack house.

"Thank you for your help," Emma said as the mailman walked along his route.

When she and Jake got back into her car, she looked around the area.

"Oh, Jake. This would be perfect for you. There's a crack house on the corner, and two doors down, there's a pawnshop. How convenient!" she chided him.

"Ha ha," he replied sarcastically. "You're so funny."

"I really didn't see anything I loved, did you?" she asked.

"I still like this one. The kitchen was amazing. And there was so much room! Besides, you wouldn't have to air-condition the second floor immediately. The master bedroom and two of the other bedrooms were on the main level. You could take your time to add the second floor. That could be the library and guest room," he told her.

"Yeah, that's true. But there's something about it I don't trust. Why would someone spend all that money to fix up the kitchen and not finish the work? I think they're covering up something," she replied.

"You think so? I could ask Rob to come over and take a look. He owns so many properties, he probably even knows this one. Maybe he'll have some input. He comes to Salisbury every so often."

"That would be great. Thanks."

"And I could move in first and do a lot of the work it needs," Jake put in. "Refinish those gorgeous hardwood floors upstairs. You know, do the painting and stuff."

"First let's see if it's worth it," Emma stalled. The idea of giving Jake a free place to stay while she was paying the mortgage, electricity, and cable sounded purely selfish to her. It sounded like the addict in Jake talking.

"Of course, I would pay rent and pay for the electricity," he added as though he was reading her thoughts.

"Jake, you don't have any furniture. No bed, no table. And how could you afford it?"

"I could pick up stuff at Goodwill or garage sales," he tried.

"Jake, do you have any idea what the electricity would cost? Especially without air-conditioning upstairs. The downstairs unit would work twenty four/seven to try to cool the upstairs. It would be a fortune."

"Yeah, you're probably right. And then the mortgage, until your house is sold. Well, I'd like to help you. Save you some money," he admitted.

"Thanks, honey. I appreciate that. But let's see what the realtor says about the AC. And I still don't feel comfortable with this neighborhood. I really loved that Victorian house in the historic district we drove by. Let's take a look at that tomorrow," Emma said.

"Which one? The one on the corner?"

"Yeah. That one was amazing and a lovely neighborhood. I'll call the realtor in the morning. Maybe we can see it."

They went back to the motel and watched television for a while. Emma took her bath, and then they made love. They had a good night's sleep; Jake only woke her a couple of times with snoring and tossing.

The next morning, Jake went to the lobby for his breakfast while Emma had her coffee and did her crossword puzzle. Then they packed and Jake took Emma's belongings to the car, including Tasha. He threw his few things into his duffle and tossed it into his truck. They checked out of the hotel, leaving Jake's truck there. Then they went downtown to see the Victorian house. They pulled up in front and parked. When they walked around the outside, they both got enthused. Emma pulled out her cell phone and called the agent listed on the sign. Surprisingly, the realtor gave them the numbers to open the lock box—over the phone.

They walked to the back door and used the pass code. The house had a lot of potential. There was a screened-in porch that led into an enormous kitchen. The huge kitchen, however, was unusable. There was water on the floor—a very bad sign. Emma estimated twenty-five thousand dollars-worth of work at a minimum to finish it. New floors, new cabinets, new counter tops, new paint, and new appliances. The rest of the house looked good. The hardwood floors throughout were in good shape. But the master bedroom had no bathroom. Emma looked carefully and saw the laundry room had once been a huge porch and backed up to the bedroom. Half of it could be used as the master bathroom, with a door into the bedroom. But that was another ten grand. The outside of the house was absolutely gorgeous. There was a pond on one side that was meant for brightly colored Koi and was surrounded with roses. The landscaping overall was beautiful. Why, Emma thought, would they spend all this money for landscaping and not fix the kitchen? She asked Jake the same question. He had no reasonable answer. She called the agent and asked the price. It was fair but not including the work. She was told it was in foreclosure, so the price wasn't negotiable.

"Well, shit," Emma muttered when she hung up the phone. She called her own agent and told him the gist of the situation. She gave him the address and the name of the selling agent.

"You're kidding me, right?" her realtor replied when she told him about the pass code.

"No. I saw the house," she told him.

"That's against the law, Dr. Weiss. I mean, really against the law. You could have been anybody. You could have stolen anything or gotten in and stayed there. They took an enormous liability by doing that," he explained.

"That's what I thought, but since I wasn't going to do anything illegal, I used the code to look. And the realtor was really rude to me. Wasn't negotiable, didn't even want to talk. She basically hung up on me," Emma told him.

"Well, I'll check into it and let you know. Oh, I got the numbers on the AC for the brick house. I was told it would be seven thousand dollars."

"Ouch! Well, check out this house and see if there's wiggle room. The kitchen has to be gutted, and a master bathroom has to be added. I'd say, conservatively, it needs fifty grand put into it. So I'd have to get it pretty cheap to justify the expense," Emma told him. "I'm on my way back to Savannah, so e-mail me or call me with whatever you find out."

With that, Emma and Jake got back into her SUV, and she drove him back to his truck. They said their good-byes, which for Jake was always difficult. Then Emma was back on the road to Savannah.

As she drove, she thought about Salisbury. Something was pushing her away from it. She wasn't sure if it was her own instincts, her conscience, or her logic that was stronger, but it was something. She thought about how long it had taken her to find her house in Savannah. She had seen dozens before making a decision. But there were several that struck her as possibilities before seeing her house. Emma wasn't getting that feeling in North Carolina. One was worse than the next, and nothing was even drawing her in. Only the last house on the corner was a consideration, but it needed so much work, and in a new town with unknown workers and unknown property values, it was a frightening prospect.

Emma decided to begin exploring other avenues. Where did she want to live? Emma loved Savannah—still did. But she had burned too many bridges and wanted a fresh start. She would get back onto the computer and continue researching. She had already researched Charleston, and that was not what she wanted. She had researched several towns in South Carolina, and they were too remote. Maybe Atlanta. She decided to check the outskirts of Atlanta to see what prices were like there.

As for Jake, Emma was confused. He seemed to be doing great, but she was waiting for the other shoe to drop. She was hopeful that it wouldn't, but knowing Jake, he'd find a way to fuck up. He always did.

Chapter Twenty-Four

At home, Emma continued to pack her belongings with the hope of selling her house. Her real estate agent in Savannah was doing very little and was showing her house too few times for Emma's comfort. She wrote the marketing information for his Web site herself. He hadn't even planned a caravan of realtors yet, which didn't give her much confidence. But he was a nice man and he tried to instill confidence in her.

She spent hours online investigating Atlanta and found some areas that looked hopeful in north Atlanta. There was Woodstock, Kennesaw, and Acworth. Emma got very lucky when she found a realtor attached to one house in Woodstock. Gary was a hard worker and understood Emma's needs. They e-mailed back and forth with listings, and Emma made plans to visit the area within the next couple of weeks.

She had done the preliminary investigation, which was to say she found that there were several Mensa groups and several synagogues in those north Atlanta areas. They had certain stores that hadn't come to Savannah yet. She didn't care about major department stores but Whole Foods—now that was important to Emma. When she lived in Fort Lauderdale, she went there at least once a week. And Atlanta even boasted Trader Joe's food store. She was thrilled.

Emma found that Atlanta had everything. Even Rosemary Daniell's Zona Rosa writing group met in nearby Buckhead every month. Marietta had a quaint downtown square similar to the many squares in Savannah. Yet from these areas, it was only half an hour (depending on the traffic) to bustling downtown Atlanta with all the culture Emma could want. It was perfect.

With the economy as poor as it had become, there were plenty of houses under a hundred and fifty thousand dollars in these north Atlanta suburbs. If the houses she saw were not complete dumps or in bad neighborhoods when she went there to see them, Emma would be much more apt to move there than to North Carolina. Atlanta had an international airport, so it would be easier for her family to visit her. The Savannah Airport was tiny and only flew small planes, so anyone who visited had to fly into Atlanta anyway and then take the little puddle jumpers to Savannah. It was more expensive and more time-consuming for them. And as far as driving went, she was five hours closer to her family in Chicago. All around, Atlanta looked like the better situation.

As far as Jake went, if he remained clean and stayed out of trouble, he could just as easily get a job in Atlanta as anywhere else. If he had this fake ID situation under control, which he believed he could, then it still wouldn't matter. If, on the other hand, he screwed up again, he wouldn't know where she was to contact her for money. Either way, her ass was covered.

While Emma was planning her first trip to Atlanta, Jake was continuing to work for Rob. He was receiving less and less respect from Rob, so Jake's ego was at rock bottom. But Jake still maintained that he had not used or even had a beer. He was happy to be taking care of himself and had planned to move into a better room. He continued to phone Emma three times a day. In one call he reported that he and Rob did drive to

Salisbury to look at the brick house Emma had liked but had suspicions about its safety. Jake told her that Rob had once owned that house and it was in bad disrepair. The updating had been all cosmetic, and the structure was in deplorable condition. Emma breathed a sigh of relief because this information took North Carolina out of contention for relocating. Other than this one important call, Jake generally called with either stupid questions like she was his mother or out of boredom with nothing to say.

"Hi, baby," he would start, and then, "I got sun burnt. What should I do?" Emma could only think, what an idiot. He's thirty-one years old! He's been on cruises with his mother. He lived in Savannah, Georgia his whole life. And he's never been in the sun before? I don't think so! Jesus, she was getting frustrated.

"Jake, this can't be the first time you've been sun burnt," she would say. "What do you think you should do?" Emma was damned if she would tell him what to do. She had to make him think for himself.

"Um, I dunno. I guess I've heard that aloe helps," he would reply.

"Yeah, you think? Aloe is what everyone uses for sunburn," she said, losing patience.

Emma was awakened early one morning by the phone. She assumed it was Jake but was startled when it was the police.

"Ms. Weiss," the officer said mildly, "my name is Detective White. We need you to come down to the police station to discuss the gun theft you filed."

"It's Dr. Weiss and certainly. I'd be happy to," Emma said calmly, this time throwing her title in his face. "When would be convenient for you, Detective?"

"Can you be here at eleven o'clock?" he asked.

"Of course. You're at the main police station on Habersham?" she asked.

"Yes. I'll be expecting you, Ms. Weiss. Thank you." He hung up the phone. Emma thought he sounded pleasant.

Emma did call Jake to tell him she was going. As soon as she told him the police called, he began to panic.

"They're sneaky bastards, Emma. Just be careful. They'll try to trick you into telling them where I am," he warned.

"Jake, first of all, I don't know where you are. I assume you're in North Carolina, but it's a big state. Don't worry. I'm sure I'll be fine. I just thought you should know."

"You're smart, that's for sure. You'll do fine. Call me when it's over, okay?"

"Of course I will. Don't worry."

The police station was not at all what Emma expected. It was one of the older buildings in Savannah. She waited in the antique lobby until Detective White came out and ushered her back. He shook her hand and smiled. He was elderly, calm, and had kind-looking deep brown eyes. His demeanor put her at ease, which was exactly what he was aiming to do. They took a tiny elevator to another floor and went into a small room. They were joined by a younger female officer. She was clearly the bad cop to White's good cop. While he did all of the talking, the other officer sat quietly watching Emma's every facial expression.

The room didn't look at all like the interrogation rooms used on television. This had no windows, no one-way glass. It was a pathetic little box with miss-matched chairs and a beaten-up old table. Detective White sat at the far end next to Emma, while the woman sat at the other end of the table. They were only five feet apart, but she left as much distance as the cramped room could muster.

"Is this the man who stole your gun?" White pulled out the mug shot of Jake from his June arrest. Emma couldn't deny the picture startled her. She only hoped that her face didn't show it. Emma definitely did not have a poker face, so she feared the worst.

"Yes," she answered. She didn't elaborate or embellish. She acted as though she were on the stand in court.

"And he was your boyfriend?"

"Yes."

"And you broke up with him? When was that?" White began to probe.

"In June."

"And you don't know when the gun was stolen?"

"No, not exactly. I heard a noise the night before I called the police. I reached for my gun, which I kept in my nightstand, and it was gone. Since I hadn't needed it before—thank God—I first noticed it missing that night."

"Do you know where Jake Stanton is now?" he asked.

"No."

"You haven't been in touch with him? You have no idea where he went?" he pushed.

"No. Once I threw him out of my house, he left. I have no idea where he is."

"Does he have any family?"

"His mother passed away early this month. His sister lives here. He has some family in South Carolina somewhere, and he has a cousin in California. I think he also has some family in Minnesota. But I don't know any of them," Emma explained. The woman at the end of the table kept quiet, even when Emma looked at her and tried to smile. She was clearly only there for observation.

"Did you know he had a woman with him in his truck when he pawned your gun?" Once again, White tried to rattle her.

"How could I know that?" Emma asked.

"Maybe because you were there with him," White reached.

Now Emma laughed. "Detective White, that is the stupidest thing I've ever heard. Why in the world would I go with him to pawn my gun? If I needed the money—which I don't—I wouldn't pawn it. And I certainly wouldn't have helped Jake steal my own gun. Look, this is stupid," she finished and refused to say any more.

"The owner of the pawnshop claims he saw Jake get into a white truck, and there was a woman waiting in it."

"Maybe it was his sister. I have no idea. Was she pretty?" she asked and laughed. Detective White was beginning to see he wasn't getting anything from Emma and gave up the ruse about a woman.

"Well, Doctor Weiss—emphasis on the doctor—when we catch him, you'll get your gun back. It's been in police custody since you filed the report," he finished and stood up, walking toward the door.

"Thank you, Detective. Let me know." And with that, the interview was over.

Once she was on the road and away from the police station,

she called Jake and told him what had transpired. She set his mind at ease by assuring him they had no idea where he was and that she had told them he might be in California or Minnesota. Emma hadn't lied. Jake's cousin was in California, and he had told her he had some family up north.

By the beginning of August, Emma made her first trip to Atlanta and she was impressed. Because she did so much driving, she had purchased a GPS for her car and she finally invested in an iPod. She bought one with so much space, she downloaded all of her audio books, all of her music, and even three movies onto it. No longer did she have to decide which books and which music to bring. It was all with her.

After speaking with Gary, they agreed on a motel in Kennesaw that was centrally located to all the houses she wanted to see. It was right off I-75, so it was convenient for the drive. They had smoking rooms, were dog friendly, and were reasonably priced. What more could she ask?

After spending the day with Gary, she was sure she had made the right selection of a realtor. He was pleasant, patient, and extremely knowledgeable. He was an investor as well and had restored houses to flip, so he knew how much it would cost to upgrade anything in a house. He had connections with electricians, carpenters, and plumbers. He was perfect. They would drive up to a house, and before they got out of his truck he would say, "This house has had a termite problem in the past. See the holes down there in the corner? That's from termites."

She saw several houses, and Gary gave her the basic tour of the area. One house—the one in Woodstock—she really liked.

It was up a long, winding driveway, and the back was forest. It was gorgeous. She imagined deer would wander onto the property in the early morning, while she had coffee on the deck. She didn't like the garage under the house, though. It meant a long trek straight up a steep staircase to bring groceries up to the house. And the basement itself was unfinished, which was where the laundry room was located. Gary explained that it would only cost three hundred dollars to give the staircase a landing in the middle so it wouldn't be so steep. But as they left the house, Emma asked a simple question.

"Gary, how would a moving truck get up this driveway?" He looked at Emma with a look of surprise and shock.

"My gosh! You know what? They couldn't. They would have to park at the bottom of the property and reload onto a smaller truck to get up there. And that's if it wasn't during the winter when it was icy. Huh!" he looked shocked.

"That would have to be expensive."

"Oh, yeah. Totally cost prohibitive," he agreed.

"I wonder how the owners got their stuff in there," Emma wondered. "Maybe they're the original owners and bought everything piece by piece. Then when they left, they sold everything at a garage sale." It was the only way Emma could figure it.

"Sounds right to me. I can't think of another answer," Gary agreed.

They looked at several other houses and left shaking hands and vowing to stay in touch and to keep looking. Nothing fit her criteria exactly, but they were all within the realm of possibility. Emma wanted move-in ready this time. She didn't want another nightmare of ten months to upgrade a bathroom, like she had in Savannah. Emma not only had to replace the air-conditioning but also had to replace all the duct work in her house in Savannah. It had cost her fifteen thousand dollars. She vowed not to get in that situation again.

    She wanted simple this time around. She no longer wanted the nicest house on the block—the one that no one wanted to leave. She wanted a home. Her home. Emma finally realized that her house in Savannah had not been for her, but to please others. She had wanted everyone else to feel at home there, for everyone else to love it. It had taken her two years to see it, but she finally saw her life in Savannah for what it was—a lie. Emma was not the spoiled Jewish American princess her house made her appear to be. It gave everyone the impression that she had an unlimited cache of money. Her jewelry, her lavish parties, her perfect wardrobe, and the continual upgrading of her house made her look that way. She wasn't that person. She only appeared to be that person, especially in small-town Savannah. No one could even find a Prada purse in Savannah, and Emma had five. It didn't matter that she had purchased them on eBay at a fraction of the price; it was still Prada. She was living like a queen in Savannah, partially because it was so inexpensive to live there and partially because she had exquisite taste that did not always mean expensive. With her vast display of Arthur Court serving pieces, her house looked like a mansion. But in reality, Arthur Court was not that expensive—it just looked impressive. Emma loved the look of it, and she also respected the company because part of their proceeds went toward wild animal preservation. She had slowly built her collection, starting in Fort Lauderdale. After buying the house, she purchased more party serving pieces, more chips and dip platters and the like. Emma was finished being the one person who gave to everyone else. She needed to start living for herself.

It was not in Emma's character to be selfish. But she was learning quickly that putting herself first was not being selfish. It was being smart. She had to start living her life for her. Not for her parents. Not for Jake. For Emma. She had to find her own peace and her own true self. Jake could take her money, pawn her jewelry, even steal her heart, but the moment he took her sense of self it would be over. She vowed it to herself then and there.

As the middle of August approached, it was clear to Emma that Jake was not going to turn himself in to the police. He was going to continue the charade. She waited for the other shoe to drop, and as she expected, it did.

She got a frantic phone call from Jake. He had moved into the better room in his building, and according to Jake, he got along well with his neighbors. But one night his neighbor accused him of flirting with his girlfriend.

"Emma, she was so ugly. I would never even think of it. But he's nuts. I didn't even think about it when I told him I was wanted by the police," he told her.

"You what? Are you stupid or crazy?" she was flabbergasted. There was his big mouth, she thought. Thump! The other shoe dropped on his head.

"Well, he told me he was wanted by the police; armed robbery. So I laughed and tried to make him feel more comfortable by telling him I was, too. Then he came back tonight, and I was going into my room and I said hello to his girlfriend. It was perfectly innocent. But I think he tipped off the police," he said, his voice shaking.

"Have they come?" Emma asked.

"Not yet but I think they will. I think I'm going to have to leave."

"How can you afford that?"

"I can't. I'd only need two weeks rent at a new place. That would only be two hundred dollars. Please, Emma. I'm really scared. And I can't go to prison. I'll kill myself first. Oh, God. Someone's at my door. I'll call you back."

Oh, shit, Emma thought. How the hell did I get involved with this? And haven't I asked myself that before? She waited. When the phone rang again, she shuddered.

"What happened?" she asked quickly.

"The police were here. They saw my ID and left. I got away with it, but they could look at the desk register in the morning. I signed in under my real name," he said frantically.

"You did what?"

"Don't. Not now. I've got to pack up my truck. Now. I'll call you from the road," and he hung up.

Emma called Cheryl to update her on the situation. She tried to keep Cheryl in the loop where her brother was concerned.

"He's had to run again," Emma told her.

"Oh, God, what now?" Cheryl asked.

"He told his neighbor he was wanted by the police, for starters," she told Cheryl.

"He really is stupid, isn't he? That's my brother. He was so smart in school and running the restaurant, but sometimes,

Emma, I swear! That boy doesn't have the brains of a collard green," she muttered. "So did the police catch up with him?"

"No. They entered his room, saw his fake ID, and bought it, from what he tells me. But he registered under Stanton. Yeah, the brains of a collard green," Emma agreed.

"You know he's going to get caught," Cheryl told her. "We've got to convince him to turn himself in before it's too late. His court date isn't for a few more days. I'll talk to him. If they catch him instead of him going to them, they'll throw the book at him. And then he'll be considered a runner, since he didn't show up for his court date. Because of his fake ID and evading the police, he could be shackled for his time in prison. Then they'll add the major charges of identity theft, fake ID, and running from the police to the one small drug charge. I mean, Emma, in any other state, the amount of drugs they found on him would have been a misdemeanor. But Georgia is a zero-tolerance state, so any amount of cocaine would be considered a felony. Even with his probation violation, he probably would have only done a year or two in prison." Cheryl explained. "But this really ups the ante."

"Try to talk him into turning himself in, Cheryl. You or I might get away with the false identity and running. We're smart enough and logical enough. Jake has too big a mouth and doesn't think his actions through. If I were in his trouble, I would become the new person and leave everything about me behind. Jake isn't doing that. He's still Jake Stanton. He can't forget that. Jake simply isn't cut out for that kind of life," Emma reasoned.

"I'll try, Emma. I'll call him in a little while. Once he's on the road. He's probably terrified right now. And knowing

Jake, he'll forget something in the room that will incriminate himself. He's so disorganized, especially when he's scared, he'll leave something behind."

"I know you're right, Cheryl. You talk to him. I'll wait until later."

So Emma waited. She had no idea where he was going or how she would get the money to him for his rent. She knew she could use Western Union but not until he landed somewhere and figured out where to send it. Not that she wanted to give it to him or even wanted to help him. Her decision had been to give him six months. If he could stay clean, stay employed, and stay self-sufficient for six months, she'd consider a future with him. When he left her in June, she had clearly told him that was the last penny he would get from her. And he had kept to that pledge. He primarily ate ramen noodles with hot sauce—the whole meal costing less than a dollar—but he had remained self-sufficient. With this idiotic turn of events that was purely his own fault, she had no inclination to help him. Emma wished Cheryl had access to money, but she knew differently.

Aaron kept Cheryl on a short leash. He didn't trust her with money—or much else. Emma was never quite sure why Aaron didn't trust Cheryl until Cheryl tried to cash a third-party check at Emma's bank. Cheryl had called Emma and asked her to cash a check for her. Emma said no, but she would meet her at the bank where Jenny was the manager. Emma assured Cheryl that Jenny would cash it for her. When they sat in Jenny's office, Cheryl started babbling about personal information—information that held no interest to Jenny and embarrassed Emma. When Cheryl finally took out the check and Emma saw it, she winced. Cheryl was actually trying to cash a check made out to Aaron. Jenny was losing patience to begin with, but when she saw the check, Jenny nearly laughed in her face.

"I can't cash this," Jenny said simply. Emma looked at Cheryl like she had lost her mind. Did Cheryl think Jenny was stupid, or was Cheryl that desperate? Emma knew Jenny would never cash it. But that was Cheryl. She was not that far removed from the con artist her brother was. Emma could see the slime beneath the surface. Jake had told Emma that Cheryl still used drugs. She could believe it. There had to be a reason that Cheryl remained with Aaron—a known recovering heroin addict who was on methadone and an overall bad human being. And there had to be a reason that Aaron didn't trust Cheryl. Emma didn't know and really didn't want to know. All of Emma's Jewish friends knew Cheryl through her children and was liked by them all. Emma didn't want to cause trouble in the Jewish community.

Emma waited for Jake's phone call and hoped it would come after Cheryl had spoken with him. Maybe she could talk some sense into that pea brain of his. But when he finally called, it was clear Cheryl hadn't called him.

"Where are you?" Emma asked.

"South Carolina. I'm going to pull off the road and sleep at a cheap motel in the middle of nowhere. Then I'll be fresh in the morning to figure out a plan."

"Jake, have you given any thought to turning yourself in? This is foolish. You'll never get away with running like this, and you'll have to run for the rest of your life. Isn't it better to get it over with? You wouldn't do that much time if you go to them before the trial date," she tried.

"I'll be more careful this time," he told her. "I won't get caught. And I can't go back to prison. I just can't." Jake wouldn't budge.

"Jake, you've got to make a complete change. If you're going to take on a new identity, you have to believe it. You have to forget about your past and who you were and become that new person. The new person who has never done drugs and never would—the new person who has never been to jail and never would. Do you understand me? You have to believe your lies," Emma tried desperately to explain to him.

"Yeah, I understand," he replied. "Right now, I'm scared shitless and I need sleep."

"Okay. Well, call me when you decide what you're going to do. And before you ask, no you can't come back here."

"Emma, I know that. Not only because you don't want me there but it's way too dangerous for me. Too many drugs, the cops will be looking for me at your place after my court date, and your neighbors will probably turn me in. Not to mention if Aaron finds out I'm there, he'll turn me over to the cops in a heartbeat. So, no. I know I can't come back."

"Well, at least you thought that through. That's a start," Emma told him.

"Yeah, even I'm not that stupid," he answered. "Lemme get some sleep and I'll call tomorrow with a plan."

Emma hung up the phone and thought, oh goodie! I can't wait to hear this one. Mr. Mensa is going to come up with a plan. And I'm sure that plan will include a check from me. Then she imagined life without Jake. It was lonely and boring. There was no laughter in her life without him. Maybe he had learned his lesson with this screw up. If he really didn't want to end up in prison again, he would learn from this experience. Fear was often the best motivator.

Chapter Twenty-Five

Within a day after Jake's court date, the police showed up at her door. The plain-clothes officer was light and friendly and asked Emma if she was, indeed, Emma Weiss. She told him yes, she was. He never entered her house; he merely pulled out the mug shot of Jake.

"Have you seen this man?" he asked amiably.

"Not since I broke up with him in June," she answered. Luckily, she really didn't know where he was. She hadn't heard from him yet.

"Thank you, ma'am," he said and walked away. Emma was shocked. That's all? No asking to come in to look around? They really don't have any interest in him, she thought. He's so unimportant, they don't even care. Well, good for Jake.

When the phone rang, it was Jake. Emma told him about the police and reiterated that they had no interest in him.

"Are you sure?" He was beginning to question her loyalty. She had given him no reason to question her.

"Of course, I'm sure. So where are you—generally speaking?"

"I'm in South Carolina. I found a room for rent, and it's not too far from Savannah. We can see each other more often and easier," Jake said it as though that would make her feel better. It didn't.

"How much is it?"

"Five hundred dollars a month. I can handle that, once I get a job. And that should be easy. There's a million restaurants here. Cash tips, no background checks."

"That sounds great. What's the person like?" Emma asked.

"He's a really cool dude. He's thirty-five and a manager at a big drugstore chain. And he has a dog! A Jack Russell terrier! She is so adorable, Emma. And what's good about the situation is he's real easygoing. Like, wherever I want to put my food in the fridge is fine or watching the big-screen TV with him. He's the perfect roommate," Jake told her.

"Does he use?" was Emma's only concern.

"No way! They drug test all the time at a big company like the one he works for!"

"Well, that's good. Okay, so how much do you need to move in?" Emma asked. Damn, she couldn't believe she was forking over more money. But what could she do? It was either give him a couple of hundred dollars or he'd move back in with her. Not a choice there. He wasn't going to live with her again for a long time. It was wrong on several levels, and Emma wasn't sure of the order. Aiding and abetting a criminal was high on the list. She wasn't going to put herself in danger by breaking the law. She didn't know if that was even at the top of the list, though it should have been. She wasn't opening her house up to him with the possibility of more theft. Emma didn't want to live that way again. Hiding her valuables, hiding credit cards, not able to keep cash in her wallet. Maybe someday Jake would regain her trust, but he sure hadn't come close to that goal yet. And Emma wasn't ready to open her heart all the way as it had once been so vulnerable. She didn't mind the occasional fun weekend—or the sex that was involved. But having her legs open and having her heart open were two different issues. Not that Emma was loose or free with sex. Hell, she hadn't had sex for three years before Jake and had only been with five men before him.

"If I can get three hundred dollars, that will cover me for two weeks of rent and food. And gas and smokes. I left before I got paid by Rob, so I'm pretty broke."

"I figured. Did the police go back to Rob's place?"

"Yeah. The next morning they were there and looked at the register. They checked my room, and I left my old birth certificate there. I think I left some other stuff, too. But they know. I have a new birth certificate with another name already, so I'm cool. And I didn't screw up with Jeremy, my new roommate. He doesn't know anything and he won't. I've learned my lesson," Jake explained.

"All right. Where do you want to meet for the check? And who do I make it out to?" Emma asked. She wasn't about to use Western Union to send him cash. She didn't trust him enough for that. He spelled Jeremy's last name, and they agreed to meet at a strip joint on the South Carolina side of the Talmadge Bridge that connected to Savannah at two o'clock that afternoon.

Once Jake was settled in his new room, he started looking for work. He began cleaning boats at a marina. He really enjoyed the manual labor. He was in the sun and working hard. He was an outgoing guy, so he became friendly with his boss. Jake's pay was ten dollars an hour without taxes being taken out, so he was making decent money. But Jake was not smart with his money. There was a sandwich shop in the marina, and he bought his lunch there every day. When he told Emma about it, she gave him hell.

"Jake, it's too difficult for you to get work, and in this economy, you need to be more careful. Hell, I can't even afford to eat lunch out every day," Emma chided him.

"Yeah, you're right, honey. I'll start packing a lunch," he promised.

"Good idea. You never know," she told him.

And Emma was right. After three weeks working at the marina, he was fired; or more accurately, downsized. They couldn't afford so many employees. Jake called and sounded crushed. He told her how much he loved the job and missed it already.

"Jake, you have to find something else. I know you enjoyed it—even when you fell in the water," she said laughing.

"Yeah, well, you try to hold one of those heavy buffers in a little boat while you're polishing the hull of a big boat. The dinghy started pushing away from the yacht, and I ended up in the middle of the water!"

"You're lucky you weren't electrocuted!" Emma said. "Especially with your luck."

"Ha ha. Well, anyway, it was fun. And I'm so tan and fit. Wait until you see me. Speaking of that—how about this weekend? Can I come down there to see you?"

"Uh…" that caught Emma by surprise. All Jake had talked about since June was Savannah was too dangerous for him. There were too many drug triggers for him. "Are you sure you want to? I mean, you said you couldn't come to Savannah because of all the dealers you know."

"I've been clean for two months and haven't even had a craving. I haven't had a beer or a glass of wine. I'll be fine.

Besides, I'll meet you at that strip club over the bridge, so I won't even have my truck in Savannah. What do you say?"

"What about the police?" she asked nervously.

"I'm small potatoes to them. They won't come back. And my truck won't be there, so they'll have no reason to think I'm there even if they drive by for some reason. We'll both be safe. And I'll duck down in the car so the neighbors won't even know I'm there," he pushed.

"Okay, Jake. As long as you spend the rest of the week looking for a new job. Don't get passive about it. You're not getting another dollar from me, Jake. This was it. No more."

"I know, baby. I know. You won't have to. When I get a new job, you'll start getting paid back."

"Right, Jake. Just like I was when you had this job," Emma got her dig in.

"I meant to this week. I swear, Emma. I was caught up, and I was going to bring you a hundred dollars. I have it on me. I really didn't think I'd lose this job. Carter swore I had job security. I never imagined I would get the ax like this," he grumbled.

"Yeah, I believe you, Jake," she said sarcastically.

"I know. You shouldn't. But I really did. Now the money will have to last until I get a new job. I'll go everywhere this week, and I'll find a good job. One that will take care us both."

"Well, good luck. I hope you find something. Keep me posted," Emma said. "And I'll see you this weekend."

Emma prepared carefully for Jake's visit. She took all of her jewelry, other than what she wore every day, and put it in her safe. She took the key to the safe and put it in her safe-deposit box at the bank. She took all the keys to the house and the spare alarm fob and put them in the safe. She took all of her good liquor and hid it in the laundry room, behind the cleaning material. She even moved all the beer into the refrigerator in the garage, hoping he wouldn't look for it there. Emma was pleased that she had already packed her valuable artwork, so Jake couldn't even find it.

She was furious that she had to take such precautions, but Emma was not stupid. Jake had been clean for two months now, but she was not taking any chances. After all, when they met he had told her he had been clean for six months. She hated the real fact that he could be lying and only wanted to visit her to get his hands on something to pawn so he could afford the drugs he might desperately crave. She could never be sure.

Once her house was in order, Emma went to the grocery. She bought ground beef and onion rolls. She had to admit, Jake made the best burgers she'd ever eaten. She made sure there were enough hotdog buns and bought his cheap hotdogs. Since Emma didn't drink milk and Jake did, she bought a half-gallon of milk. She added a few of his favorites, some fresh fruit and ice cream. Emma flat out refused to buy Spaghetti-Os. She did buy steaks for grilling and fresh green beans—the only vegetable he would eat.

All Emma could really think about was her neighbors. She was sure if they saw him, they would call the police. Not because they hated Jake but because they loved Emma. When she picked him up at the strip joint on the other side of the Talmadge Bridge that connected Savannah with South Carolina, he looked so good that once again, she forgot all the negatives.

When they neared her house, Jake scrunched himself down in his seat so no one could see him. She drove right into the garage and closed the door before they got out. No one saw him.

They decided to take a swim before dinner. It was August in Savannah and ungodly hot. The blue of the pool against the moss-laden oak trees and setting sun looked too inviting. They put on their swim suits, brought an ashtray to the side of the pool, took plastic glasses with ice water to the pool, turned soft jazz music on all the outdoor speakers, and waded into the pool. It was glorious. Emma had the Jacuzzi jets on the steps turned to full power, so they sat in the warm water opposite each other, letting the jets relax their muscles and their minds. Together, they paddled to the deeper end of the pool—which, in Emma's pool, was only five feet. Jake held onto her, and they were quickly wrapped around each other. Emma's long hair was clipped on top of her head so it didn't get wet, but Jake wanted to see it flow. He pulled the clip out of her hair and watched the blonde hair flow through the water. She looked like an angelic mermaid.

They kissed passionately, and Emma could feel the hard need in him pressing against her. He untied the halter top of her bikini and tossed it onto the pool deck. He began to nuzzle her neck and breasts.

"I love you, Emma. I don't want to live without you," he murmured. She had lost her voice and merely purred her response. Running her hands down his tanned and muscled chest and arms, she nearly came right there. She wrapped her legs around his waist and bit lightly on his shoulder. Finally, he pulled off his trunks, and Emma thought, thank God. He gets the idea. She was so sure he would take her right to the edge and leave her dissatisfied like he had done so often in the past. But he pulled off her swimsuit bottoms, and once again, she wrapped her legs around him. This was perfect, she thought. Since Jake was so much taller than Emma, it was difficult to make love in the shower, but the pool was ideal. They made love—quietly—right there. Her neighbors were classic busybodies, so if they made too much noise, her neighbors would surely know what was going on. Especially Mark, right next door. He often worked in his backyard and had been known to poke his head over the fence to say hello. Or worse, his fifteen-year-old son might be playing basketball back there. But it was quiet next door.

Their lovemaking in the pool was a first for them, and Emma hoped not the last time. It had been amazing. When they were spent, they floated to the edge to light cigarettes and take long drinks of their water. Sated and happy, they decided they were also starving. Burgers would definitely fill the bill. Jake wrapped a towel around Emma first, and then himself. Emma grabbed their suits and threw them in the dryer, and then went into her bathroom to start the long process of blow-drying her hair. She put on a lace tank top and shorts. Unsure as to whether or not Jake would be up for another romp later and knowing she had to take a bath later anyway, she wore plain cotton underwear. When she left her bathroom, she found Jake in the kitchen preparing the burgers.

"Hi there," she said with a smile. At that moment in time, she felt a twinge of happiness seeing him standing in her kitchen.

"Hi, yourself," he replied. He was wearing a sleeveless tank top and shorts, as well. She wanted to eat him up more than the burgers.

"What can I do to help?" she asked.

"I think I've got it. What do you want with your burger?"

"Some chips is fine. You want some baked beans? I can get those ready for you," she offered.

"Yeah, that sounds great, baby." He was busily adding spices and making patties. She still snuck up behind him and put her arms around his waist. Then she playfully grabbed his adorable ass. "Hey!" he laughed. "That's cheating."

"Couldn't help it. Those fluffy biscuits of yours were looking too squeezable," she said laughing. Emma loved using that term of endearment because Cheryl had used it on him when he was a kid. She knew it mildly annoyed him, but it was too appropriate. He had buns of steel, but they did remind her of fluffy biscuits.

"Well, instead of playing with my buns, how about getting the hamburger buns out of the fridge?"

"Party pooper!" she mock-pouted.

"That's me," he laughed.

He took the meat out to the grill and fired up the gas. As was his custom, he sat smoking a cigarette, staring at the burgers. Emma generally put the meat on the grill and went into the kitchen. Not Jake. He watched over his cooking every second. Maybe it was from all that rib cooking he had done at his restaurant was all she could think.

They enjoyed their huge cheeseburgers in the great room in front of the TV. They caught Cash Cab, the first time they'd seen it together in months. Then Jake introduced her to a show she had never seen before, and she was immediately hooked. Family Guy was an adult animated comedy that came on at seven o'clock, and Jake insisted she watch. People either loved the Griffin family or hated them, but Jake knew his Emma. They had the same taste. From that night on, Emma TiVo'd every episode of Family Guy. Eventually she would buy the entire series on DVD.

They played Scene It, they played pool, and watched one of Emma's top five favorite movies of all time, Tune in Tomorrow. Jake loved it. The entire weekend was exactly like that first night. They made love, they ate good meals, and they played. Jake never touched a drink and never left her side. It was one of the best weekends she had ever had. Emma couldn't believe it was Jake that gave her such a great time.

Jake found a new job quickly. He took a cooking job at a burger joint. They served sandwiches, fries, and beer. He was not happy with it, but it paid the bills and the food was free. He got into several arguments because it was assumed that he knew how to make everything on the menu. With Jake's picky eating habits, there were several items he had no clue about putting together. Club sandwiches were his nemesis. With his refusal to eat lettuce or tomatoes, he had no idea what a club sandwich even was. His boss thought he was a moron. Who doesn't know how to make a club sandwich? Or a Reuben? His boss didn't understand Jake at all.

When Jake would call during his break, he would whine continually. His ego couldn't take the abuse, but Emma couldn't blame him. This time it really wasn't his fault. He had such a shallow food palate; it wasn't fair to be angry at him for it. His boss should have been a little more patient and explained how to prepare the foods that Jake didn't know already. She was sympathetic when they spoke.

What Emma also learned that scared the hell out of her was he was also given free alcohol. With his evening burger, he too often had a glass of wine or a beer. Even though Jake was not an alcoholic—he didn't need a second drink—it had proven to be enough to push him to crave cocaine. Emma was scared to death. He had been doing so well, she thought. Combining the alcohol with his damaged ego could push him over the edge.

When he called, she told him as much. He swore he wasn't using and still had absolutely no craving.

"It was only one glass of wine, baby. It's nothing. I've been clean for three months, and I'm not about to jeopardize that. My sobriety is too important to me," he said.

"Then you shouldn't be drinking," she said firmly. "You know that spirals you down the wrong path."

"I know. To be honest, I didn't even enjoy it. I won't drink any more, okay?"

"Jake, if you want to stay out of trouble and keep the police out of your life, don't take any chances. Just remember, you're driving illegally. If you get pulled over for anything—a broken tail light, not using your turn indicator, anything—you're fucked. Remember?" she lambasted him. "A DUI and they would throw away the key. Keep that in your mind with every sip."

"Shit. I know you're right. I don't know what I was thinking. It was free, so I just—shit!"

"Yeah, well, don't forget the situation you're in."

Chapter Twenty-Six

During the month of September, Emma and Jake met discretely many weekends. He had been clean for four months, with the exception of his occasional glass of wine or single beer after work. Sometimes when she picked him up across the bridge, Emma could smell the alcohol on his breath, but it didn't seem to make a difference in their activities. In the past, he had he used alcohol to cover up his cocaine use, so he wouldn't be able to perform sexually. That wasn't a problem. They had fun, swam, and he had his normal hearty appetite. If he was keeping secrets, Emma couldn't see them.

During the first visits to Savannah, Jake's nerves were on edge. If the doorbell rang, he ran to the back of the house for fear it was the police. It was usually Ray, who was terribly depressed over his impending divorce from Samantha. He would sit on the sofa, smoke Jake's cigarettes, and vacilate between tears and anger. Or Steve would drop in to give Emma support and Jake advice. It appeared to be the Savannah way. People didn't call before they stopped by—they just knocked on the door. But each time, Jake panicked. Emma was jittery as well, knowing that he was wanted by the police in Savannah. She finally taped a black napkin over the beveled glass in the door so no one could see inside. After a couple of these weekends, their guard was down because the police didn't seem to care about Jake.

Emma took another trip to Atlanta, but this time it was for

two reasons. House hunting was a priority because she had to know for sure where she would settle down once her house sold. But this time she went to see a famous psychic. The woman was referred to her by a close friend of hers in Savannah who was a writer. The psychic only took appointments from referrals—no walk-ins and no strangers. She didn't advertise because she didn't need it. She had famous, dedicated clients.

Emma met with Mary the afternoon she arrived in Atlanta. She sat in a chair across from Mary, who sat at a desk. Emma was determined to give nothing away. She would let Mary see what she could see without any help. Mary's first words were, "Your books will be published." Hmm. That was interesting. Emma hadn't told her about her writing. Then Mary told Emma that she was moving.

"You're moving to Atlanta, aren't you? Oh, this is where you belong. It's your place." Mary told her. Emma had not said a word about meeting with her realtor the following day, and she hadn't even settled on Atlanta. "You're in a relationship, but you're troubled. He's going to use drugs again during the holidays," Mary told her. "And you're wondering if he'll get caught. Yes, dear, he will."

Mary told her several other pertinent, personal facts. Information that no one could know. As Emma wrote the check for fifty dollars that her friend had told her was Mary's fee, Mary stopped her.

"Emma, the fee is $125. But I'll tell you what. You give me that check and dump this guy of yours now, we'll be square. If you dump him now, you'll sell your house in December. If you don't, it won't be until spring," Mary told her.

Emma couldn't do it. She knew it was right but she wasn't

emotionally ready. She wrote a second check for seventy-five dollars and slid it across the desk. "I'm sorry, Mary. I'm not ready."

"I understand. It's a tough decision."

The rest of Emma's trip was successful. She found a house that she liked. It was small, but it had a great deal of potential with some paint and minor changes. The problem was it was in foreclosure. She would have to wait and see if she could buy it. She told Gary to make an offer. The next day he called her back and said it was already sold. But at least Gary was clear on what she would buy and that she was a legitimate buyer.

As October began, Jake received an odd phone call. He was asked to interview for a management job with a small franchised restaurant chain. He thought it strange because he didn't remember putting in an application with them. Someone must have referred him was all he could figure, but he was ecstatic. This was finally a job that could actually become a career. He interviewed for the job, and shock of all shocks, he got the job. He called Emma with the good news.

"Honey, you're not going to believe it, but I just got hired as manager at your favorite hamburger joint! Manager! Salary and benefits! Is that fantastic, or what?"

"That is great! I'm so glad. When do you start?" Emma replied with equal enthusiasm. Jesus, maybe he really was on his way toward becoming a stable adult. If he could stay out of trouble, which it looked like he was, she might have a future with him. Of course, they couldn't get married. Cheryl told her he had stolen one identity and made up another, so exactly who would she be marrying? A phantom, a ghost, a nonentity. But he assured her that he would be able to take what he had and make a real identity from it. Emma did a bit of her own research and didn't see how he could do it without a boatload of money. It would cost thousands to get a real false identity, and you had to know the right people. Jake certainly didn't. But according to her research, if someone could get a birth certificate that could pass for authentic, he could go to several states and get a real driver's license. With the driver's license, the trick would be to get a real social security number. But how a thirty-one-year-old man could convince the Social Security Office that he had never been assigned a number was beyond even Emma's imagination.

"I start on Sunday. And the best part of the job is if I do well and they like me, they'll pay for me to open a franchise in another city. It would be all mine to run. Isn't that awesome?"

"Absolutely. Hey, don't forget to get Halloween night off. Remember the party? God, I've been waiting all year for this party—ever day since I went last year with Ray and Sam! Remember when I bought the costume in Chicago? That was months ago. I already talked to Ray about it, and he said it was okay to bring you and Steve," she reminded him.

"No problem. Besides, even if I'm late it'll be okay," he answered.

"And the food at the party is so great! Sweet Potatoes caters it every year."

"It's still two weeks away so don't worry, baby. I'll be there. My boss is such a great guy. He's smart and patient. You'd really like him," he said enthusiastically. "I start Sunday at ten thirty in the morning. He wants me there early so I can study the menu and train. But hey, the only thing I really have to remember is their ten thousand varieties of milk shakes," he laughed.

"You're kidding!"

"No. With the flavors they have, there are like ten thousand possibilities of combinations. You know, like mint chocolate or strawberry banana or, I don't know, mango pineapple," he told her.

"Wow! And I thought thirty-one flavors was a lot! So I could get a pina colada milk shake?"

"Yeah, pretty much anything you want."

"Sounds like fun," Emma told Jake. "As Joe would say, don't fuck up!"

"Yep, that's what he would say. I owe him that much for everything I did to him," Jake reminisced sadly.

"Yeah, you do. Will I see you this weekend?" Emma asked.

"Sure. I'll just have to leave either Saturday night or really early Sunday morning," he told her.

"It's probably best if you leave Saturday night. That way you get a good night's sleep and don't have to rush in the morning. How far away is the restaurant from your house?" Emma asked.

"Oh, that's the best part! It's a quarter of a mile away! No using a ton of gas in that guzzler of mine! I could practically walk there," he added.

"We'll have to celebrate. How about we grill steaks for dinner Friday night? Oh, wait, who am I talking to? We'll order a pizza!"

"Oh, baby! You know me too well," he cooed.

"Yeah, I think I do," she agreed.

Their night together was fine. Fun and frolic. There was little he could manage to steal, so she was safe. He didn't have the key or the combination to the alarm system, so he couldn't take her car and sneak out. She even kept her car keys in her purse, hidden in the closet. Normally she kept her keys in a bowl by the door but not when Jake came over. She had learned her lesson.

The night that he had made drug deals from her house he had somehow managed to turn off the alarm without waking her. Since she learned that, she made sure he couldn't even find a remote control for the alarm system. Emma was far from trusting him, if she ever would. She thought she could detect his lies, but he was good. When he needed to lie, he did a good job at it. Hell, he could be lying to her at that very minute. Did he really have this new job? She would find out on Sunday or Monday. She would call the restaurant and ask for him. She would introduce herself via phone to his boss and give him her number.

Jake actually made it working full-time until Halloween. He got the day off and drove all the way to Savannah specifically for this annual Halloween soiree. The party was at a fabulous mansion on the water, and the Victorian home was decorated to the tens for the holiday. It was catered and they had two open bars. Emma couldn't wait. She had bought her costume months ago in Chicago with Jake, so he knew how important it was to her. Emma picked up Jake late that afternoon, and he plopped tentatively on the love seat, while she fussed over her French maid costume. Unfortunately, Jake was now suffering from a new ailment—hemorrhoids. If it wasn't poison oak, it was hemorrhoids. He was complaining and moaning like a little girl. He whined that he was in so much pain, he couldn't bear it.

When Steve arrived for the party dressed as a pirate, he sat down and talked to Jake first. Jake figured that since Steve was gay, he would know about hemorrhoids. He did. Steve gave him excellent advice.

"Jake, you have to run bath water as hot as you can tolerate it and stick your butt under the running water. The key is to be on your knees to take the pressure off your butt. That will take down the inflammation. And don't lie down like you are. Elevate your feet. Here," and Steve walked over to Jake and put a pillow under his thighs to take some of the pressure off his rear end.

"Oh, that's better," Jake sighed.

"See, you need to take the strain off your butt," Steve explained. "The same with the bath. Don't sit in it. That won't help. If you turn your back to the faucet and let the water sluice down your backside, the heat will make it feel better." Steve was patient and calm. He watched Jake's face to be sure his advice was registering. It seemed to be, so he patted Jake's shoulder and said, "You'll be okay, big guy."

Emma and Steve went into Emma's bathroom so she could help put the finishing touches on Steve's eye makeup. He wanted a Johnny Depp pirate look. He borrowed one of Emma's big silver hoop earrings and he was set. Emma was dressed as a French maid, feather duster and all. When they walked back into the den, Jake was still not dressed.

"What's going on?" Emma asked. "Why aren't you dressed?"

"I'm not going," he pouted. "I'm in agony."

"Well, for Christ's sake, Jake. Why the hell did you come all the way here if you weren't going to be my date at the party? You know how important this is to me. I've been waiting all year for it!" Emma was furious. He was taking advantage of her. He had her house, her food, and God knew what else. Was he looking for something to steal?

"If you're really going to be that upset, then fine. I'll just go," he threatened.

"Yeah, I'm really going to be that upset. Why the fuck did you drive all the way here if you weren't going? Why didn't you stay home and be a miserable bastard by yourself?"

"You know it's been bothering me all week," he defended.

"Oh, and that's better? You've known all week that we couldn't have sex, you weren't going to the party, we couldn't do anything, and still you came? God, you're as selfish as ever!" Emma quickly grabbed her purse and stormed out with Steve. "I'll be back—eventually. Don't wait up!" She slammed the door behind him. Then quickly apologized to Steve for her outburst.

"Honey, you never have to apologize to me," he told her. "He's the one who's being a selfish baby. Jesus, Em. When are you going to have enough of his games? You know I love you and I support whatever you decide, but haven't you given him enough chances?"

"Yeah, I have. I don't think I'm going to be able to stomach it much longer. I know that if he does drugs one more time, that's it. It's over. I couldn't take it. That's assuming he hasn't done any coke already. He swears he's been clean since his arrest in June. But do I know for sure?" Emma said as they got into her car to meet Ray at the party.

"No, you don't," Steve reluctantly told her. "You can't know for sure. I've known addicts, honey, and they're expert liars. It's their lifeblood. If you're asking my opinion, I don't think he's using. He's too calm. He'd be much jumpier if he was using. But will he? The minute we left the house he could have made a call and had it delivered."

"Thanks, pal. That made my night," Emma retorted.

"I'm not trying to scare you, sweetie, but it's possible. Not likely but possible. I think he was genuinely in pain and wanted to wallow in it," Steve told her. Emma changed the subject.

"God, I hope I can find this place. I went last year, and it was so amazing. Okay, I know it's off Waters, and Ray said it's just past the Truman Parkway. I remember it's on the right and there's a really long driveway to the house," Emma said half to herself.

"I know where it is. There's a lot of those huge mansions up ahead on the right. Okay, there," he pointed. "You probably want to turn right at that corner." She followed his directions and saw the drive. There were tiki torches lit all the way up to the house.

"Yep, this is it. Wait 'till you see the house! It's Victorian and absolutely gorgeous. I would kill for the kitchen alone. The dining room seats twenty-four!"

"Ooh! Sounds fabulous!" Steve said in his most gay voice.

"And the pool! It's amazing. Then you go past the pool and there's a bridge to a dock that sits right on the marsh. The whole property is great," she said stepping out of the car and ducking under the live oaks to walk toward the house. "For the party they have a live band and it's catered by Sweet Potatoes.

Awesome food." They walked into the grand entrance, and Steve's mouth nearly dropped open. The high ceilings and wood floors made the house look even bigger than it was, even with more than a hundred people milling about. Emma and Steve walked straight back through the house to the patio beyond. The wrap-around porch was covered and had tables set up with glorious food. Sweet Potatoes was a family-owned restaurant that specialized in Southern cuisine. Their trademark dish—other than their various sweet potato dishes—was lemon collard greens. They were scrumptious.

"Let's take a look around and grab a drink before we eat," Steve suggested. They walked over to the outside bar (as there was a bar set up in the game room, as well), and each grabbed a beer.

"I'll be damned if Jake is going to ruin my evening," Emma said as she took a swig from the bottle. "I'm going to have fun and flirt. And wearing this little outfit, I should get my flirting reciprocated," Emma pushed up the bra on her low-cut maid's uniform. There wasn't much fabric at all. It was low in the front and very short, showing off her bosoms and long legs. She wore fishnet stockings and black spike heels. She had done her hair in an up do, with the little white lace doily atop. Her lips were fire-engine red, as were her fingernails.

Emma loved Halloween. It was the one night of the year she could be bawdy. She could be whatever she wanted. She didn't have to be herself at all. But as she thought about the holiday, her angered simmered. She should have her man at her side, making sexy comments and protecting her from other men. She was downright pissed off that he had not only blown off the party but blown her off as well. She also knew damn well the costume wouldn't get her any sex.

"Damn straight, sister. You flaunt those girls!" Steve agreed. "I hope you get picked up by the most gorgeous guy here—or I do!"

"Well, one of us should get lucky. Ah, speaking of lucky, there's Ray," Emma pointed. He was already pretty well trashed. Ray sat cross-legged on the ground in front of the band. He had a blank expression on his face, and his eyes were partially closed. "I guess we'll have to wait until he comes out of his trance."

Eventually Ray joined Emma and Steve at a table, where they were eating. Ray never ate a bite. He was getting so skinny, Emma hardly recognized him. They talked for a while, Ray asking where Jake was. Emma told him the truth.

"Oh, darlin'," Ray said in his native Savannah accent, "you shouldn't be here in that outfit without him. I might take advantage of you."

"No, you wouldn't. You're still hung up on Sam," she said with a small grin.

"Yeah, you're right," and a tear spilled down his cheek. He and Sam were an odd couple from the time Emma had met them. Sam tossed Ray out every six months, but it looked like this time was the last. She had finally actually filed for divorce.

Emma and Steve remained seated and watched all the costumed people. It was great fun. These were mostly wealthy people, and they could afford elaborate costumes. She couldn't help but think about how Jake would enjoy people watching. The shithead! God, he was still so selfish, she thought. Emma wanted to stay out as late as possible. She wanted him to suffer—and wonder. She decided she wouldn't even consider leaving until Jake called her.

Emma and Steve took a tour of the house. It was owned by friends of Ray's—actually customers of Ray's, when he worked at Jaycee's Café. The man was a prominent doctor in town, and his wife enjoyed life as a doctor's wife. The house itself was magnificent. The upstairs, she finally saw, was as beautiful as the downstairs. There were several bedrooms, a library, and a master suite that put Emma's to shame. It was as big as her great room and had a full-length balcony overlooking the pool and the marsh. She imagined having her coffee on that patio, doing her crossword puzzle, and gazing at the water. There was a huge Jacuzzi in which at least four could probably fit, on one side of the master bathroom. On the other side of the bathroom was a glassed-in shower with eight showerheads. A double sink sat in the middle. On the far left side was a small, separate room for the toilet and bidet. The enormous walk-in closet was between the shower and tub, taking up the whole wall and went fifteen feet back.

"Oh, Steve! I want that bathroom!" she cooed.

"Ditto, sweetie."

Disturbing their fantasizing over the house, Emma's cell phone rang. At nine thirty, Jake finally called.

"When are you coming home?" he asked.

"When I damn well feel like it," she answered.

"I'm sorry, baby. I didn't think it was so important to you. But now I wish I'd gone."

"You would have had a good time. Too bad! And you're full of shit. You knew how important it was to me. I've only been talking about it for six months. See ya," and she hung up.

"Steve, why the hell did he come to Savannah? It wasn't to

see me—that's for sure. We ain't havin' sex tonight—that's another for sure. So why? Just to be an equal pain in my ass?"

"Sugar, I couldn't tell you. Maybe when he left home he thought he'd be okay. If I felt like he did, I sure wouldn't leave my home. I wouldn't want to be a burden to others. I know how painful hemorrhoids are, and I would want to be left alone," Steve replied.

"Well, I wish he had made that decision. I know he's not helping his cause by being a selfish child. But Jake is not known for his good judgment," Emma said as they decided to leave despite Jake.

"Nope. He's definitely one light bulb short of a chandelier."

When Emma and Steve returned home, Jake was exactly where they left him. Plopped on the love seat with his legs propped up on the pillow.

"Did you eat?" Emma asked him, while Steve sat down on the sofa.

"Yeah. I had hotdogs and baked beans. And a peanut butter sandwich," he replied.

"Peanut butter? Now that was clever," Steve put in. "Jake, the last thing you want with hemorrhoids is constipation. Hello? Constipation, pressure, pain?"

"Oh, yeah. I didn't think of that," Jake answered.

"What's new?" Emma tossed into the mix. "When do you ever think before you act?"

"I know, I know. Be nice. I'm in pain," he whined.

"Then why the fuck did you come here? So I can have the same pain in my ass as you do?"

"So how was the party?" Jake asked.

"It was awesome," Steve told him. "You missed the best party of the year."

"I wish I'd gone instead of lying here feeling sorry for myself," Jake said.

"Too late," Emma ended the conversation. "I'm going to change."

"And I'm heading home. I love you, sweetie," Steve hugged Emma.

"I love you, too. I'll talk to you soon," Emma answered.

"And you," Steve pointed a finger Jake. "If you need anything, just call me. Okay?"

"Thanks, man. And thank you for taking Emma. At least she wasn't alone."

Once Steve was gone, Emma glared at Jake. She was disgusted.

"I'm going to take a bath and go to bed. I suggest you sleep in the guest room. I had every guy at the party asking me to clean his house—as long as I wear this costume. My own boyfriend hasn't said a word about how I look. Since we're not going to have sex, I'd rather you slept in the other room."

"I'll sleep on the couch," he muttered. "Watch TV for a while and go to sleep. Look, I'm really sorry, Em. I love you."

"Yeah, right. This is almost as bad as when you had poison oak. You're a spoiled child when you are in pain. You knew that before you came here. Why did you come?"

"To see your face," he answered quickly.

"Well, you've seen it. Now you can leave." With that she walked out of the room and into her bedroom.

Chapter Twenty-Seven

Jake's hemorrhoid problem persisted well into November. What exacerbated the problem was Jake's job. Since getting the job as manager of a restaurant, he was on his feet all day, which put all the pressure on his butt. Jake called Steve to ask for advice.

"Jake, I explained this to you on Halloween." Steve explained the whole routine again with total exasperation. Was this guy a total moron? Steve thought. I already told him. Jeez!

"Thanks, Steve. I really appreciate your help, man," Jake answered.

"No problem, Jake. That with Preparation H should get the problem solved quickly. If it doesn't, you'll need surgery. I had it done. What a hemorrhoid actually is, is a blood clot. It's nothing to fool around about. If it isn't gone by the end of next week, you'll have to go to the doctor. Call any time you want, Jake. I'm here to help," Steve said, as he hung up the phone. He silently prayed there would be no more calls.

When Emma spoke with Jake, he told her he had talked to Steve.

"He gave me really good advice, baby. I'm going to do it tonight when I get home."

"I hope it helps, Jake. Steve wouldn't steer you wrong," she told him.

Jake called Emma the following day, still complaining. But once again, what was new. He lived to complain. Jake thought he was going to die because he had a cold. Emma actually had to take him to the Emergency Room once because of a stupid head cold. And Emma had a hemorrhoid once. It only itched. She used some Preparation H and she was fine. She also didn't need to tell the whole world about it. But this was Jake she was dealing with.

"Did you do what Steve told you to do?" she asked first.

"Yeah, I took a really hot shower and had the spray aimed at my ass. I also tried a hot bath to soak it," he told her.

"Jake! That's not what Steve told you to do. You did the exact opposite of what he told you! What is wrong with you?" she chided him.

"I did?" he asked innocently.

"Yeah, you did. He told you specifically to sit on your knees with your butt under the faucet. The shower put more pressure on the hemorrhoid by standing up. Jesus, Jake. Do you want to go to the hospital and have it cut out?"

"No. Absolutely not. Okay, I'm a dumb shit. I'll call you later," he ended the call abruptly.

Emma called Steve and told him what had happened. He was, to say the least, annoyed.

"What is wrong with that boy? Why does he ask for advice and do the opposite? Is he just fucking stupid?" Steve said.

"I'd say that's probably the reason. Steve, I'm losing patience here. Maybe he's not doing drugs, but I've never seen someone make so many bad decisions. It's like he was never taught how to think. I know his mother did a lot of his thinking for him but my God! He's not a child. He should know how to add two and two by now!"

"Well, he certainly can't. Sweetie, patience is neither of our virtues. Maybe we're assuming too much. I mean, I had that long conversation with him about higher power in the universe and recommended he write in a journal…"

"So did I," she interrupted.

"He won't do anything to help himself. He doesn't listen," Steve said with frustration.

"I know. He's so bound to fuck up again," she said.

"I think he needs to fuck up," Steve agreed. "I think his self-esteem is so low, he has to find a way to ruin even the good things in his life. He can't stand being successful. Look at you, for example. He has a gorgeous, smart, loving woman, and he's throwing it away. I don't think he believes he deserves any success. Certainly not you."

"He's told me that from the beginning," Emma said to Steve. "He's never believed that he deserves me."

"And he's right. He doesn't."

"Thanks, sweetie," Emma said.

"It's the truth. You deserve so much better than Jake. You deserve a man who will treat you with respect and love. Someone who will give to you, not only take from you. Honey, you're not eating. You're not sleeping. What exactly are you getting from this relationship?"

"Sex – when he wants it. Ego, I guess. I mean, look at him!"

"Sweetie, you need to look in the mirror!" Steve added.

"Why couldn't you be straight? Or I be a man? We'd be perfect together!"

"If only you had a dick!" he laughed. "But Emma, if I went for women, you'd be tops on my list. I'd fuck you in a heartbeat!"

"Thanks, Steve. You're the best. I love you," Emma said.

"I love you to, sweetie. I'll talk to you soon. Keep me posted," he hung up the phone.

By Thanksgiving Jake's hemorrhoid was finally gone and he drove to Savannah for dinner. Emma met him at the strip club over the bridge and she drove him into Savannah. Since neither of them really liked turkey and Jake didn't like any of the traditional trimmings, Emma made her own version of Thanksgiving dinner. She baked a chicken, made a rice casserole that was her mother's recipe, and green beans. She made biscuits and homemade pineapple pie, another of her mother's recipes. A recipe that she was not permitted to share outside the immediate family. Pineapple pie had become a Thanksgiving tradition since Emma's mother was allergic to most fruit (including apples) and most nuts. So pineapple pie represented Thanksgiving to Emma.

They ate at the dinner table, which always made Jake uncomfortable and made Emma rather ill. At the dinner table, even with classical music playing and candles lit, Jake still wolfed down his food. There was no conversation, no slow enjoyment of the meal. Most families have a leisurely dinner, talk about their day or the world, and take at least an hour to enjoy a festive meal. Not Jake. Unless the television was in front of him, he quietly ate his meal as though it were his last.

He spent the night, even though he had to go to work the next day. He didn't have to be there until noon, so he stayed. They did make love but it was quick and not fulfilling for Emma. It was Jake's pleasure that was paramount in this sexual encounter. If Emma didn't know better – and maybe she didn't – he had used drugs in the past week. He was turning back into the selfish person he had been.

Jake continued to work at the burger restaurant and enjoyed it. He was working at the counter making milkshakes and getting tips for his friendly manner and good job. His boss appeared to be happy with his work and saw a future with Jake. All was going well. Emma saw very little of him, due to his long hours but Jake's future was more important to her. If he could stay clean and hold a job for more than a month, that was Emma's top priority concerning Jake.

Suddenly, Emma got a call from Jake. He was panicky and speaking quickly.

"There was a robbery at the restaurant, Emma. Five hundred dollars was stolen. I left it on the desk and forgot to put it in the safe. When I got home, I remembered I hadn't set the alarm and went back really late to turn it on. The money was gone. The police have been there and they're sure I did it. I went to the police station to answer questions, and I swore I didn't do it," he explained.

"Did you do it?" Emma asked.

"No! I swear to God, I didn't!"

"What are you going to do? How can you prove your innocence?" Emma asked. She knew damn well he did it. There was no way on earth he would voluntarily walk into a police station. Even he wasn't that stupid. He would have to know they could fingerprint him, and Jake was basically a coward. His story didn't add up.

"I don't think I can prove it. They're waiting for the results from the security camera before they can arrest me. I'm probably the only one caught on film, but maybe the person who did will be on there. I won't know until tomorrow. I think I'm going to have to leave. I called my boss and he sounded like he believed me, but the police are going to convince him that I did."

"Jake, why don't you wait until tomorrow to see what happens? If you really didn't do it, the truth will come out. I believe that. You love that job so much and your boss. It doesn't make sense that you would jeopardize it all for that small amount of money," Emma told him. She was sure he took it, but she was trying to get through to him what a stupid stunt he had pulled. "Have you talked to Cheryl?"

"Yeah, I told her. She didn't believe me either. I'll wait until morning, but I'll probably have to leave here. I can't afford to take a chance. Maybe you're right, and they'll see on the video who really did it, but I doubt it. With my luck, it'll be my face on that video."

"Jake, if you do decide to leave, I'm not paying for another room for you. I just can't. You've fucked up too many times, and I'm not funding another one. If you need money for rent, you'll have to get it from Cheryl," Emma told him.

"I'll talk to you in the morning. Hopefully it'll all be okay," he said and hung up abruptly.

Emma immediately called Cheryl, her best source of information about Jake. Jake would confide in Cheryl before he'd tell Emma, and she could get more of the truth about Jake from Cheryl.

"Hey, Cheryl," Emma started. "So I hear Jake already called you. What do you think?"

"He did it. He swore he didn't, but I know my brother. He did it. I wish he would 'fess up already. He won't. I pushed and pushed, and he wouldn't give," Cheryl told her.

"I thought the same thing. There's no way in hell that Jake would waltz into a police station to give a statement," Emma added.

"Exactly! This whole story is so fake. It reeks of lies. He's talking about going down to Florida. Like, right over the border," Cheryl told her.

"Well, I'm not paying for another one of his fuck ups. I just can't, Cheryl. If you can come up with the money he'll need for the room, then he can go wherever he wants. But I won't do it," Emma told her. "And he'll have to ask for money or else we'll know he stole the five hundred."

"I'll help him, Em. You've done enough. It won't cost but a couple hundred bucks for two weeks, so I'll find a way. I just can't tell Aaron. Don't worry. I'll take care of it," Cheryl promised.

"Thank you so much. If he could manage to keep a job long enough to get a paycheck, he could afford this himself. But if he took the five hundred…" Emma never finished the statement.

"Yeah. If he took it, why does he need money from either of us? He couldn't possibly have spent five hundred dollars on drugs. So where did it go?"

"This stinks to high heaven, Cheryl. I'm sure he took the money, but what did he do with it?"

"I'll find out. Jake can't keep a secret from me," Cheryl assured her.

"Okay. Meanwhile, we wait."

"Yeah, we wait."

The next morning, Jake was terrified and on the road. He had thrown all his belongings into his truck—again. He was driving south. He called Emma.

"I'm on the way to Florida. The police were at the house this morning. My roommate got rid of them. Told them I wasn't there. I was right. My face was the only one on the video, so I'm fucked. Officer James called me and asked me to come back into police headquarters. He was so cocky. He said he always got his man."

"What did you say?" Emma asked.

"That my favorite movie was Catch Me if You Can. Fuck him and his 'I always get my man' shit." Jake answered glibly.

"Good work, Jake. Get him not only looking for you but piss him off even more. And by the way, Jake, Tom Hanks did catch Leonardo DiCaprio in the end of that movie," she chided.

"Yeah, but not for years and this asshole isn't going to be looking for me for years over five hundred dollars. I told him I was innocent and to talk to my boss. But I called my boss, and he said he believed me and I should come to work today. I know they're going to grab me. He's setting me up."

"I still believe you took the money, Jake."

"Well, I didn't. If I did, I wouldn't be broke, would I? I'm owed two weeks' salary, and now I can't get it," he complained. Emma changed the subject, seeing it wasn't going anywhere.

"So where are you going?" she asked.

"I'm meeting Cheryl at the supermarket. She's bringing money for my rent. I found a place just over the Florida border. The woman lives with her parents so she can take care of them. Her ad said she also includes dinner with rent. So that saves even more money for me. And I have a job interview in two days. It's for a water purification company. Straight commission but I can make a lot of money. I used my roommate's computer all night and got the call this morning. Maybe things will finally turn around for me. For us," he added.

"Well, that all sounds good. Jake, why don't you turn yourself in? This is getting ridiculous. You can't hold a job, you keep screwing up, and you've had to run twice already. Do you really want to spend the rest of your life like this?"

"I have to, Emma. I can't go back to prison. I can't. I'll get my act together, Emma. I promise. I know I'm meant to do something meaningful with my life. And I know you're meant to be a part of it. I'll call you when I'm settled. Okay? Please, Emma. I can't live without you. I'd rather die than lose you," he wept.

"Okay, Jake. I'll talk to you soon," she hung up.

Emma needed help. She was beyond the ability to deal with this situation alone. Emma had been raised to cope with life, to be rational and reasonable and logical. It wasn't working. She thought about actually seeing a therapist, but that didn't feel right. If she started with a therapist, it could take weeks before they arrived at the meat of the problem. A therapist would want to start with the beginning, and Emma didn't need help with her parents and her childhood. She needed help about the now. The most intelligent, stable, and aware person she knew was Steve. Maybe he could help her. Emma could always opt for a professional if Steve didn't have the answers, but he was the best start. She called him and asked if he had time to go to lunch. Emma wanted someplace neutral and quiet; somewhere with no phones or dogs. Somewhere they could talk quietly. Steve agreed to meet a local coffee shop near her house.

"I'm so glad you agreed to come to lunch, Steve. I'm in over my head," she confessed. She told Steve about the latest disaster.

"Oh, sweetie," he said sympathetically. "I'm so sorry. I really hoped he would get his life together. That being on his own two feet would change him."

"Me, too," and tears began to fill Emma's eyes. She realized at that moment, that there was still a piece of her heart that belonged to Jake. She tried to eat her lunch but found her appetite was gone.

"You still love him, don't you, sweetie?" Steve asked and held her hand.

"Well, at least some of me does. I remember the great times. The fun and companionship and being part of a couple. I remember how excited I was to be getting married. You know, the idea of a wedding. Shit, Steve. I've got to stop this," she whimpered.

"I know how you feel, Emma. It all seemed so happy in the beginning, but now you've become a victim," he explained to her.

God, he was right. How could she not have seen it? She had become a textbook victim in this relationship. As smart as she was, Emma had been blinded by the fun, by the sex, and by her own ego.

"I am, aren't I? He's turned me into a victim. And that's not who I am. I mean, I've never had an abusive relationship in my life. Not really. So why am I taking on that role now?" she asked.

"You're parents weren't abusive? No past relationships that

were abusive? Usually it's a pattern. You grow up feeling like a victim, so you continue the pattern into adulthood."

"No, not at all. My mom loves me, my stepfather loves me, and my dad loved me. I've never had a romantic relationship that was abusive," she answered after she thought about that one.

"I always thought that you and Jake were reliving a relationship from a past life that demanded payback. He owed you and you owed him. But sister, you've made your payment in full. He hasn't. For some reason though, you're still paying. You need to find the strength to stop being a victim. You deserve better, and he doesn't deserve any more," Steve explained. As Emma listened to him, she could hear the love in his voice. There was no anger or reproach, only caring.

"You're so right, sweetie. Where do I find that strength?" she asked.

"It's in you already. You have it. You own it. You need to talk to yourself and retrieve it. I know you, Emma. The strength has just been overpowered by love and by trying to save him. First, you have to admit that he's hopeless. You can't save him. No one can. It's not a weakness in you. Sweetie, if anyone could have saved Jake, you could have. But you need to realize that he's not capable of being saved. Then and only then, will you be able to stop being a victim," Steve told her.

When Emma left the restaurant, after she hugged Steve tightly and told him how much she loved him, she walked to her car. Her steps were a little lighter. Her heart was a little lighter. She needed to write—to take her own advice and write in her journal. That, along with Steve's advice, should enable her.

I am not a victim, Emma wrote in her journal when she returned home. I don't deserve this treatment. I am Dr. Emma Weiss. Strong, independent, intelligent. Jake may have stolen my heart in December, but this is almost a year later and he has not reciprocated anything in this relationship. He just keeps taking and taking. It's time for me to do what's right and move on with my life. I once wrote that if he took my sense of self, I would end it. Well, he's taking it. I no longer have the peace of mind I always had, and I can't live with that. I still care a great deal about Jake, but I'm more important. I have to save myself. I have to live with myself forever, and Jake will have to live with what he's done.

Chapter Twenty-Eight

It took a couple of days before Jake was settled enough to call Emma. He had moved into the house in which he was renting a room. Sylvia Brown, the woman who owned the house, was—according to Jake—probably in her late fifties, and her parents lived with her so she could care for them. Sylvia was a smoker, which was good luck for Jake. He could actually smoke in his room and wouldn't be given grief about the smell of smoke on him or the occasional stray ash. Sylvia cooked a family dinner every night, and Jake was included as family. Since Jake looked clean-cut and wholesome, Sylvia had no reason to distrust him. He was friendly, helpful, and sweet. She quickly adopted him as a surrogate son, and Jake was wonderful with her elderly parents. He had spent enough time in the nursing home visiting his mother that he developed an easy rapport with the elderly.

He went on an interview with a water-purification company two days after he arrived in Florida. He was offered the job immediately, since it was straight commission. He spent much of his day studying the information they gave him and went on a few sales calls with experienced salesmen to get the pitch down properly. When he called Emma, he was enthusiastic.

"Oh, Emma! I think everything's going to turn around for me now. Sylvia is terrific. She treats me like family. And the job, even though it's straight commission, should get real money coming in quickly. The first paycheck I get, I'll send to you," he promised.

"Jake, do you think I believe that? Yes, I got the one check from Mercedes for a hundred bucks, and I know that was tough for you. But I haven't seen a penny since then. Look, I really hope you do well, but the psychic said you'd never be able to hold a job. It looks like she's right," Emma said.

"Honey, I feel in my gut that this is going to work. And I won't quit. I owe you so much, and no matter what, I'm going to pay you back. If it takes my whole life, I'll find a way."

"Then you would have given me the five hundred you stole," she said.

"I didn't steal that money!" Jake said, still arguing his innocence. God, Emma thought, he really thinks I believe him! What an idiot.

"Right, Jake."

"So can I come up to see you? Maybe you could be my sales call so I could try out my skills. I can use Sylvia's truck, so no one will know it's me," he added.

"Why would she let you use her truck?" Emma asked.

"Because hers gets better gas mileage than mine, and she doesn't use it that much. She's nice that way."

"She's a fool," Emma said. "If only she knew that you don't have a legal driver's license and you're a felon. Not to mention you're running from the law and you're a drug addict."

"Recovering drug addict, you mean. I've been clean for six months. Come on, baby. Give me a chance. I know I can make it," he pleaded.

"Sure, Jake. Let me know when you can come. We can role-play your sales pitch and—whatever," she told him.

"Sex would be a good whatever," he tried.

"Yeah, it would be helpful."

"I can probably make it up there this weekend. I'll let you know. I love you, Emma. I won't lose you," he ended the conversation. He didn't realize that it was probably too late.

When Emma saw Jake for the first time since running from South Carolina, he looked different. He looked beaten. Although he tried to act normally, she could sense a change. He kissed her and held on to her for longer than normal. He played with her dog, Tasha. He set up his equipment to test her water. He screwed up his demonstration several times, and they both laughed.

"I don't think you should say 'fuck' every time you make a mistake," Emma replied, giggling.

"I won't. And I'm going to learn this shit backwards and forwards. I'll be able to close my own deals in another week. And you know, it really is a good system. It takes out all the impurities in the water for the entire house. Not only from your sink faucet and refrigerator but from the whole house. You'd actually be using the same water to wash your face or take a shower that you get from that one little faucet. It's pretty awesome," Jake explained.

"Sounds terrific. Too bad my house is for sale. Maybe in the new house."

"We can hook it up anywhere, and it has a lifetime guarantee," Jake told her. If only love had a lifetime guarantee, Emma thought.

"So what do you want for dinner?" Emma asked.

"Whatcha got?"

"Sausage and steaks in the freezer," she told him.

"How about I make some spaghetti and sausage? And you can make a salad with it for yourself. Does that sound okay?"

"Sure. That's fine."

While Jake cooked dinner, Emma sat on the sofa with the television on. She tried to focus on the questions on Cash Cab but couldn't concentrate. She decided to make her salad, so she wandered into the kitchen.

"Tasha's already been outside and I fed her," Jake told her as she strolled in.

"Thanks." They were so uncomfortable together. Not cold, just—distant. Like they were strangers. They ate dinner watching television, as usual. They played a game of Scene It, but after one game, Jake had enough. She put a movie in the DVD, and for the first time, Jake didn't like it. They played a few games of pool. Eight-ball, then nine-ball, and then eight-ball. Nothing seemed to satisfy either of them.

When it was finally late enough, Emma went to take her bath. She lounged longer than usual in the ginger bubbles. She sang along with the soundtrack to the movie version of Chicago. Jake walked into the bathroom to see her.

"Hello, gorgeous," he said as he sat on the toilet seat and watched her shave her legs.

"Hi, yourself," she replied playfully. "Wanna come in and play?" Emma blew some of the bubbles at him. Then Tasha pushed her way inside, long golden tail wagging. "You wanna play?" she asked Tasha and blew and handful of bubbles over the dog's head. Tasha leapt to catch them, tail wagging furiously. "See, Tasha likes to play."

"I'd rather wait until you get out to play," Jake said.

"Yeah? You think so?" Emma taunted.

"Oh, yeah. Definitely. God, you're beautiful. I can't believe some of the things I've done to you. I want to make amends to you. I can't do that with Mom or with Joe, but I can with you. I'm going to make tonight perfect and only for you," he promised.

He kept his word. Once Emma was toweled dry and moisturized, she brushed her waist-length hair, and he pulled her down to him on the bed. He always preferred her either naked or in regular underwear to wearing something blatantly sexy. He took his time, kissing every inch of her soft, warm skin. He parted her thighs and pleasured her with his mouth, pleasuring himself with her tremors and sighs. He ran his mouth up her flat belly, and she wrapped her long legs around his waist. When he entered her, the feeling was hard and slick. They knew each other's rhythms so well, it was easy to orgasm together. At least when Jake hadn't used drugs it was easy.

"Wow!" was all Emma could say.

"Yeah, wow!" he replied as he got out of bed to do his ritual cleaning. No cuddling, no afterglow. "Can I get you something?" he asked as he pulled on his pajama bottoms and walked toward the kitchen. "I'm starving."

"Um, yeah. A banana would be good," Emma asked. And as she heard the microwave ding, she knew he was making either hotdogs or reheating the leftover spaghetti. She hoped for hotdogs because they didn't give him indigestion and nightmares. But he couldn't pass up the spaghetti. He sat in bed eating spaghetti with hot sausage from a small bowl. Emma broke off a piece of the banana and ate it delicately.

"Can you turn on the TV?" was all he said.

"Sure. Here," she handed him the remote. He glanced at the television, then put the remote control down on the bed. Instead of turning on the television, he turned toward Emma and began to talk. This shocked the hell out of Emma.

"I'm really sorry for everything I've done to you, Emma. I want to tell you the truth about everything, but before I do, I want you to know that I really love you. I don't want to live without out you. I don't know if I can. You're all I have left, other than Cheryl and I can't depend on her. Not like you. Or Joe or Mom."

"I have a lot of questions, Jake, if you'll really tell me the truth," Emma sighed.

"Shoot. I promise to tell you the truth."

"The robbery here at the house. Did you do it? Or how did it happen, is the better question," she asked.

"Okay. My cousin and his girlfriend did come over. He had cocaine with him, and I didn't have any money. I told him to go into your bedroom and told him where you kept your jewelry. He took a few things—just enough to pay for the cocaine. His girlfriend must have been listening, and after I passed out, she went to town in there. I mean, he wouldn't have taken your purses or anything. But I didn't know her at all. Since she did the drugs with us and helped empty your bottle of scotch, she probably went into your bedroom and went shopping. I have no idea who she even is," he explained.

"And the dog eating my jewelry?" she asked.

"I had taken those two pieces a few days before we got the dog. I didn't know what to do. But when we got the dog and she was so wild, I took her into the office and played tug-o-war with the bag they had been in. She took a big bite out of it, and then I left it on the floor. After that, I panicked. I figured if the dog was gone, then I would be off the hook. So I took her back to the animal shelter. Besides, you might not find it for a few days. I was high as a kite and not thinking."

"So that poor dog may have been put to sleep because you had to have drugs?" Emma accused.

"I hope not. Really, she was a beautiful dog. I pray that someone else adopted her," he said.

"The five hundred dollars from the restaurant?" She was going to get it all if he was going to tell the truth.

"Yeah. I took it. I was desperate for money. I had lost my first job and didn't have enough for food and gas. It was sitting there at the desk, and I stopped thinking. I took it without considering the consequences," he finally admitted.

"But Jake, you loved that job. You were comfortable with your boss and with your roommate. Why did you throw it all away?"

"Emma, I think I just felt so worthless—like I didn't deserve the good things in life. The same as I don't feel I deserve you. I find a way to fuck up anything good. Maybe by realizing that about myself, I can change it." Tears started flowing down his cheeks. His crying was certainly pitiful, but Emma was trying to remain strong. She had found the strength within her, and even Jake's tears wouldn't break her.

"Have you been using?" she finally asked, assuming he would lie.

"Yes. Just small amounts and not for three days before I see you. I can't lose you, Emma. I just can't. So I stay as clean as I can when I'm going to be with you." He was still sobbing.

Emma's emotions were a jumble. She wanted desperately

to put his head on her chest and stroke him like a child. She finally understood his mother. Emma, too, wanted to coddle him; to soothe him. But this was not her son, and he was not a child. Jake Stanton was a man, and he had asked her to marry him. He wanted to spend the rest of his life with her. Emma clearly understood at that moment, how impossible that was and how right Steve had been. Her logical side began to win over the emotional. She found that she was no longer angry. She felt nothing vindictive. Most of her feelings were betrayal and exhaustion. The betrayal was painful but oddly did not result in hostility. It was the deepest anguish she had ever felt. And she was physically, mentally, and emotionally drained. Emma felt as though she could sleep for a week. If it weren't for Tasha—a defenseless and dependent animal whom she loved more than life itself—she would do just that, sleep for a week. But Jake was still in her bed, and she had to get through this visit. Finally she replied to Jake.

"I'm tired, Jake. I'm really tired. Let's get some sleep, honey," she said as she forced a smile. She kissed him good night, and he turned on the television at a very low volume.

Jake woke up before Emma and quietly called Tasha to his side.

"Come on, girl. Let's let Mommy sleep," he whispered to the dog. He let Tasha outside and fed her. Then he fixed a bowl of cereal for himself and took it into the great room. Jake turned on the television and ate. He waited for Emma to awaken.

When she finally wandered into the kitchen to turn on the coffee maker, she didn't realize how late it was. It was ten thirty! She poured a mug of coffee, adding cream and sugar and inhaled the aroma before taking the first needed sip.

She took her mug of coffee downstairs to the great room, where Jake was sitting quietly.

"Good morning," he said with a big smile.

"Good morning," she answered. Emma was not a morning person, so she was not talkative before that first jolt of caffeine. She took out her crossword puzzle and tried to get her brain functioning. "Did you sleep well?" she looked up from her puzzle and asked Jake.

"Yeah, I did. I don't think I talked or anything. Did I?"

"No, not at all. You didn't even snore," she answered.

"I'm glad. You seemed to have gotten a good night's sleep."

"Uh huh." She continued her puzzle. Jake knew by now that she was not ignoring him; she was only trying to wake up.

When she was finally awake, she went to her room to put on some clothes. She threw on jeans and a lightweight sweater. It was mid-December, and even in Savannah, it was chilly. Looking at her calendar, Emma realized it was the first night of Chanukah. Since she was no longer friends with Kathy, she would not have any company. She would light her menorah herself. Jake had to leave that afternoon to return his landlady's truck to her and to go to work. So she would be alone. That was fine with her. Emma wasn't in the mood to make a big Chanukah dinner this year.

When Jake left, he kissed her tenderly and hugged her tightly. He promised her the next time he saw her he would bring a big check. She laughed and told him she hoped so.

"Well, Christmas will be in another week and a half. Why don't you come for Christmas Eve and I'll make a great Christmas dinner?" Emma offered.

"That sounds great. I love you, baby. I'll see you then." And with that, Jake was gone.

Emma spent the next week in inner turmoil. She had several phone calls to make, each of which she made reluctantly. She went shopping for a ham, green beans, and found a recipe online for a bourbon glaze. Miss Ellie came to clean on Wednesday, and Emma was happy to see her. Christmas Eve was the following night, so when Ellie left, Emma gave her a Christmas present of a hundred dollars. She thanked her for all her hard work and her friendship and wished her a merry Christmas.

Emma was ready for Jake's visit. She didn't buy any Christmas presents for him since he had demanded she not do it.

"I've taken enough from you, baby. I don't deserve or want any gifts from you," he told her.

"Okay, honey, " she replied.

He called from the road to let her know what time he'd be arriving. It was about a two-hour drive, and he wasn't leaving home until close to three o'clock. When he called, it was already five o'clock, and he said he was still two hours away.

"Where are you?" she asked.

"Hinesville, Georgia," he answered.

"What are you doing there?" she asked. She knew the answer but she asked anyway.

His voice was slurred, and he was speaking rapidly. He found a dealer in Hinesville, and he had used. On Christmas Eve! Emma was disgusted. "You used, didn't you?" Before he could think, he answered.

"Yes. I'm so sorry, baby."

"Don't worry about it. We're not eating dinner until tomorrow night, so you'll be fine," she answered sweetly. Then she raced to the phone to make a few last-minute calls.

When Jake came to the door, he looked like hell. The open twenty-four ounce bottle of beer was probably still in the truck, as well as small remnants of the coke he had just scored. He looked as high as she'd ever seen. He kissed her, missing her mouth.

"I gotta take a shower," he muttered as he took his duffle bag into the bathroom with him.

"Sure, honey. I understand." Geez, he was really out of it. She listened to the bathroom door and heard no singing. When the shower was off, he dragged on his pajama bottoms.

"I'm going to take a nap, okay?" he said, already walking to the guest bedroom.

"Of course, honey," Emma replied.

When the knock on the door came, Emma nearly jumped out of her skin, even though she knew who it was. She opened the door and held her finger to her mouth to keep them quiet. Two uniformed police officers walked in, followed by Detective White from Savannah and the detective from South Carolina. Emma quietly pointed and led them to the back bedroom.

The uniformed officers stood aside, while the two detectives opened the door to Emma's guest room. He was sound asleep and was startled awake.

"Jake Stanton, you're under arrest," Officer White was given the lead since he was local. He read Jake his Miranda rights and began rattling off the charges. "Let's see here, Jake," he looked at the list he'd compiled, "you're under arrest for DUI, two counts of possession of a controlled substance—since we found what we believe to be cocaine in your truck just now, multiple probation violations including the theft of Dr. Weiss's handgun, evading the police, grand theft in both Georgia and Florida, which includes the robberies of the homes of Dr. Emma Weiss and Mrs. Sylvia Brown, and the vehicles owned by the aforementioned, assisting in the burglary of the Bed Depot, falsifying identification, and identity theft. Since you'll be drug tested as soon as you're booked, I'm sure there will be another count of probation violation added. Detective Singer? Would you like to finish?" Jake was being handcuffed by the uniformed officer, and he was alert enough to be crying.

"Jake Stanton, you are under arrest for the burglary at Cheeseburgers, Inc. in Bluffton, South Carolina, and for running from the police investigation. You have the right to remain silent..." and Detective Singer finished reading Jake his Miranda rights. "We'll get you when Detective White and whichever detective they assign your case in Florida are finished with you."

Emma stood in the hallway listening, tears running down her cheeks. She didn't feel a sense of justice and certainly didn't turn him in to the police for revenge. She realized that the only way karma would be served and she could move on with her life as the true Emma Weiss was to be sure Jake would be where he belonged—in jail. Not only for her own peace of mind but for the memory of Big Joe and Jake's mother Mimi, and even for Sylvia.

Sylvia had been one of her phone calls, after she had spoken with the police and organized his arrest. After she had spoken with this woman, she learned that Jake had been stealing from her. Emma phoned the Florida police after speaking with her.

Emma assured Sylvia that the police would have him in custody by Christmas. Sylvia was so grateful, she began to cry.

Emma sobbed as they took Jake away in handcuffs, but she knew she had done the right thing. She couldn't utter a word to him. There were no words left to say. If no one else was, Emma was proud of herself. She had finally found her strength and used it to save herself. She could now move with her soul intact and the karmic circle closed.

EPILOGUE

With Jake in jail and sentenced to twenty years in prison, Emma breathed a sigh of relief. She was grateful that he could no longer hurt her or others. She had done everything in her power to keep him from going to prison, but it hadn't been enough. When the police report included the grand theft, she was reimbursed some forty thousand dollars from her insurance company. They had cancelled her, but with Jake in jail, she could probably get new insurance. Jake's truck was returned to her, and she sold it for three thousand dollars. At last her life was in order, but it was time for her to begin again. She sat quietly in her new house.

Emma had left Savannah without leaving a forwarding address, and her new phone number was unlisted. Steve was the only person in Savannah who knew her new address. Steve had actually come to her new home the day of her move to spend the weekend helping her unpack and settle in.

She sat on the back porch of her charming little house, overlooking a small forest of pine and crepe myrtle trees. There was no Spanish moss to be seen, and that suited Emma just fine. Tasha happily romped through the grass, sniffing the trees. Emma sipped her coffee, and rather than work her crossword puzzle, she turned on her laptop computer. The first word she typed was Addiction. And with that, she began the book about her months with Jake. Maybe, just maybe, if she wrote the story of how she became involved with an addict, gone through the hell of living with him, and had come out the other end whole, she would be able to understand how a woman like her had fallen in love with a man like Jake in the first place, and in doing so, she might also help others.

www.ingramcontent.com/pod-product-compliance
Lightning Source LLC
Chambersburg PA
CBHW030302080526
44584CB00012B/411